A School for Politics

Early America
History, Context, Culture

Jack P. Greene and J. R. Pole
Series Editors

A SCHOOL FOR POLITICS

COMMERCIAL LOBBYING AND

POLITICAL CULTURE

IN EARLY SOUTH CAROLINA

REBECCA STARR

The Johns Hopkins University Press

BALTIMORE & LONDON

THE JOHNS HOPKINS UNIVERSITY PRESS
2715 North Charles Street
Baltimore, Maryland 21218-4363
The Johns Hopkins Press Ltd., London
www.press.jhu.edu

Library of Congress Cataloging-in-Publication Data will be found at the end of this book.
A catalog record for this book is available from the British Library.

ISBN 0-8018-5832-1

For
BETTY AMELIA PERRY KIRK
(1913–1993)
and for
AMY AND FRANCIS STARR

CONTENTS

       IN THE NEW REPULIC, 1783–1800 • 136

       CONCLUSIONS • 161

       APPENDIX: STATISTICAL METHODS • 167

       NOTES • 169

       ESSAY ON SOURCES • 203

       INDEX • 211

Acknowledgments

I've accumulated such a mountain of debt during the production of this long-gestating work that no acknowledgment can fully meet the extent of my obligation or express the measure of my gratitude. There are many more not named here, who know who they are, and without whose help creating this book would have been a far more difficult task. I am grateful to my teachers at the University of South Carolina, where the idea for a study of Charleston's cosmopolitan merchants began, and especially to George C. Rogers Jr. and Robert M. Weir. George Rogers's broad knowledge and unswerving instinct for the meaning of South Carolina's history set me on a true course from the beginning. Many of the ideas developed in this book began life in lively exchanges with the creative mind of Rob Weir. He taught me to ask questions in unusual ways. I hope he will not want to disavow what I have made of them.

J. R. Pole supervised the D.Phil. thesis that found a politics in commercial lobbying. He gave sound advice and encouragement throughout, always pushing me to look for the broadest implications of my story. My D.Phil. examiners at Oxford University, Duncan MacLeod and Daniel Walker Howe, made of my viva voce examination a learning session for revising for publication. Harry Pitt of Worcester College, Oxford, Robert Weir, and James Henretta of the University of Maryland all read the manuscript at various stages, pointing out many lacunas and offering valuable organizational advice.

The years of original research that went into this study have left me indebted to many institutions, libraries, and foundations. Walter B. Edgar gave me generous support at the Institute for Southern Studies, both while a master's degree student at the University of South Carolina and afterwards. Several summers spent as an associate fellow in the Institute allowed time to research and consult with others interested in the history of

South Carolina. The staff at the Department of South Carolina Archives and History at times must have thought I lived there, so much time did I spend in the search room. The staff and especially the director Alan Stokes at the South Caroliniana Library let me sift through innumerable manuscript collections in search of relevant nuggets, often suggesting sources that saved me valuable research time. This same patience and support was offered by David Moltke-Hansen and his staff at the Charleston Historical Society and at the South Carolina Library Society, Charleston.

The British phase of my research was supported in part by student grants from the Vice Chancellors of the British Academy, by an Oxford University Overseas Student grant, and by faculty research grants from The Cheltenham and Gloucester College of Higher Education. British repositories that gave indispensable assistance include the staffs and directors of the Rhodes House Library and the Bodleian Library at Oxford University, Nottingham University's Manuscript Library, The Central Library, Bristol, The Bristol Merchant Venturers Society, Sheffield Public Library, The Commonwealth Institute, London, the British Library, the London Public Record Offices at Kew Gardens and Chancery Lane, and the public record offices of Gloucestershire, Bedfordshire, and Avon (Bristol) Counties.

Throughout the work I have enjoyed excellent company and intellectual stimulus from fellow students, professional colleagues, and personal friends. They include Connie Schulz, Jane Squires, Ed Beardsley, Lacy Ford, James Lamb, Billie Burn, Hartmut Pogge von Strandmann, David Medalie, and Melanie Ilic. Julie Bugler heroically word processed all the statistical data for the original study from handwritten drafts. Latterly, the critical eye and ruthless standards of Robert Brugger and the staff at Johns Hopkins University Press have made a book of a manuscript.

Finally, I owe a debt to my mother, Betty Amelia Perry Kirk, which I can never repay. A spunky widow, she brought me up to believe that I could do anything if I tried. Right or not, I absorbed her faith or I would never have attempted an academic's life. Mostly, she taught me that love never abandons nor ends, a belief I have had no reason to discard. She did not live to see this book finished, but without her it would have had no beginning, and she is fully present in it. This book is dedicated to her, and to her grandchildren and my children, Amy and Francis Starr. I hope each knows why they deserve a page in the book to themselves.

A SCHOOL FOR POLITICS

THE PROBLEM OF SOUTH CAROLINA REVISITED

There is something undeniably attractive about South Carolina's history. Drawn to the state's dramatically disruptive role in the events of the antebellum period, scholars have repeatedly tried to unravel the "problem" of South Carolina. As early as 1820, the state seemed to possess a unique (read deviant) political culture with a prickly politics as its effective side. Historians long have asked why South Carolina's politics were so obstructionist, its politicians so petulant. The quick answer, of course, was slavery and the necessity to defend the institution against growing national disapproval.

Yet the problem of South Carolina becomes more puzzling still when one discovers that, as method at least, the state's antebellum politics was not new. The pattern later called a problem stood unnoticed and almost unremarked on from the early days of the new Republic. Indeed, its roots lay in the mid-eighteenth century.

If, for example, one looks at South Carolina while it remained a dependent in Great Britain's vast commercial empire, one finds that this small, politically weak colonial power repeatedly challenged His Majesty's government, winning concessions time and again in a pattern that became entrenched from as early as 1767. From undramatic beginnings—routine petitioning and informal pressure on Whitehall and Parliament for imperial trading law exceptions during the colonial period—Carolina's leaders gradually moved to a politics of self-conscious confrontation on the floor of the Continental Congress, Independence Hall, the Constitutional Convention, and finally in Congress itself. Along the way South Carolina's leaders evolved a patterned opposition politics and a radical leadership style that gained authority and audacity with each successive use.[1]

During the same half-century, the size and composition of South Carolina's political community changed radically. Shorn of its prerevolutionary harmony, South Carolina's elite cultivated a politics of stability at home, where jarring interests and potent social divisions forebode as much conflict in its internal government as could be found in any other state. How did this politics come to be, how did it work, and why did it persist? In this period of rapid growth, of revolution and government-building, what were the sources, methods, and means by which such a small, socially diverse state created an internal politics so harmonious and an external politics so relentless as to be famous for both?

Since the problem of South Carolina has not been approached from a standpoint of process before, existing studies provide incomplete answers. Two other factors—periodization and the way the question has been formulated—truncate present interpretations. Historians of the nineteenth century, with an eye on the Civil War, highlight South Carolina's radicalism, its tendency to desperate remedies, and look to a unique nineteenth-century political culture to explain it.[2] These studies make a promising start at identifying eighteenth-century social and political preconditions. But by focusing on the nationally intensified period from 1820 to 1860, they overlook the fact that this same politics was at work much earlier in the state's history.

In the hands of historians of ideology, the republicanism thesis has been fruitfully mined for the period from 1800 to 1860 to explain why the state's upcountry yeomanry supported a radical movement in which they had little material stake.[3] The dearth of work on republicanism for early South Carolina suggests the weakness of the impulse, at least among lowcountry South Carolinian leaders, even at the high tide of Federalism.[4] Although they could employ the rhetoric of republicanism when it suited them, republican values alone do not explain why Carolina's leaders repeatedly used disunion talk to force negotiated compromises.

For historians of slavery, the centrality of race and race relations has dwarfed all other interpretations. Although it may help establish a cogent reason for white collectivity, by itself neither slavery nor a covert fear of slave rebellion explains the pattern of South Carolina's resistance or why the state's leaders could argue for free trade in 1790 with the same intensity and rhetoric of disunion as they had in 1774 and in 1832.[5] For these reasons, historians of the new cultural history, with its broadened conception of the forces of historical change, should look to an earlier period[6] and to factors previously overlooked or dismissed as irrelevant for the answer to the problem of South Carolina.

Before going further, it is important to declare that this study neither claims nor attempts to explain the causes of South Carolina's secession in 1860. This analysis ends in 1800. The object of this book is to interpret the development of South Carolina's politics to the time of the early Republic. Similarly, this study does not supplant but rather augments the already well accepted social explanations for the character of South Carolina's early politics.[7] The approach used here identifies a new source for South Carolina's early political culture, one that describes the dynamics of its politics more concretely. Perhaps this account will prove suggestive enough to open new lines of inquiry from a new angle of vision.

Because the problem of South Carolina was ultimately so dramatic in its national consequences, more work has concentrated on the state's political radicalism than its remarkable political unity, but the two are inextricably linked. Both also have a long pedigree. Growing ties of kinship, friendship, and marriage among lowcountry elites in prerevolutionary South Carolina founded a genuine social homogeneity and supplied the solidarity so essential for an organically harmonious politics.[8] A longing for lost harmony will account for why South Carolinians turned to a restorative politics in the postrevolutionary period, but it will not explain how South Carolina's leaders sustained a working harmony during the revolutionary crisis, when its own social and economic bases fractured among merchant, planter, and artisan classes. Nor does it explain how, when the political community widened after Independence, the old leadership successfully defused conflict between itself and an increasingly aggressive and vocal backwoods elite.

For all that they have added to our understanding of the political culture of South Carolina, both the social and ideological analyses overlook the fact that the way in which people do things, including their politics, may have an important formative influence.[9] People become attached to the way they do things, long after the original, pragmatic reasons and context for devising those procedures have vanished or changed. If the method continues to work on new sets of problems, it becomes a familiar routine, valued for its own sake. Those who use it may come to discern in it the workings of fundamental principles that they feel a moral stake in protecting. If this politics, this formula for problem-solving, produces an internal politics that reinforces a longing for social harmony, so much the better. If it produces an external politics that somehow sets its practitioners apart and makes them appear more formidable than their actual military, economic, or electoral strength would warrant, they may even come to take pride in it.

Whatever the case, South Carolina's politics in its formative period was worked out by men who did not know that a revolution against Britain, let alone a revolution against other Americans, would one day come—and probably would not have approved if they had. Working backwards from the assumptions and conditions of the antebellum period, one finds an agenda not yet written. Enmeshed in the assumptions and conditions specific to South Carolina in the last half of the eighteenth century, South Carolina's leaders crafted a politics that suited the state's needs from the materials at hand. This study seeks to interpret the patterns and processes that provincial politicians developed in the day-to-day experience of practicing the informal politics of their imperial commercial trade lobby and the formal politics of provincial self-government. Why did these two politics merge in the revolutionary crisis? How were they transformed by Independence, when self-rule and widened gaps in the political community created new stresses that demanded flexible solutions? Once the "South Carolina model" of political problem-solving evolved, how did it differ from that of the other states? Only at that point can the state's unproblematic (for itself) politics be said to constitute a potential problem for the rest of the nation.

This inquiry asks to what extent South Carolina's problem (that is, its distinctive politics and political culture, where the definition of political culture has been broadened to include habitual patterns of political behavior) owes its origins to method and process. The state's colonial commercial and political relationship with Britain suggests that informal, interest group political practices provided a psychological and methodological framework for the future.

Having no representation in Parliament to push for legislation more favorable to the colony's considerable rice and indigo trade, South Carolina's great planters and merchants (who were also its provincial political leaders) developed a trade lobby in conjunction with British merchants and manufacturers involved in the Carolina trade. From these undramatic beginnings, a body of political practices and habits of mind, a radical style, and a conception of enlightened group interest developed and eventually came to typify South Carolina's approach to politics, both state and national, persisting long after Independence. Put another way, the mind and methods of lobbying entered South Carolina's political culture and came to shape it.

Of course, a trade "lobby" was not so called in the eighteenth century. I use the term in this study to describe a kind of political activity pursued by groups joined by some common interest. "Interest" was the term most often used at this time to refer to some sphere individuals shared by virtue of their livelihood, religion, political beliefs, or ethnicity. Hence, the "merchant" interest, Quaker interest, Rockingham interest, or Irish interest. These interests were informal and unorganized, but could be mobilized for political action into interest groups or lobbies when the defining interest was threatened. Lobbies were always out-of-doors, since organized indoor opposition to the Crown still smacked of treason in this period.[10] In a commercial state like eighteenth-century Britain, trade lobbies were the best developed of the interest groups. This was particularly true for South Carolina.

Once enmeshed in South Carolina's politics, the lobbying tradition became an unconscious interpreter of contingent events and a program for response. During the prerevolutionary period, the lobbying tradition contributed a powerful methodological paradigm for South Carolina's self-satisfied elite leaders, who were flatly dismissive of "airey theories" of political philosophy. Only in the postrevolutionary period, when social homogeneity (with its common tacit assumptions) cracked, did South Carolina's leaders experiment with conscious, articulated ideologies like republicanism.

Political structure being but a short step from political culture, South Carolina's lowcountry elites carefully tooled the committee system of the greatly enlarged, newly independent lower house in order to deflect social conflict into the system, where it could be thrashed out behind closed doors. Through the appointive powers of the Speaker (invariably a member of the old elite), committees became a forum for sharing power with underrepresented groups and interests without formally restructuring the legislature. As a channel for conflict, the committee system offered an alternative to another political structure, the party system, whose modern form (two-party politics based on the legitimacy of institutional conflict) did not achieve permanent status in state politics until the twentieth century. The party system's divisive potential on the state level, and its divided appearance on the national level, made it a nonstayer if not a nonstarter in such a political culture. On the national level, South Carolina's senators, congressmen, and delegates to national conventions as in the past could still behave as a sometimes beleaguered, sometimes belligerent lobby group dealing with an imperious foreign power.

Five key events demonstrate the lobbying tradition at work in revolutionary and republican South Carolina's internal and external politics: the legislature's reception of the Massachusetts circular letter in 1768, the colony's nonimportation movements of 1769 and of 1774, the constitutional debates in Philadelphia, and the ratification debates in Charleston in the late 1780s. An emerging theory of interest representation appears in the pamphlet literature of 1794, a response by lowcountry leadership to the populous backcountry's demand for legislative reapportionment based on numbers only.

Once entrenched, the lobbying tradition had profound intellectual consequences. The basic assumption of the approach—that the claims of interests are important in making law—had an impact on the assumptions behind the type and apportionment of representation in the state legislature. A correlative idea emerged—that interests and not individuals were the basic units of the state. On them government operates, and they stand in equality to each other. Such a view meant that the rights of minorities might legitimately supersede those of absolute majorities (an idea later elevated by John C. Calhoun into the doctrine of the concurrent or "constitutional" majority). The basis of a lobby's strength, its ability to present the appearance of unity (regardless of internal divisions), affirmed the idealization of the social value of harmony to a greater degree than elsewhere. Indeed, the word "harmony" infuses the political discourse of the period.

South Carolina's internal conflict resolution politics compares interestingly with representative states from New England, the Middle Atlantic, and the upper South. How well did the politics of harmony sustain its powers for limiting faction during the troubled 1780s and 1790s relative to methods developed in other states? Extending the social and political comparison to the West Indies further emphasizes South Carolina's distinction from the mainland by pointing to the similar nature of its "Caribbean" experience, even though the state did not make a "Caribbean choice" on the question of Independence.

A word about boundaries is in order. This study focuses on the machinery of South Carolina's politics in the early Republic, how it was acquired, how it worked, and how it was transformed into a unique configuration by 1800. While this study does not carry its specific inquiry into the nineteenth century, its implications suggest that Carolina's colonial schooling in an opposition politics acquired out-of-doors led to a politics of single-mindedness in which means at times overdetermined ends. In such a politics, a "pressure group" strategy to pursue or protect vital interests set its practitioners on a collision course of action. When the tactics of persuasion failed, success depended on the greater power's willingness to yield to avoid disaster. If the greater power would not yield, South Carolina's leaders could either accept an undesired outcome (a move likely to invite faction at home and bring their fitness to rule into question) or take more dramatic action. Although rare in this early period, South Carolina's leaders could and did play the lobbyist's trump card: withdrawal to halt negotiations. South Carolina's radicalism is not so unreasonable as it has been portrayed. But short of that outcome, and in the vast middle ground over which political thought and action could range in the day-to-day brokering of power, the interest group approach to problem-solving proved flexible and effective.

This book concentrates on politics, white political elites, and political culture. While South Carolina society, white and black, forms an essential background, this study's focus is not social groups, but political groups, both formal and informal. Lobbies, networks, interest groups, and their managers are the protagonists. Parliament, Congress, the state legislature, and the various extralegal committees and associations that formed the revolutionary government and protogovernment are the settings in which their story is told.

In selecting biographical subjects through which to follow the workings of my argument, I have concentrated on persons who might be termed "major minor" characters in South Carolina's revolutionary and confederation politics. This decision is partly owing to the existence of a suitable body of papers on the Lloyd, Champion, and Farr families of South Carolina and Bristol. But it is also based on the belief that showing the pattern at work in secondary characters demonstrates more convincingly that the method, attitudes, and ethos traced here penetrated throughout South Carolina's elite leadership, without creating the impression that there were never divisions within that group. There were indeed divisions and exceptions, but the general strategy by which the leadership core held the state on a chosen course is the one I describe.

As the ideology paradigm is proving insufficient to explain all the sources of political thought and practice in American history, I think an analysis of patterned political behavior offers a new approach to explaining the problem of South Carolina. A politics, too, can have a pedigree. Analyzing the political strategies and habits of some long ago merchants and commercial planter politicians may at first glance seem a tedious and uninspiring task, with little (if anything) to contribute to the great questions of America's history. But the nagging consistency of these patterns suggests compellingly that South Carolina's entrenched political practices carried an unwritten text of values, attitudes, assumptions, and opinions, and supplied an important grammar for subsequent political discourse.

PART ONE

LOBBYISTS AND THEIR STRATEGY

One

SOUTH CAROLINA'S ELITE ON THE EVE OF THE REVOLUTION

Much has been written about the lowcountry gentry. Sometimes described in terms of a landed, even feudal aristocracy, or a country gentry on the order of England's county families, South Carolina's wealthy elite were actually intensely pragmatic men on the make in a bustling commercial world. Especially after the successful introduction of rice culture in the 1730s, the colony's merchants, planters, and the lawyers who tended their affairs put aside earlier political quarrels and plunged into the business of getting rich. Although the ultimate social ideal remained that of a gentleman planter, they grasped the nettle of marketplace realities with unusual zest, living the life of West Indian nabobs from its profits. These same men, mostly interrelated by blood or marriage, filled the seats of the colonial Assembly. A visitor in 1773 noted that proceedings were so informal as to give more the appearance of a social club than a parliament. Politically and economically fixed within the British mercantile system, this "vast cousinage" shared a culture of commerce that formed the backdrop for the system of informal, interest group politics that South Carolina was even then evolving to serve its needs.

By the mid-eighteenth century, the coastal settlement that was South Carolina had achieved a social homogeneity, a political stability, and an economic prosperity that the other American colonies could well envy.[1] This achievement was due to a number of factors. Religious disputes early in the century, though never critical, did lead to political factionalism that was resolved in the ascendancy of the Anglican party. That group subsequently absorbed its Huguenot rivals into the elite through marriage and business connections. The end of the long Yamessee War and the founding of the buffer colony of Georgia in 1732 secured the colony's southern frontier. Concurrently, the colony's long dispute with an inefficient and neglectful proprietary government ended. South Carolina became a royal colony, and the land office, closed from 1719, reopened in 1731 to a rush of land-hungry Carolinians. The development of rice culture in the early 1730s, unquestionably the most important factor behind South Carolina's new stability, created an export boom that transformed the colony into the West's leading rice supplier and made its planters and merchants rich.[2]

Just how rich deserves elaboration. Between 1722 and 1762, the annual compound growth rate of mean personal wealth in the colony's most populous district, Charleston, was an "astonishing" 2.0 to 2.2 percent. To make the same point another way, on the eve of the American Revolution, the mean total wealth per inventoried wealthholder in the Charleston District was £2337.7 sterling or $126,844 in 1978 U.S. dollars. The next wealthiest region in America was Annapolis County, Maryland, at £660.4 sterling per inventoried wealthholder, or less than 30 percent of the Charleston figure.[3]

The Carolina elite were not only rich; they were socially homogeneous. There is an assumption among historians of colonial America that the planting class looked down on merchants. The error has been repeated so often that it has become common wisdom. The fact is that in prerevolutionary South Carolina, the elite unquestionably included merchants. In 1773, a New England traveler to Charleston, commenting on the characteristics of the gentry, observed that "the gentlemen (planters and merchants) are mostly men of the turf and gamesters."[4]

One obvious source of the error lies in modern historians' confusion about the eighteenth-century meaning of the term "merchant," which, indeed, was sometimes misapplied. A merchant was in foreign commerce, not in retail sales, wholesaling to retailers, or keeping a shop. He might be "in the trade" of one commodity or other, or to one market or other—hence, wine merchants or Carolina merchants—but he was not "in trade." He might be a "trader," but he was not a "tradesman." The introduction to a 1763 London merchants' directory addressed the problem of terminology in a way that clarifies the issue for historians:

> After a strict and impartial examination of all the printed Lists of Merchants and Traders of the city of London, that have been hitherto published, I find myself obliged to declare, they are extremely imperfect; several persons being inserted as Merchants, who have not the least pretence to that very honourable title, in any shape whatever: others again are denominated Merchants, who keep retail Millinery and Haberdashery Shops, merely because they have, perhaps once or twice, imported some

trifling commodity, and made a few entries at the Custom-house. In a Commercial State it is highly necessary that the Merchants, who are its chief support, should be accurately and definitely pointed out, for the benefit of Foreigners, and likewise of such considerable Wholesale Dealers as may find their account in applying to them for the several commodities they import, instead of purchasing of the Warehousemen, who often style themselves Merchants, for the very purpose of selling to persons who are more considerable than themselves; whereas their proper business, to pursue the regular channel of Trade, is, to supply the mere Retailer. In the following sheets I have endeavoured to form a just barrier between the Merchants, and the Warehousemen and Shopkeepers, by admitting some into the List of Merchants but such as are so in every sense of the word.[5]

Another source of error is the agrarian bias of the country/republican ideology school as worked out in modern historiography. Application of such theoretically dichotomous aggregates as land, independence, and virtue versus commerce, dependence, and corruption across the spectrum of occupations grounded in either agriculture or trade, has collapsed the very real differences in status within those categories as well as assigning, inappropriately, social superiority to one and inferiority to the other.[6]

If the merchant occupied an inferior social status in South Carolina, what did Charleston audiences of 1764 make of the profession's favorable portrayal in George Lillo's popular 1737 play, *The London Merchant?* The play's main character, Thorowgood, instructs his apprentice Trueman about the merchant's new place in English society. "As the Name of Merchant never degrades the Gentleman, so by no Means does it exclude him."[7]

Maria, as Thorowgood's daughter and sole heir to his wealth, is marriageable to a lord. But when her father thinks it is only on that account that noble lords pay him attention, Maria answers, "The man of quality, who chooses to converse with a Gentleman Merchant of your Worth and Character, may Confer honour by so doing, but he loses none." The merchant, moreover, may claim as much civic virtue for his profession as the landed gentry.

When Spain threatens war, it is the merchants who save the country. As Thorowgood explains to his apprentice and the audience, "Merchants, as such, may sometimes Contribute to the Safety of their Country as they do at all times to its Happiness."[8] While it is tempting to dismiss the entire thing as sentimental nonsense, yet one Charleston merchant named his plantation "Thorowgood" and two South Carolina-built trading schooners bore that name as well.[9]

In South Carolina, at least, the most immediate and probably the most significant reason for the mistake is the fact that, after 1790, the merchant's status did indeed diminish, although the very richest continued to be held in high esteem. This decline was due to the postrevolutionary influx of foreign British (including the despised Scots) and later northern merchants, who squeezed out native merchants too short of capital to compete during the troubled 1780s.[10]

These new merchants did not understand the old ways of doing business. When their "sharp trading practices" became the substance of commerce over the "honourable exchange" that was integrally a social as well as an economic relation during the prerevolutionary period, merchant status declined. The issue of relative social status among the rich in prerevolutionary South Carolina did not turn on the source of wealth, but on the activities required to sustain each.

Another reason for the exodus of native merchants from commerce into planting was simply the greater profits to be made in agriculture, particularly after the introduction of cotton culture in the 1790s. Almost all those merchants who did amass a fortune invested it in land and slaves, just as they had in the prewar period, where the annual returns could far exceed the 9 to 13 percent profits to be made from trade. This shift by the elite nearly exclusively into agriculture, plus the arrival of less desirable men into the formerly respectable role of merchant, is at the bottom of the nineteenth-century depreciation of trade.[11]

But in the period of political culture formation under review, Carolina merchants and planters (and certain professionals like lawyers and physicians, if wealthy) enjoyed an equivalent status, whose chief criterion was wealth. Intermarriage among them was so common that the Carolina elite has been called a "vast cousinage." These social and familial intertwinings helped ensure the political stability that economic prosperity underpinned.[12]

Interrelated by blood and marriage, the lowcountry elite frequented each other's houses on long visits, met each other in church, and socialized together in Charleston's network of more than forty social and fraternal clubs. Most held memberships in several at once. It is not surprising that the lines between their public and private lives should become blurred, and that membership in the provincial Assembly that they dominated should seem like just one more aspect of their social lives.

While visiting Charleston in 1773, Massachusetts politician Josiah Quincey Jr. remarked that from his observation of a day's session at the South Carolina Commons House of Assembly, the proceedings more resembled a meeting of a social club than a legislature. "The members conversed, lolled, and chatted much like a friendly jovial society, when nothing of importance was before the house: nay once or twice while the speaker and clerk were busy in writing the members spoke quite loud across the room to one another. A very unparliamentary appearance."[13]

Informality in a procedural sense also marked the Assembly's manner of doing the colony's business. Informal procedures ensured that politics proceeded less competitively than in governments where open rivalry determined leadership and decision-making. The colony's revenue and sheriff offices, for example, were appointive rather than elective, a policy that assured deferential attitudes from political hopefuls.[14]

Even the elective seats in the Assembly were filled by self-perpetuating cliques taking turns in office. Of the twenty-two individuals elected for the six seats from Charleston (St. Philips and St. Michaels parishes) in the eleven royal assemblies that sat between 1760 and 1775, all but three (86%) won reelection from Charleston at least once. Eleven (50%) won election from other electoral districts when not sitting for Charleston.[15]

The postrevolutionary election record of Charles Cotesworth Pinckney illustrates the ease with which the elite continued to rotate the available offices among themselves. After representing St. John Colleton in the previous five royal assemblies and in the First (1775) and Second (1775–76) Provincial Congresses, he sat for St. Philips and St. Michaels parishes (Charleston) in the Second General Assembly (1776–78). He then won election from both St. Philips and St. Michaels and St. George Dorchester to the Third General Assembly (1779–80), but chose to sit for the latter. In 1782, he won from both St. George Dorcester and St. Helena parishes to the Fourth General Assembly (1782). Despite not taking up either seat, he won again in St. George Dorchester as well as St. Philips and St. Michaels parishes for the Fifth General Assembly (1783–84). This time he chose to sit for Charleston. He represented the city parishes in the House in the Sixth (1785–86), Seventh (1787–88), and Eighth (1789–90) General Assemblies and in the Senate in the Eleventh General Assembly (1794–95). He was elected by the voters of St. Thomas and St. Dennis parish to the Fourteenth General Assembly (1800–1801), but declined to qualify for the House. Instead, he represented St. Philips and St. Michaels parishes in the Senate.[16] In all, Pinckney won election from seven different parishes to both houses of the Assembly, where officeholding resembled a game of musical chairs.

As for leadership roles, although the planter majority set the tone for society and numerically dominated the House, it was merchant and lawyer members who claimed the forward ranks. As they were always in a minority, their prominence can only be explained by their greater political activism. Eugene Sirmans has calculated that of the twenty-two men who emerged as leaders of the Commons House of Assembly between 1733 and

1751, eleven were merchants, six were lawyers, and one was a doctor; but only four were planters. Moreover, since three of the four planters held leadership for one year only, granting them four leadership positions actually exaggerates their importance. Similarly, between 1751 and 1763, the twenty-seven House leaders included fourteen merchants, six lawyers, five planters (but three were leaders for one session only), one doctor, and one placeman. Merchants dominated the front ranks of House leadership until 1770, at which time lawyers assumed an increasingly important leadership role.[17]

Merchants and lawyers sought leadership responsibilities for several reasons. Living in Charleston, they found legislative attendance much less burdensome than planters did. Lawyers, often ambitious young men who lacked family influence, sought to advance their social standing through public service. The Pinckney and Rutledge families achieved social and political prominence in this way. Young or newly arrived merchants might also seek social advancement in this way, but even socially established merchants saw that the mercantile community had special economic interests that could be protected if not advanced in the Assembly. But as planters always outnumbered them, merchant and lawyer leadership can only be explained by their greater political aggressiveness against a background of planter acquiescence. Even so, when issues of clear-cut interest conflict between trade and agriculture did arise, the planter backbench majority usually roused itself to vote them down. However, these instances became increasingly rare after about 1740, so the planter members remained content to let the merchants and lawyers control the proceedings, so long as their interests were not abused.[18]

It may be too obvious to state, but at least in terms of their commercial relationship to England (which for lowcountry white South Carolinians was the primary economic relationship), merchants and planters had identical interests. Whatever legislation benefited the rice and indigo trade—a direct vent for rice to foreign markets, for example, or the exclusion of competing foreign indigo from domestic (British and British colonial) markets—benefited the planter in the form of higher prices. Similarly, measures directly benefiting the planter's export, such as crop subsidies or drawbacks (a customs rebate on reexported goods), meant more capital to pour into expanded plantation operations, which in turn meant increased business for the slave trader and importer of essential English-made farm implements. These measures were not determined by the provincial legislature, of course, but local concurrence and support for them had to be in place.

This only explains why planters would not generally oppose merchant leadership, particularly in imperial matters. It does not indicate that planters understood the marketplace or accepted its values in their political culture. And while merchants did not seek public office as merchants only, it would be surprising if the attitudes and practices acquired in a commercial political economy should not be their first point of reference for much of their political thinking. But why should a commercial cast of mind be acceptable to (let alone characteristic of) planters?

The thought-provoking work of T. H. Breen on Virginia's largest tobacco growers suggests a way of entering the mental world of the great Virginia planter, which can then be contrasted with that of the South Carolina planter.[19] Taking an anthropological approach, Breen suggests that in the "culture" of tobacco growing, a planter's primary relationship was to his crop. His daily life was organized around it and his daily conversation consisted in it. His life's role, his self-esteem, his sense of independence, his values and attitudes, even his relationships with his neighbors—in short, his whole identity—were formed by and anchored in a self-contained plantation world sustained by one plant: tobacco.

Shaping his view of the larger world by his local experience and habits of mind, he personalized the business side of the staple, seeing his relationship with his merchant in faraway England as a "favor" granted to his commercial "friend." Even his perception of indebtedness was transformed into a social relationship, a favor between friends. When the 1772–73 financial crash forced merchants to tighten credit and press their colonial clients for payment, Virginia planters felt it as friendship betrayed and a slight upon their personal honor. These qualities of mind are essentially agrarian, communal, and anticommercial.

Extrapolating from the agricultural experience to the political realm, Breen goes on to suggest how the tobacco experience conditioned planters for the reception of radical country ideology. The mentality of independence fostered by an autonomous plantation economy resonated with the primary tenet (political independence) of country ideology, making it an ideology with a compatible worldview. Moreover, incommensurable perceptions about the meaning of debt and credit relations between planters and British merchants threatened the planter's cherished sense of independence and created a psychological stress that could only be interpreted as merchant tyranny.

Finally, tobacco itself came to be seen as an enslaving staple, harmful to the land and its people, "a culture [said Thomas Jefferson] productive of infinite wretchedness." Tobacco culture, in other words, was an agricultural analogue to the radical country view. Here Breen draws a useful distinction between country ideology in its descriptive sense (that is, as a general model for social thinking), and "radical" country ideology (the political ideology described by Bailyn and Wood).[20] Tobacco culture did not invent radical country ideology; rather, it stocked the shelves of Virginia's political culture with an agrarian language of analogous values and stresses, so that on the eve of the Revolution, the two discourses merged and planters spoke of tobacco, merchants, and Parliament as though they had all conspired to rob them of their liberty.

Even as South Carolina's native merchants' commercial world was ruled by a country etiquette of social relations, so the mental world of South Carolina's planter elite, in marked contrast to that of Virginia's tobacco planter gentry, was far more urban, commercial, even bourgeois. For South Carolina's planters (although they did manage to become revolutionaries), the rice and indigo growing experience lacked the radical potential of the tobacco culture experience of the Chesapeake.

Unlike Virginia's tobacco growers, planters were not in daily contact with their crop. More like Caribbean sugar lords, they were absentees, spending up to nine months out of twelve in Charleston, South Carolina's busy port, commercial, and social center. Here they built elaborate townhouses as their chief residences. (The plantation house was usually a serviceable, unimposing building. The grand plantation "big house" was a nineteenth-century phenomenon.) For them the quaint saying that the Ashley and Cooper Rivers meet at Charleston to form the Atlantic Ocean expressed a psychological truth about the world's center. The year was governed not by the growing seasons, but by Charleston's social seasons.[21]

It began in February with the races, which culminated with the famous Carolina Jockey Club trials for purses of up to £1000 sterling. Many a fortune was won or lost on the day's outcome. Daily races held at the Quarterhouse and Newmarket and at the York courses kept the gentlemen's gambling instincts active. When interest in horseflesh paled, there was always cock fighting and cards.

Society also offered more genteel pursuits. The Saint Cecilia Society held weekly concerts played by the best musicians obtainable. Theater was extremely popular, and in 1773–74, the American Theatre Company gave Charleston arguably the colonial stage's most brilliant season, producing some seventy-seven plays, farces, and operas. Dancing, too, was a favorite pastime, and the Assembly [Society] met twice a week during the season to entertain the ladies and gentlemen with dining, dancing, and cardplaying.

"Pray, what is your Assembly about—Dancing?" punned Henry Laurens to an East Florida legislator in 1763. "Ours [the General Assembly] breaks up next week for that and another amusement [horseracing] which you know is due to us in February."[22]

What the town's amusements didn't supply, Charleston's many social clubs did. The city had more private and charitable societies than any other eighteenth-century American city. Most gentlemen belonged to several. Some were purely social. Quincey mentions "cards, feasting, and indifferent wines" and conversation at the Monday night and Friday night clubs. Others turned on a patriotic or charitable feature, such as the Sons of St. Patrick and the Mt. Sion [Academy] Society, for deserving sons of backwoods planters. But all included feasting and entertainments and were essentially social in nature.[23] This highly interactive, interconnected, cosmopolitan social world was a far cry from the solitary, independent, rural world of the Virginia tobacco grower.

Entertaining at home (where most of Charleston's social life took place) had a similar tone of bourgeois sociability and display. Many guests wined and dined at sumptuous tables. Meals were highly ritualized, formal affairs, featuring elaborate toasts, stylized manners, and genteelly conventional conversation. Especially revealing from the point of view of planter attitudes to law and public policy was this subject's absence from table talk. Political discussions at table were discouraged by all present as positively impolite. Discussion of issues might develop into a discussion of political principles with more heat than light to shed. This practice was probably not simply a nonexclusionary mannerism adopted in the company of ladies, but reflected an aversion for a speculative approach to politics.[24]

Mark Kaplanoff's study of South Carolina planter-legislators in the 1790s notes a positive antipathy toward political philosophy. We have no records of legislative debates, but in their public discourse planters constantly denigrated political theories and theorists. Charleston's most acid critic noted that "the gentlemen (planters and merchants) are mostly men of the turf and gamesters. Political inquiries and philosophical disquisitions are too laborious for them." This is not to say that South Carolina planters were uninterested in politics; but, believing that law is the outcome not of speculative but of practical reasoning, chose to approach public business in a day-to-day, ad hoc, and deliberately nonideological way.[25]

In ordinary discourse, planters' conversation followed a commercial track. "The general topics of conversation," observed Josiah Quincey, when not of Negroes, "are of the price of indigo and rice. I was surprised to find this so general."[26] Planters' psychological distance from the crop production side of their livelihood is easy to understand. Overseers took charge of the daily running of plantations, even when the planter was in residence. The view we have of the planter from diaries, letters, and ledgers is that of a manager, keeping accounts of productivity, statistics on slaves, and balance sheets of profits and losses.

Every plantation typically had a small office building flanking the main house, where the master spent the main part of his working day. Full-time absentees, such as Ralph Izard, put even this much of the planter's role in the hands of another, thereby doubly abstracting himself from an agrarian context. It is not surprising, when one contemplates the style of life he had to support and his relative noninvolvement with the cultivation side of things, that the planter's primary relationship to his staple was not as a crop but as a commodity.

James M. Clifton, whose study of antebellum rice culture in South Carolina is based on the most complete set of plantation records in existence, writes that "even in the colonial era, South Carolina rice plantations were already factories-in-the-field . . . [with] monetary profits the chief concern of the owners." Quite different indeed was this from eighteenth-century Virginia tobacco plantations—described by one planter as "little Fortress[es] of Independency."[27]

Clifton's market-minded planter image is supported by the comparative work of John E. Crowley, who finds the lowcountry attitude toward land both more liberal (that is, less agrarian, or "feudal") and more commercial than that of the South Carolina backcountry, the Chesapeake, the Middle States, or New England for the same period. By analyzing testamentary strategies for the 1730s, 1760s, and 1790s, Crowley finds that patriarchal trends evident in other inheritance studies for the colonial period, such as favoring males over females, eldest sons over younger sons, and limiting the widow's right in real property were progressively attenuated in South Carolina. Land was not a patrimony to be kept together to ensure the next generation's wealth and social status, but a volatile commodity in a highly commercialized economy.

In fact, propertied families in lowcountry South Carolina usually had more wealth in slaves than in land. Consequently, they willed both land and slaves in ways to ensure maximum liquidity and to achieve the movement of assets between land and commerce with minimum restrictions. Hence, the tendency in both custom and law (South Carolina was the only royal colony to abolish entail before the Revolution, and most nearly to approach absolute equality for the sexes in its reformed law of intestacy after Independence) was to limit hereditary restrictions that could complicate the availability and reliability of credit.[28]

Moreover, planters (although predictably more patriarchal) over time became more like merchants and tradesmen in their testamentary treatment of land.

> The low interest in status from land was characteristic even of the colony's [planting] elite. The practice of building mansions on plantations had lapsed by mid-century, and was not renewed until the turn of the century. Meanwhile, architectural interest focused on townhouses. David Ramsey measured this inconsequence of South Carolina's architecture outside Charleston by the absence of brick from any but public buildings. Few plantations had names before the 1790s, and real estate was usually devised by references to general acreage or specific location without the homestead itself being identified.[29]

With their recent overseas wealth, their abstraction from day-to-day crop production, and self-conscious cultivation of urbane sociability, the merchant-planter elite of South Carolina were more analogous to West Indian nabobs than to Virginia planter aristocrats. Although frequently characterized as a landed upper class, such characterizations are either contradictory (one-quarter of all colonial planters listed Charleston as their residence, while three-quarters of the merchants and traders owned slaves) or anachronistic (nineteenth-century developments extrapolated to the eighteenth century).[30]

The lowcountry colonial South Carolina planter and merchant drew his social status from wealth. Whether based in land, slaves, or commerce, the important features of wealth were its abundance and the character of the relations necessary to sustain it. Hence, growing a crop lacked the symbolic power it held in the Chesapeake. In South Carolina's intensely commercial agriculture, getting the best return on the crop was what counted. The planters are "full of Money," quipped Henry Laurens, and they wanted more. Only a group who understood, accepted, and approved of market values could have cooperated to hold back their rice crop (as they did in 1755) in order to inflate its price. Henry Laurens complained to his Bristol correspondents that "A great deal [of rice] is now ready for Market, but the Planters don't choose to part with it hoping something may turn up still in their favour."[31] Hence, the elite merchant or planter of South Carolina could and did avow a code of gentlemanly, country etiquette in business dealings, while at the same time taking a liberal, commercial view of his property.

Of course, getting rich was the first requirement for social success in South Carolina. But for colonial planters and merchants of enumerated crops like rice and indigo, getting rich meant working within the restrictions of Britain's imperial system. Trade and politics were inseparable in such a political economy. Because it supplies the best example, the story of rice will be told in the next chapter, but indigo can give a brief introduction to the constraints that affected a crop's profitability, and within which merchant-planters had to plan political strategies.

Indigo was the colony's second largest export. Exports grew from 112,900 to 662,000 pounds exported between the years 1747 and 1772. The crucial year, 1775, was actually South Carolina's biggest year ever, when the colony exported over a million pounds' dry weight of the product.[32] Indigo was the perfect complement to rice. Not only did it thrive in the Carolina climate and soil, its growing season occurred during the off-season for rice. Thus, precious labor could be kept productive throughout the year.

The commercial success of indigo can be traced to several factors, among them war policies and the doctrine of mercantilism. The War of Jenkins Ear that merged into the War of the Austrian Succession (1739–43), and which closed British ports to Spanish and French goods, gave Carolinians a virtual monopoly on the English indigo market and dramatically stimulated sales.[33] James Crockatt, a leading Charleston merchant until 1739, afterwards a London merchant, and a future agent for the colony, stimulated interest in the crop in England and production of the crop in South Carolina with publications on indigo culture in 1746 and 1747.[34]

When the Treaty of Aix-la-Chapelle in October 1748 cut sharply into South Carolina's exports by reopening international trade, Crockatt responded with a campaign to obtain relief for the Carolina growers. He produced another pamphlet, *Reasons for laying a Duty on French and Spanish Indigo, and Granting a Bounty on what is made in the British Plantations,* which he distributed among members of Parliament.[35] Concurrently, the Carolina merchants of London presented a petition requesting a crop subsidy to Parliament.[36] Despite some opposition in the pamphlet press,[37] the bounty bill passed.[38]

While international trade policies doubtless played a role in the overall development of Carolina's indigo industry, for the individual planter it was the subsidy that made the crop so profitable. Based on the average market price of 30 shillings currency per pound that Carolina growers obtained for their product between 1747 and 1777, the six pence sterling (3.5 shillings South Carolina currency) per pound bounty boosted returns by 11.6 percent.[39]

Both rice and indigo owed their favored status in Britain's commercial system to the effects of lobbying. Bit by bit, careful but insistent pressure by South Carolina planters and merchants in conjunction with British merchants who profited from the trade won exceptions to the prohibitions against direct shipment (in the case of rice) and special protective legislation (in the case of indigo). On the part of all concerned, the exercise was wholly one of economic interest. But the method, if not the motive, was a political one, and the lessons of lobbying were not lost on Carolinians, whose chief experience in foreign affairs before the Revolution was to be as commercial lobbyists.

DEVELOPING THE CAROLINA TRADE LOBBY, 1707–1769

In a parliamentary system in which every blade of grass and every acre of land had an elected spokesman, other forms of wealth had no such direct representation. The problem, therefore, for eighteenth-century British and colonial merchants and market-planters was how to get Parliament to pay attention to their commercial needs. The answer was a trade lobby.[1]

The concept probably originated in the right to petition for redress, and while the petition remained the standard form of address, in the hands of lobbyists its mode was subtly transformed from a plea into a politely insistent form of bargaining. Not only commercial interests, but religious dissidents and other unrepresented outsiders practiced interest group politics. Quakers, for example, used very sophisticated, and quite secular, methods for drawing Parliament's attention to their particular problems not shared by the empire as a whole.[2]

But in a commercial state such as eighteenth-century Britain undeniably was, merchants' lobbies inevitably became the most powerful and most fully developed. They began in the late seventeenth and early eighteenth centuries as loose congeries of British merchants specializing in one or another of the American trades. They quickly grew to transatlantic proportions, broadening their constituency to include their colonial merchant correspondents and their market-producer clients.

If, on the American side, the corresponding merchants were merely agents of British houses (as in Virginia) rather than merchants with businesses indigenous to the province, the lobby remained an English operation and had no real impact beyond England's boundaries. Nor would Virginia's great planter-rulers, embedded as they were in an agrarian cast of mind, have been receptive to what was essentially an alien, commercial discourse.

In contrast to Virginia, South Carolina had a thriving merchant community, a market-minded planter elite, and an intensely commercial economy. Moreover, the presence of a class of indigenous merchant and market-planter politicians that formed the colonial side of the network meant the means for spreading interest group politics as a formal strategy into the local political culture was in place. Hence, commercial lobbying, although originally devised as a craft to cope with commercial problems only, became by the late 1760s a familiar, accepted, available, and largely successful means for coping with political problems as well.

South Carolina, of course, was not alone in having a vital native merchant community.[3] Philadelphia's highly developed merchant class, however, deferred both socially and politically to the newly minted gentry (many of whose families made their fortunes in trade only to distance themselves from it), thereby placing themselves among the ruled. Whatever ideas, attitudes, or administrative techniques from the commercial sphere they might have adapted to politics, therefore, remained untapped. The same is even more true of New York, where surviving records of an active Chamber of Commerce attest to merchant vigor and political potential. But the very existence of a separate merchant organization indicates a sense that business and government existed apart. New York, like Pennsylvania, was ruled by an elite that, despite party rivalries, considered government the province of its leisure class.

In New England, despite a powerful merchant class in Boston, a dispersed government on the township system prevented anything like a single, secular influence gaining predominance, and particularly not an urban, commercial, merchant-dominated interest, as representation in the General Court was weighed heavily in favor of rural populations.

South Carolina, on the other hand, possessed a unique combination of conditions that predisposed it to the reception of commercially originated ideas, attitudes, methods, and models: an urban center (Charleston), where all government, administrative, trade, and social power focused; a socially homogeneous merchant-planter elite; a native merchant elite, accustomed to local political leadership; and a society and politics still open to men of capital and enterprise. These conditions, plus the chance element of timing, which found a nonideological political culture maturing alongside a culture of commerce, inclined the strategy of lobbying to fall naturally, equally, and almost imperceptibly into the context of both, where it provided a behavioral language available and, because already acceptable, legitimate for a future discourse.

By the final decade before the Revolution, the Carolina lobby had developed from a London-centered and -directed interest on the order of the West Indian and Chesapeake models, to a bipolar organization operating on two fronts. By the late 1760s, a vital Charleston lobby emerged whose native merchant and planter members at first imitated but finally innovated on the techniques of its London teacher. Energetic and successful, the Charleston lobby spread its methods and attitudes among a receptive planter majority, finally becoming a behavioral paradigm for subsequent political problem-solving.

The emergence and character of the lobbying strategy are traced in three sections. The first section describes the development of an organized, London-directed Carolina lobby around the long-term campaign to free the rice trade from the restrictions of the Navigation Acts. The second section traces the development of a local lobby, organized to do battle with a corrupt customs official. The latter experience supplied vital leadership experience as well as the opportunity to innovate on traditional lobbying practices. For South Carolina, it marked the maturation of a self-conscious, organized lobby politics as the method of choice for political problem-solving. The third section considers the contribution that other earlier lobbying experiences, not related to overseas trade, and directly involving assemblymen (and their out-of-doors rivals) in a considerable amount of lobbying, may have made. Might not such a domestic experience, logically closer to the state's political culture than the commercial sphere, better account for the behavior described here? The question is explored using the land speculation dispute of the 1730s.

I

The beginning of South Carolina's mercantile lobby can be traced to 1712, when the legislature passed an act appointing the colony's first permanent agent to Parliament. The act's preamble acknowledged that trade was the colony's foremost concern, since the act's purpose was to remove "the pressure which the Trade of this colony now lies under . . . by a fair and impartial representation of the same to the Parliament of Great Britain."[4] It is worth noting that what is being represented is not persons, but interests.

Although the agent subsequently came to represent all of the colony's interests (at least those recognized by the Royal Assembly) before Parliament, initially at least he was South Carolina's first paid trade lobbyist. The agent received his instructions from a legislative Committee of Correspondence. He then laid the colony's concerns before the Board of Trade, an agency that acted as a clearinghouse for all the various complaints and demands coming from all the agents of His Majesty's plantations in America. Because local merchants could not claim the agent as their sole advocate with the Board of Trade, they soon found it advantageous to supplement this official channel with an informal network of British (chiefly London and Bristol) merchants engaged in the Carolina trade.

An inspection of the Board of Trade and parliamentary records shows that a Carolina lobby existed in London from about 1707.[5] It had no formal organization, but grew out of routine daily associations at the Carolina Coffee House and along "Carolina Walk" at the Royal Exchange. Here merchants gathered to conduct business, exchange news, receive letters, and occasionally mobilize in response to their Charleston counterparts' request for political assistance. They might circulate petitions, promote interest in certain issues, notify their fellows of hearings, or organize a group to appear before the Board of Trade or a parliamentary committee.[6] It was not unusual for merchants to solicit assistance from other trade lobbies, where an interest was shared, in order to expand the base of support for the issue at hand.[7]

On their side of the water, Charleston merchants individually wrote to their London business "friends" about their concerns, but before the 1760s, did not find it necessary to organize locally. Indeed, Robert Pringle, a prominent merchant of the 1740s and 1750s, claimed Charleston's mercantile community was too internally divided to sustain collective action. A case in point occurred in 1744, when the Commons House of Assembly's planter majority pushed through a tax bill to which merchants took exception. Writing to his brother and trading partner in London, Andrew Pringle, Robert complained that the new law required local merchants to swear to an oath "which is Levell'd internily against the Trading people of this town & which no Trading Person can clearly Swear to."[8]

Initially cooperating in opposition to the measure, Pringle and his fellow Charleston merchants petitioned the governor against the bill immediately upon its passage and planned to carry the fight for disallowance to the king and Privy Council. But within two months, the merchants' consensus had disintegrated. The petition either never materialized or failed to garner enough signatures, for "a Great many [now] draw back and won't subscribe to it, so am afraid will Drop & that here will be nothing done in it, & is like all the Rest of Our Carolina affairs where People are never steady or unanimous in any one thing."[9]

Andrew Pringle, a member of the Carolina lobby in London, responded with the suggestion that Charleston merchants organize and fund a local pressure group on the London model. Robert replied, "Your observation on Raizing a fund for the Defraying of Expence of public Operations in Behalf of Trade or other Merchants in the Plantation Trade is certainly verry good & just & which Could I prevail on People here in Trade To join and agree on would be greatly for the advantage of this Province & the Trade thereof." But, Pringle went on, "there is not a place perhaps in the Brittish Dominions where there is so little Good Harmony, Sociableness, & Unanimity Amongst Persons in Trade as in this town of Charles Town."[10] Had such an organization been formed, it would have been the first provincial Chamber of Commerce on record.

The problem of merchant divisions that Pringle described was endemic to any local issue where interests were affected differently. In 1764, for example, the Commons House of Assembly passed a Negro Duty Act that imposed a heavy tax on all Negroes imported after 1765 and forbade importation after 1766 for three years.[11] Henry Laurens, prominent merchant member of the Commons House, claimed the bill was the work of a "junto" and strove to delay a vote until "the general voice of our constituents might be heard." But there was no general voice, since the duty favored some traders and hurt others. It was inimical to the slave trade, but could be counted on to drive up prices in the short run. Laurens pointedly asked House member Samuel Brailsford, who was in the Bristol slave trade and supported the bill, if he planned to sell any more Negroes "at the Crisis." Laurens himself opposed the bill as he was both expanding his own planting operations and investing in land for speculation, and feared the prohibition would slow settlement and cultivation. Other merchant-creditors, however, supported the bill since the prohibition would enable established planters to clear their debts. Hence, merchants' divisions were not to be wondered at.[12]

But while internal discord may have precluded unified action on home issues, the transatlantic lobby, focusing on imperial trade policies and dominated by the London side of the trade, went forward with considerable long-range cooperation and success. As their junior partners, Charleston merchants observed the methods of successful lobbying while they slowly acquired the confidence they would later need to assume a lobbying posture of their own. One outstandingly instructive success among all the lobbying efforts was the ongoing effort to obtain favorable concessions on rice trade restrictions.

Rice had been freely exported to Europe until it was designated an enumerated commodity in 1704 and thus restricted to English bottoms and English ports by the terms of the Navigation Acts.[13] This measure was a serious disadvantage to South Carolina. England consumed very little rice, so most of it had to be reexported to its natural markets in northern Europe and the Iberian peninsula. In the latter case, the added freight costs, plus lost sales to Italian competitors (the indirect route to Catholic countries meant that rice harvests could not reach those markets in time for Lenten sales, and occasionally spoiled en route), were crippling southern European trade.[14]

In 1705 and again in 1717, Joseph Boone, the colony's agent, tried to obtain a parliamentary act permitting direct shipment to points south of Cape Finisterre, but without success. The chief reason for South Carolina's 1712 statute creating a permanent agent paid by the legislature was to attempt to remove rice from Britain's list of enumerated goods altogether and relieve "the pressure which the Trade of this colony now lies under."[15]

In 1722, British merchants trading with Carolina, Spain, and Portugal sent a petition supported by Horace Walpole, auditor general of plantation revenues and a member of Parliament, to the Board of Trade. The board presented it to the House of Commons and the Treasury, but neither acted.[16] In 1724, South Carolina's agent, Samuel Wragg, made the case for rice again, this time couched in a protest against a bill restricting South Carolina's trade to British-built ships.[17]

Finally, in 1729, the London merchants, supported by a petition from England's second largest city and port, Bristol, presented their case directly to the Treasury. At last a bill was brought into Parliament, becoming law in 1730. While the bill was in committee, Wragg appeared as a supporting witness. Since Wragg had made the same case unsuccessfully in 1724 in his capacity as colonial agent, Charleston merchants could not have failed to note that Parliament responded more readily to unified group pressure based on economic and voting-block power.[18]

While the new law exempted rice shipped to ports in southern Europe, markets in north Europe, Africa, and the French, Dutch, and Spanish settlements in the Caribbean and South America remained closed. Pressure to extend the exemption act to these markets began almost at once. In 1734, South Carolina's agent applied to the Georgia Board of Trustees for assistance. Lord Egmont responded in writing that the board "should always contribute our endeavors for the advancement of the interest of Carolina," but no bill was forthcoming.[19] Again, in 1744–45, South Carolina agent Peregrin Fury and Georgia agent William Knox submitted petitions to the Board of Trade, along with a merchants' petition "of the like nature," but the Commissioners for the Customs to whom they were referred turned down the appeals.[20]

The commissioners recognized that this request threatened to virtually abrogate the navigation laws. In their report to the Board of Trade, the Lords Commissioners of the Custom pointed out that "the granting of what was desired would require such great alterations in the laws relating to the Trade of Plantations, they could not take it upon themselves to judge how it might affect the general trade and navigation of this Kingdom."[21]

There the matter rested until the events of the Seven Years' War presented a new opportunity to reopen the question. Inspired by the new markets rice found in the captured islands of Guadeloupe, Martinique, St. Lucia, and Cuba, the agents for South Carolina and Georgia in 1763 let loose a new spate of memorials.[22] Just who wanted to keep the captured islands, who wanted to trade them for Canada and Florida, and why, is still a matter of conjecture. The West Indian lobby has been credited with shaping the final decision, although West Indian opinion was divided. Younger planters on the make wanted to keep them, but more established (and more politically powerful) planters, fearing increased competition, wanted them returned.[23] Ultimately, national security and distrust of France tipped the scales, yet the commercial consequences loomed large and brought out numerous opposing interests, who used what influence they could muster to press their arguments forward.[24]

The South Carolina rice interests, who saw an opportunity to legislate away the remaining trade restrictions on their crop, were among them. Indeed, the captured islands represented a considerable commercial asset. In 1762, rice exports from South Carolina to Guadeloupe exceeded 1,500 barrels, and in 1763 Havana took off 1,490 barrels, but the 14,000 barrels estimated by a London merchant to have been consumed by the foreign islands in the possession of Great Britain in 1763 seems too high. Carolina traders in London benefited in several ways: in added freights for their ships, in increased inter-island trade, but chiefly in attracting Spanish specie, since any foreign bullion acquired by colonials found its way into their pockets as commissions on purchase of English manufactures.[25] Therefore, when the terms of the Treaty of Paris returned these islands to France and Spain in exchange for Canada and Florida, merchants on both sides of the water were jealous to retain the trade.[26]

Charles Garth, South Carolina's agent from 1762, first approached the London merchants for a direct rice trade bill, but found them unwilling to forfeit their commissions for reexporting to the northern European markets. Once the request was pared to foreign markets in the Caribbean, South America, Madeira, the Canaries, and other African islands only, London's Carolina traders willingly lent their support.[27]

This hurdle cleared, objections were raised by the colonial agents and trade lobbies for some of the northern colonies whose wheat trade might be hurt.[28] The debate delayed a decision for over a year and must have doubly offended South Carolinians, both for the delay and because wheat, being unenumerated, already enjoyed free export to any port in the world. No doubt John Rutledge remembered it ten years later, when he led South Carolina's delegation in radical opposition to the Continental Congress's 1774 Association draft agreements, which barred rice but not wheat from export. The 1774 episode must have seemed to Rutledge to be nothing more than a replay of this earlier, purely interest-motivated struggle.[29]

When the arguments of the wheat trade interest had been overcome, a bill was brought in and the exemption (for rice exports from South Carolina and Georgia) became law in 1764.[30] Since the Board of Trade had disapproved a petition from the colonial agents of South Carolina and Georgia on February 14, 1764,[31] but gave their approval when the London and Bristol lobbies joined the action, it must have been clear to Carolinians that the key to success lay in unified interest group politics, and not in the less influential work of the colonial agents alone, although when working with the merchants they did supply crucial leadership and coordination.[32]

Actually, there were at least two political lessons available from the lobbying experience, one theoretical, the other tactical. As we have already seen, South Carolina's merchants and commercial planters were of a market cast of mind. With one more intellectual step, some may have seen power as only a commodity that was unequally distributed. In the power relationship with Westminster, Carolinians had virtually none. Legislation offered a remedy for the *effects* of unequal power, but not for the power imbalance itself. Carolina's merchant and planter leaders might petition; they might even press. These tactics did not question the underlying principle (sovereignty) or structure (the state) of power. But inherent in the practice of bargaining for relief from its effects lay the coiled idea of renegotiating power itself. The problem at this point, however, was not to devise a new theory of power, but to find a means to alleviate its undesired consequences. Such thinking, moreover, was unlikely to be accepted by minds suspicious and a bit contemptuous of theoretical questions, those that asked "why" instead of "how."

The other lesson, the more immediate one of technique, spoke to the "how" question. Success lay less in persuading Parliament of the abstract justice of their requests (no request, no matter how just, would be entertained if it ran counter to the interests of Britain) than in convincing first the various ministerial commissions and then Parliament that the lobby spoke for many, and that they spoke in a single voice. It was obviously important that outwardly the lobby appear united, harmonious, confident, and purposive. Yet lobby leaders must be alert to inward divisions, constantly aware that secondary, but often quite jarring, interests within the group must be negotiated in such a way that the common interest remain first. Lacking the power to coerce, lobby leaders chose balancing, trade-offs, and co-option (and sometimes cruder methods of social or professional ostracism), juggling internal strains with one hand while holding up a mask of unanimity with the other. South Carolina's merchant and planter politicians became deft at both.

Consequently, by 1765, Charleston's leadership had learned that a fragmented position was a weak one. One way to foster unity in the ranks was to balance representation at the top. It may be only a coincidence, but South Carolina's delegation to the Stamp Act Congress consisted of a merchant, a lawyer, and a planter—the three major economic interests of the lowcountry elite. And the twelve leaders of the Commons House of Assembly between 1762 and 1765 included four merchants, four lawyers, and four planters.[33]

These examples of interest representation from the three main occupational groups in the ruling population indicate that lobbying principles were taking hold among political elites. (The mechanical interest would soon be represented on local committees, but no artisan ever achieved a place among the leadership. That group generally united behind an elite figure like Christopher Gadsden, who acted as their spokesman.) However, the homework on learning the fundamentals of lobbying as a strategy was largely completed by the mid-1760s.

II

While provincial lobbying practices would doubtless have continued to mature without it, one more crisis occurred that conclusively demonstrated the power of the lobby as a political problem-solver, that validated its reception, and that ensured the strategy's perpetuation as a political paradigm. That crisis was set in motion on March 20, 1767, with the arrival of the colony's new customs collector, Daniel Moore.[34]

Moore arrived in Charleston at a time when South Carolina's government was gaining ground along several fronts by bringing home as much control over its internal affairs as possible. In order that the colony might choose its own sheriffs (necessary to meet backcountry demands for courts and jails), the General Assembly was negotiating with the colony's

Crown-appointed provost marshal to sell his office to the province for £4,000 sterling. Efforts to secure repeal of the 1764 Currency Act, which hampered domestic trade by restricting the money supply, seemed to have a good chance of succeeding. Charleston itself was in a euphoria of self-congratulation, having joyously celebrated the first anniversary of the Stamp Act repeal only two days before. Business was booming, and Charleston merchants could afford new chariots and the finest Madeira wines for their own tables.[35] They had bid a respectful farewell to acting custom's officer Edwards Davis, who despite having to follow in office the extremely popular (and indulgent) Hector Bereger de Beaufain, and despite some tensions over enforcing new regulations, had handled his office with restraint and tact.[36]

But merchant confidence based on past satisfactory relations with customs officials was soon shaken. Barely a fortnight after his arrival, on April 4, Moore charged the merchant Paul Townsend 20 shillings currency to execute a hemp certificate, a service for which no fee should have been assessed. Again, on April 16 and 18, Moore improperly charged John Ward and another merchant, Aaron Loocock, for bounty certificates. Then, on May 14, Moore demanded 21 shillings to register a plantation schooner, a small plantation-to-market vessel, for which no registration was required.[37]

On May 16, Moore ordered the schooner *Active*, owned by the merchant James Gordon, seized for not having the proper clearances. As the schooner was used wholly between Winyah (Georgetown County) and Charleston, entirely within the waters of one province, it was outside the terms of the 1763 Navigation Act requiring such clearances when provincial boundaries were crossed. Vice Admiralty Judge Egerton Leigh dismissed the charges when they came before him, but certified that seizure had been made with "probable cause," meaning there had been reasonable grounds to believe that the vessel was in violation of the law. Therefore, Gordon had to pay all his costs in the suit and could not countersue for damages.[38]

These incidents, and numerous lesser ones, at last galvanized Charleston's merchants into a political action group. They chose a "Committee of Seven," consisting of important export merchants Gabriel Manigault, John Neufville, John Chapman, John Gordon, Thomas Shirley, and Henry Laurens, "in the Name and on Behalf of the whole."[39] On May 26, this select committee met with Moore to express their grievances and to propose establishment of a mutually agreed-on schedule of fees to avoid future disputes. Moore responded with assurances, but later alleged that the committee's true purpose was to reform the customhouse, an impertinence he promised to answer by reforming Charleston's trade.

The personal confrontations between Moore and the merchants escalated throughout June as the excessive and capricious fees continued. The issue peaked in late July, when Moore ordered the port's searcher, George Roupell, to seize two vessels belonging to Henry Laurens, the *Wambaw* and the *Broughton Island Packet,* for lack of lumber bonds. In both cases the lumber was used for ballast on the return trip from Laurens's Alatamaha, Georgia plantation. In the former case, however, the lumber was also intended for sale in Charleston. Since there was not a customhouse within thirty miles of Alatamaha, Laurens attempted to compensate for sailing without a bond by obtaining a certificate signed by two local magistrates. The bonded certificate set forth these circumstances and further declared that, immediately on arrival in Charleston, Laurens would enter the lumber's value at the customhouse and pay the fees. Moore, however, refused to accept the certificate as a proper instrument, and ordered the schooner and its cargo libeled.[40]

The case of the *Broughton Island Packet* differed from the *Wambaw* in only one particular. The firewood laden for the return voyage was intended for ballast only. When both cases went before the Vice Admiralty Court, Judge Egerton Leigh ordered the *Wambaw* and her cargo condemned and sold at public auction. Leigh accepted the ballast argument in the *Broughton Island Packet* case, but did not certify that there had been "probable cause" for the seizure. This left Roupell open to a damage suit, which Laurens forthwith filed.[41]

Three days after the Laurens trials, on September 3, the assistant judge to the Court of General Sessions, Robert Pringle, ordered Moore to post a recognizance bond. It was related to a June 16 information action filed by merchant John Logan against Moore for extorting fees. Rather than post the bond, Moore fled the colony sometime between this date and September 8, when he arrived in Savannah. He claimed he fled from mob action (Henry Laurens tweaked Moore's nose outside the customhouse, to approving shouts of merchant onlookers), but he probably also knew he had little chance of an acquittal from a local jury.[42]

The grand jury did indeed bring in a true bill of indictment against Moore on October 3. But the merchants, now thoroughly unified in their anger and alarm, could not relax. Although Moore was gone, he raised charges against the merchants' lobby in a letter to the Treasury before his departure and in a memorial to the Treasury after his arrival in England. Fearing that unless they made their case in London Moore would be sent back among them to resume his tactics of economic terrorism, the merchants seized the initiative.[43]

Their first stratagem was to gain the endorsement of the colony's legislature, in order to give credibility to their complaints and to broaden their constituency, in theory at least, to the colony's entire British manufactures-buying population. On September 29, the Committee of Correspondence for the Commons House of Assembly addressed a letter to the colony's agent, Charles Garth, recommending the merchants' cause to him since "the Committee look upon the whole Province to be much obliged to those Gentlemen, for their steady Opposition to the Extortion and Rapacity of an Officer . . . in His Majesty's Customs."[44]

Since a colonial lobby could not mobilize voting power or warn of reduced customs as could the London lobby, it turned instead to the weapon of buying power. (Note, too, that this provincial legislative committee acted like the colonial equivalent of the Board of Trade, receiving complaints, choosing among them, and assigning them to the proper agency. This point will be enlarged on in chapter 6.)

The merchants' next move was to hire their own agent (they chose Garth) and set up direct correspondence with him. The merchants did so in a letter setting forth their case in detail. True to the lobbying methods learned from their London correspondents, the Charleston merchants proposed to act as suppliers of information only. "Unacquainted as we are with the Mode of proceeding in such cases, we rely more on the Detail of Facts with which we have furnished you."[45]

True to another traditional lobbying method, the merchants presented the case in terms meant only to explain Moore's illegal infringements on their interest. They did not link their case to any larger principles of liberty. Such a connection would have shifted the ground from interest to ideology, grounds that most commercial men considered entirely unrelated to either a business lobby's actuating principles or its goals.[46]

The merchants appointed a smaller committee, perhaps the six men who represented them with Moore. This core group was responsible for coordinating the local campaign against Moore, for conducting correspondence with Garth, and for setting up and administering a war chest to cover Garth's fee and expenses.[47] One hundred and eleven merchants—Charleston's entire trading community—signed the initial letter to Garth. Only Miles Brewton abstained because of a family connection with Moore.[48]

This display of solidarity cannot be fully explained by simple uniformity of narrow economic interest. Captain James Hawker, a deponent in the case by virtue of his command of His Majesty's Ship of War the *Sardoine* that seized the *Active*, alleged that the letter was carried door to door and signatures demanded without a reading. Those who protested were "in their own

Phrase, to be marked as Black Sheep."[49] By using ostracism both to enforce a policy and as a judgment, the merchants' association was acting in both a legislative and a judicial capacity, and, in a very rudimentary sense, was erecting a new political structure. Here we can discern the first faint outlines of the lobby as a protolegislature, a point developed in chapter 5.

These intimations, however, were probably not obvious to the participants. Rather, they were following the lobby behavioral model, which, in the hands of the London merchants, had demonstrated such success. Unanimity added effective weight to argument; hence, even so crude a tactic as threatened ostracism was acceptable if applied to obtain the necessary consensus.

Having obtained a consensus among the merchant community, the lobby then sought to expand its base. For this purpose, the most formidable weapon in the lobby's arsenal proved to be a pamphlet campaign, beginning with a tract entitled *A Representation of Facts*. Some forty-three pages long, the pamphlet described the dispute with Moore through a series of documents, vouchers, and affidavits. Although Henry Laurens was its principal author, some twenty-nine merchants (over one-fourth of Charleston's entire trading community) either supplied direct testimony or subscribed as witnesses.

The pamphlet's style was well chosen. Avoiding the weaknesses of polemics, the pamphlet based its case on documented evidence and presented it in dispassionate language. One wonders if John Rutledge, the fine legal mind who later chaired the committee of detail for the new federal Constitution and was among the lawyers retained by the merchants' lobby, might not have devised the format.[50]

Once printed, *A Representation of Facts* was privately distributed. In keeping with traditional British lobbying methods, no appeal to the public was made. No notice of the pamphlet's publication was placed in any Charleston newspaper. Instead, the merchants' committee sent twelve copies to Charles Garth, presumably to be distributed to members of the Board of Trade or the Treasury and other potentially sympathetic government officials. Laurens distributed at least nine copies among his British correspondents. Presumably, other merchants did likewise.[51]

The lobby would not depart from tradition by going public until the next year, following the seizure and libel of yet a third vessel belonging to Henry Laurens called the *Ann*. Shifting the focus of the struggle with customs from Daniel Moore to Vice Admiralty Judge (and Attorney General) Egerton Leigh, and using the same documentary format as the earlier pamphlet,

Laurens compiled an account of the ship *Ann*, which he published first in Philadelphia in November 1768.[52] He was not satisfied with certain editorial deletions made in the Philadelphia edition, and so reissued an expanded version in Charleston shortly afterwards that contained a summary of the merchants' difficulties the year before.[53] Laurens had come to believe that all British merchants' interest, not merely that of Charleston, was at stake. As he put it, he hoped the case of the *Ann* "will not be called Mr. Laurens', but the case of the British merchants trading to America."[54]

Broadening the base of support to include merchants not directly interested in the issue was not new, but this time Laurens also attempted to enlist public opinion for the cause. He placed notices of the publication and sale of *Extracts* in Boston, Philadelphia, Charleston, and London newspapers.[55] By the time of the publication of *Appendix to the Extracts,* his fifth and final pamphlet on the subject, Laurens aimed at distribution "through the principal Towns and Cities on the [American] Continent" and abroad.[56]

During the trial of the *Ann,* Judge Leigh made several sarcastic references from the bench to Charleston's "Patriotic Merchants," whose motives he clearly doubted. He threatened to prosecute the lobby for "Maintenance and illegal Combinations," alluding to Moore's allegations that he was denied an adequate defense because the merchants had retained all the colony's most able counsel, and that the town's remaining lawyers had resolved among themselves not to plead on the part of the Crown.[57]

Leigh's remark struck a nerve on several levels. One was the eighteenth-century independent merchant's distaste for the whole concept of "combinations" as experienced in trade. Monopolies (such as the greatly disliked East India Trading Company) both threatened his independence and smacked of unfair competition. The second level had to do with the lobby's nonideological role already discussed. The third involved the eighteenth century's general execration of "party" politics. The merchants denied that their lobby had political goals and that any of their actions were motivated by a party spirit. "Merchants have always labored for harmony," protested Henry Laurens, and never had the group acted from "an affected Patriotic Zeal . . . [in order] to keep alive the flame of discord and opposition."[58]

But the nerve of merchant honor was not the important one, or at least not the legally significant one that Leigh meant to touch. Maintenance, according to Coke, "signifieth in law a taking in hand, bearing up or upholding of quarrels and sides" by persons who have no legitimate interest in the civil proceedings.[59] In Leigh's view, no lobby could have standing in law. Moreover, since the case was against a Crown official, Leigh viewed the lobby as the equivalent of a formed, and therefore unconstitutional, opposition to His Majesty's government.[60] But despite Leigh's misgivings about the lobby, the case ended with an acquittal for Laurens. Leigh did certify a probable cause for the seizures, however, leaving Laurens feeling robbed of redress for the expense and injury.

The publication of *Appendix to the Extracts* concluded the long dispute that began with Daniel Moore and continued in the confrontation with the vice admiralty judge. For Laurens personally, the long controversy propelled him from a conservative merchant into the moderate Whig camp, among the men who would later strain across the gap between striving for redress to a commitment to revolution. For the Charleston merchants, their lobby succeeded to their fairest expectations, and apparently without help from its London side. Moore was dismissed from his post in the summer of 1769, and Egerton Leigh's ultimate resignation from the bench struck a blow to the concept of plural officeholding in South Carolina.[61]

Hence, the Charleston lobby, although matured by the Moore and Leigh episodes, was clearly the offspring of its London model. It adopted, at least initially, the English view of a mercantile lobby's legitimate concerns, its sphere of action, and its advisory and supportive role toward government. It experimented with certain departures, however, which had important political implications. One was that of carrying the campaign to the public. The lobby previously had restricted its appeals to informational tracts placed in the hands of government officials appointed to handle such matters. The practice was an implicit acknowledgment of government's sole authority, an unmistakable mark of mercantile deference. An appeal to public opinion, however, expanded the definition of a lobby's constituency to an entire consuming population, thereby adding an unsubtle economic (and potentially socially unstable) factor, a move that shifted the lobby from a petitioning to a pressure group.

Second, although popular sovereignty could not have been in the minds of the Charleston merchant leaders, the idea that political authority requires the people's consent slept comfortably there. The recruitment of popular opinion shifted the lobby from the status of a quasi-governmental agency and ally toward an early version of extraparliamentary formed opposition. Carrying the campaign to the public marked a key transitional phase in the conversion process of lobby politics to a general politics with a representational character.

One reason why the Charleston lobby changed in these small but extremely significant ways was because it was no longer strictly a merchants' lobby (see table 2.1). Among the papers forwarded to Garth by the mer-

Table 2.1
CHARLESTON LOBBY OF 1767

M = Merchant   P = Planter   L = Lawyer   S = Shipowner
A = Apothecary   B = Banker   Mfn. = Manufacturer

| | | COMMONS HOUSE OF ASSEMBLY SERVICE | |
| | | PERIOD OF | NO. OF ASSEMBLIES |
NAME	OCCUPATION	SERVICE*	ELECTED TO
Henry Laurens	M/P	1757–85	17
William Brampfield	M		
Thomas Ferguson	P	1762–86	18
David Deas	M/P	1749–75	4
John Deas			
Thomas Savage	M/P/S	1768–84	8
Thomas Smith	M/S	1751–55	2
John Gordon			
Thomas Gadsen	M/P	1762–65	2
Andrew Marr	M		
Thomas Bee	L/P	1762–88	18
Jno. Dawson	M/P	1776–99	3
Isaac Motte	P	1772–90	13
Ben. Guerard	L/P	1765–86	6
James Firkin			
M. Brewton	M/S	1765–75	8
James Skirving	P	1768–75	3
James Laurens	Mfn.		
George Livingston	P	1776–84	3
Richard Berisford	P/S	1749–64	3
Thomas Loughton Smith	M/P	1771–73	5
William Ancrum	M/P	1779–80	1
Isaac Mazyck	M/P/S	1736–70	23
Gabriel Manigault	M/P/S	1733–54	6
John Neufville	M/S	1775–83	6
John Champneys	M		
William Price	M/S		
John Ward	M/P/S	1772–83	9
William Brisbane	A/M/S	1749–54	2
William Maxwell	P/S	1762–65	2
John Edwards	M	1772–80	8
Thomas Smith	M/B	1769–75	6
Samuel Wainwright	P	1757–60	1
Robert Philp	M		
Benjamin Smith	M/P/S	1747–63	21
John Logan	M		
William Logan	M/S	1783–84	1
George Thomson			

*Some service not continuous

Source: W. B. Edgar et al., eds., *Biographical Directory of the South Carolina House of Representatives*, Vol. 2, *The Commons House of Assembly, 1692–1775*, and Vol. 3, *1775–1790* (Columbia, S.C., 1974, 1984); *Laurens Papers*, III. 30n, 523n; IV. 251n; V. 492, "The Remonstrance to Mark Robinson," December 4, 1767.

chants' committee was a copy of an anti-Moore remonstrance signed by "divers inhabitants of the Province," together with a petition for relief addressed to Governor Charles Montagu. We may consider the remonstrance's thirty-eight signers as core members of Charleston's lobby, since they responded to a newspaper advertisement inviting persons with an interest in the Moore affair to assemble at Dillon's Tavern. Not all were merchants. Some of the signers were planters and lawyers (many of whom were part owners of ships), an apothecary, and one moneylender. An analysis of the signers by occupation and public office gives some idea of how widespread the knowledge and practice of lobbying methods were among the political leadership by 1767.[62]

The Moore affair affected the local interest so broadly that by the time of the formation of the so-called merchants committee, lobby membership actually included a fair proportion of men who were exclusively planters (14%) and several lawyers with large planting interests (5.5%). Most of the lobby were or had been members of the Commons House of Assembly. The largest category was that of merchant with planting interests (55%). Those who were exclusively merchants comprised only 17 percent of the total.

Governor Montagu noted that Moore's opposition was broader than the merchants' only when he reported to Lord Shelburne that "merchants and planters objected to several fees levied at the customhouse" and that Moore had been unable to obtain an attorney's services because "no other Lawyer here would be concern'd for him, lest they should disoblige the Merchants and Planters."[63]

The important thing to these South Carolina merchant-planter politicians, however, was that they had discovered an informal method and a structural model for dealing with imperial problems, on the one hand, with implications for handling constituency problems on the other. Each successful use reinforced the pattern, so that it became the rational, habitual, "paradigmatic" way of organizing to meet new challenges. It is not necessary to analyze what is already an acceptable method to all. Only the cause in which it is enlisted need be scrutinized. In these questions (questions beginning with "why") radical country ideology or any other sort of ideology might play (although at this point it did not) as important a role in South Carolina as elsewhere.

Indeed, the lobby mentality shared certain assumptions with radical country ideology. Both assumed human nature to be self-interested and that power was never willingly shared. Moreover, since all final power in both political and imperial trade questions had always lain with London, the lobby developed few interior brakes on its behavior. As a politics, and in the hands of an impotent minority, the lobby had radical potential.

In the Moore and Leigh affairs of 1767–68, however, the lobby as a process, although relatively young, was clearly a highly effective set of plays in the delicate business of negotiating concessions in an empire that had to juggle commercial and imperial interests. In its structure, method, and attitude, the South Carolina lobby sat comfortably alongside the gentlemanly values of the elite's socially derived and wealth-sustained political culture. The lobby by 1768 was a largely unexamined and unarticulated behavioral trope—a commercial analogue for the South Carolina variety of the country tradition. The lobby model for political problem-solving can be described as a convention, not an ideology. Through long usage, a convention may become a tradition.[64] How the lobby tradition developed into a politics will be explored in chapters 5 and 6.

III

Finally, in arguing for the importance of the transatlantic lobby as the formative experience that produced the "South Carolina" model of politics, one must consider instances of lobbying taking place in the period before the 1760s and unrelated to the commercial lobby. Several local issues cropped up in the early part of the eighteenth century that involved an intensive lobbying of Parliament by the Assembly itself as well as by out-of-doors opponents. These experiences might well be considered to be a good deal closer to the state's evolving political culture. Land and paper money are two such issues. Paper money created disruptions throughout the colonial period, but the land speculation disputes of the 1730s make a manageable example.

Underpinning the great land boom of the 1730s was the township scheme, which promised to secure the southern frontier with an influx of new settlers; the 1720s growth in rice prices, which increased demand for good rice acreage; and the reopening of the land office, which released land hungers pent up for over a decade. At stake were large tracts of lands claimed under "baronial patents" granted during the proprietary period but never actually laid out. Many planters, leaders in the Commons House of Assembly, had bought rights to these lands and wanted the titles validated. In 1731, Royal Governor Robert Johnson signed a quitrents law that did just that, even though the Crown, seeking to encourage immigration, opposed engrossment of large tracts for speculative purposes. Johnson, who had been accused of attempting to engross land inside township boundaries intended for immigrants, may have been colluding with Commons leaders.[65]

On the opposing side stood the colony's surveyor general, James St. John; his deputies, Dr. Thomas Cooper and Benjamin Whitaker; several landowners in the affected area around Port Royal; and several assemblymen (among them Dr. Cooper) elected to work for a disallowance of the Quitrents Act. St. John and Whitaker (themselves probably complicit in land fraud through their silent partnership in a land speculation company) had resurveyed the disputed lands and sold some of them.

The St. John faction won the first round by obtaining the Board of Trade's recommendation to the Privy Council to repeal the Quitrents Act. The Commons House launched a countercampaign aimed at the Privy Council through its provincial agent and influential London friends. When the St. John's faction petitioned the Commons House to stop what they considered illegal land sales, the House retaliated by arresting St. John, Cooper, and even their lawyers for abridging its privileges. Chief Justice Wright, who issued habeas corpus writs to free the imprisoned surveyors, their lawyers, and several other luckless sympathizers, found his salary refused by the Commons House for several years afterwards, while petitions for his removal flew to London. Some of the dissident assemblymen elected to protest the land program in 1732, 1733, and 1734 were denied their seats by the Commons House committee on privileges and elections.

The rights and wrongs of the dispute have never been fully clarified, but the energy with which both sides marshaled a lobby to attempt to influence the Board of Trade and the Privy Council is undeniable. The difference for this discussion is twofold. First, the crude aggression of elite House leaders to squash opposition shows no comprehension of a lobby's potential for handling constituency problems. None of the finer points of interest reconciliation appear to have occurred to the ruling elite. And while each side argued in London that its view best served the colony's public interest, no pretense was made at home by assemblymen that the exercise was anything but a power struggle by the ins to defeat the outs over a matter of considerable private profit. Second, the opposition's momentum dissolved in the face of arrest and the Assembly's success with the Privy Council. A newspaper dispute in the *South Carolina Gazette* ended inconclusively in 1733, and by 1736 Benjamin Whitaker had regained his seat in the Commons House. No remnant of either "lobby" remained.

This early example of interest group activity does show that the individual elements of the lobby's craft were well known to South Carolina's leaders. And for sheer high-handedness, the Assembly's behavior is hard to beat. Yet both these factors, a touchiness about its privileges, and an elemental familiarity with the rudiments of lobbying may as easily be said to help account for the commercial lobby strategy's ready reception into the province's political culture. However, the integration of these elements into a systematic strategy, available for repeated use, failed to develop before the 1760s, and neither did the constituency conciliation refinements that would finally transform the strategy into a politics.

PART TWO

THE SCHOOL

THE CAROLINA LOBBY ABROAD, 1765–1774

It is doubtful that members of commercial lobbies thought of their activities as a politics, let alone an opposition politics. Indeed, they explicitly denied a political purpose, always stressing that interest alone was the sole object of their activity. One problem, then, is to trace the metamorphosis of the Carolina network from a group with strictly commercial reforms in mind to one acting from more principled motives for change.

A second problem is more prosaic. If one is to argue that the lobbying strategy became the politics of choice for native Carolina political leaders, one needs to show some of them hard at work as lobbyists on the British side of the network, from which strategic planning and leadership emanated. Here was the school in which the lessons of lobbying were to be learned firsthand.

For both these tasks, I have chosen a prosopographic approach to the events of the revolutionary crisis, broken down into two periods. This chapter covers the structure of the Carolina lobby and its drive for expressly commercial reforms in the 1765–74 period. The following chapter covers the 1774–76 period (to the failure of the merchants' petitions and the Rockingham secession from Parliament), and recounts the shift toward more principled goals. It is during this second period that the Carolina lobby takes on the character of a *political* opposition, and it is at this point that the network's British-American linkages begin to break down.

To demonstrate the links by which the lobbying strategy spread from England to South Carolina and to identify which events and in what ways lobbying in England contributed to an oppositionist politics in South Carolina, we turn to the Carolina lobby abroad.

The British side of the lobby consisted of native Carolinians living in England, British merchants in the Carolina trade, and the politicians and literati who desired a negotiated solution to the imperial crisis short of absolute submission. Active participation in this network taught Carolinians the tactics and flavor of out-of-doors opposition. Further, through a connection with Edmund Burke to the Rockingham Whigs, Carolinians could observe and assimilate tactics of parliamentary opposition as well.

By 1775, all colonial eyes (and, subsequently, most historians' eyes) were focused on the powerful London merchants committee (and Carolinians could be found on that scene as well). But between 1765 and 1774–75, from the Stamp Act agitation to the merchants' petition drives of 1774 and 1775, it was the less well known Bristol lobby that provided crucial initiative and organizational support in the effort to bring Parliament to the table.

At the transatlantic nexus of this group stood two men, John Lloyd, Charleston merchant, planter, and member of the General Assembly, and his brother-in-law, Richard Champion, a Bristol-Carolina merchant and chief political aide to Edmund Burke. Thanks to the survival of a scattered body of sources, we can piece together the structure of the Bristol-Carolina lobby from this nexus.[1] Using Lloyd and Champion as our window, we can follow the network's strands as they radiated outward, connecting South Carolina with the London American merchants' lobby, as well as that city's network of intellectuals, pro-American journalists, booksellers, other colonial agents and their networks, miscellaneous individual Americans attempting to make a difference, and even Parliament itself, all caught up in the events that swirled toward the Revolution.

Born in Bristol in 1735, John Lloyd resided in South Carolina by at least 1760, when he signed a farewell address to Governor Lyttelton with seventy-five other Charleston merchants. With two other former Bristol merchants, George Inglis and George Abbott Hall, Lloyd founded a merchant house in Charleston in 1759 that was thriving within a very few years. After Hall left the firm in 1764, the partnership continued first as Inglis and Lloyd, and then as Inglis, Lloyd and Company, until 1773. Through his marriage to Ann Branford in 1764, he became connected to the socially and politically prominent Smith, Branford, and Savage families of Charleston.[2]

Earlier generations of Lloyd's Bristol family had been Quakers, but his immediate family, or at least Lloyd himself, can no longer have been, since he engaged in the slave trade, served in the militia, and was married and buried outside the community. We may speculate, however, that the Quaker community's high degree of political awareness and tight religious interest group organization may have made an impression on Lloyd.[3]

His successful climb in South Carolina resembled that of the talented and ambitious young men of the 1730s and 1740s who arrived in Charleston with some capital, a few connections, a sense of enterprise, and boundless energy. But by the 1760s, Lloyd's success was unusual both for its rapidity and degree, since lowcountry South Carolina had by this time developed a clearly defined, if not closed, elite. By 1768, Lloyd possessed sufficient fortune and status to be elected to the Commons House of Assembly from Charleston. Jack Greene has identified him as a House leader in the 1768 and 1769 sessions (of less importance than a Henry Laurens or John Rutledge to be sure, but unusual for so recent an immigrant), where he served on several major committees. He probably achieved some local recognition for his role in the Moore affair of 1767. He was an active and visible member of the merchants' lobby in that dispute, and was one of the twenty-seven merchants who supplied affidavits for the pamphlet, *A Representation of Facts.* Lloyd with John Chapman, one of the "Committee of Seven" in the Moore dispute, subsequently headed a similar committee chosen to negotiate a customs fee schedule agreement with Moore's successor, Peter Handasyd Hatley, acting once again "on Behalf of the Whole Body of them [the merchants of Charleston]."[4]

Lloyd's family were no strangers to government service, although it was chiefly the sort won through influence. His brother Caleb's appointment as stamp distributor for the port of Charleston in 1765 came through family connections with Lord Hyndford,[5] and despite Grenville's intention to appoint only persons born in the colonies.[6] Naturally, he became a target of patriot enmity. It was doubtless fortunate for John's later political career that Caleb conveniently died in 1767, a result, according to his sister-in-law, Sarah Champion, of the distress suffered by Caleb's "naturally grave" and sensitive temperament during Stamp Act disturbances.[7] As Richard Champion wrote in a letter of condolence to his wife's brother, John Lloyd, "He was not formed for public life." Both John Lloyd and Richard Champion, however, clearly did possess temperaments and ambitions for public affairs.

Richard Champion's political significance in his own right has been overlooked because historians have only considered his political life as a fringe on Edmund Burke's career.[8] No one has seen Champion's importance either as a link in political networks to America or his potential as a vehicle for opposition theory and practice. Champion's papers have been chiefly exploited by economic historians for what he can reveal about eighteenth-century overseas trade[9] and by art historians for his contributions to ceramics. Champion was an early producer of hard paste porcelain on the

Cookworthy process, a patent he successfully defended in Parliament against the claims of Josiah Wedgwood.[10]

Champion's business association with William Cookworthy began in 1768. After a brief period of china manufacture in Plymouth using kaolin from his property in Cornwall (a property Champion retained for its superior clay), Champion moved the business to Bristol in 1770. There he founded a china house with a new partner, Joseph Harford, and began exporting overseas, trading to Carolina with correspondents probably arranged by his brother-in-law, John Lloyd. Champion was soon able to leave the manufacturing end of the business to Harford while he expanded his merchant trading operation. He imported rice from Carolina, tobacco from Virginia, and wheat from Pennsylvania, and exported a variety of English-made goods (including his own) to those places, but he traded mainly with South Carolina.[11]

Champion either visited South Carolina or met visiting South Carolinians while still a bachelor living in the Islington home of his father, Joseph Champion, a wealthy Carolina merchant in London.[12] In a letter to his friend John Lloyd in 1763 (Champion did not marry Julia Lloyd until 1764), Champion mentions hearing of the marriage of "a [South Carolina] lady whom I was particularly attentive to, as it might have been my lot to be well acquainted with her. I mean *Miss Izzard* (sic)." She married into a noble family, but Champion thinks she might have been happier with a more "mediocre" connection, meaning, it appears, himself.[13] If so, Champion had a high estimation of himself, for in South Carolina, as the tour guides say, you couldn't do better than to marry an Izard.

Champion was certainly an ambitious man, who felt himself disadvantaged by the lack of a gentleman's classical education. He advised his half brother Joseph, a student at Cambridge, to pay particular attention to the study of history and elocution, skills essential for a career in public affairs. In this and other letters on the same theme, Champion's tone is tinged with regret for lost opportunities; having been early committed to a life of commerce by his father, the result was this "narrow Sphere of Life in wch. I have moved having been a constant bar to me." His desire for the credentials conferred by a gentleman's education is further betrayed by his adoption of the classical pseudonym "Valerius Publicola" for a newspaper essay.[14]

Unable to seek political office on his own, he plunged into politics as a sort of campaign manager, linking his abilities to organize and deliver merchant support with the needs of aspiring (and promising) candidates in search of a seat. He is probably the Mr. Champion who, in early 1770, organized with one Joseph Squire a mercantile interest in Plymouth, then tried (unsuccessfully) to enlist John Wilkes as the group's candidate.[15]

Although it did not last, Champion had an early and enthusiastic admiration for Wilkes, an enthusiasm he imparted to his entire household. When his daughter's inoculation-induced case of smallpox produced a suggestive number of spots, his sister Sarah Champion (who lived in Champion's household until her marriage) wrote, "She was so lucky as to have exactly *forty-five spots;* such a circumstance just at this period, had she been a Boy, might have foreboded great things."[16] Perhaps Champion did play some part in Wilkes's political saga. It is suggestive that the December 1769 grant of £1500 sterling subscribed by the South Carolina Commons House of Assembly to the London Bill of Rights Society to pay Wilkes's debts was drawn two-thirds on Richard Champion and his partner, Edward Brice, and only one-third in London.[17]

The fact not only suggests some association between Champion and Wilkes, but also points to Champion's connections in South Carolina's politics. Brice and Champion had once before acted as the province's bankers when, in 1766, the House ordered a statue of William Pitt sculpted in London to honor his efforts in the Stamp Act repeal.[18] These links undoubtedly came through the Lloyd brothers, first Caleb and then John. Before his appointment as stamp distributor brought him down, Caleb had been a respected Charleston merchant and local officeholder. Through Caleb, the Carolina Assembly in August 1765 had requested Champion to obtain prices for sculpting several figures intended to adorn the pediment of South Carolina's statehouse.[19]

It is unclear whether Champion took an active part in Bristol's movement for repeal of the Stamp Act, but he certainly expressed strong opinions on the subject.[20] His objections, like those of other British merchants and politicians, however, were wholly commercial, and reached only after the colonies had made known their objections. Indeed, from the moment of the act's passage Champion worked assiduously for Caleb's appointment to the distributor's post in Charleston. He assured Lloyd of his "intention of purchasing of any person who may have obtained the place" ahead of Lloyd. When Lloyd did obtain the post, Champion and his china manufacturing business partner, Joseph Harford, acted as security for Lloyd's bond of office.[21]

We may conclude Caleb Lloyd's story here. He wrote Champion on October 11, 1765, about the first stirring of discontent in Charleston, and by February 1766, had offered £300 sterling for a deputy to serve in his place, but could find no one "hardy enough" to accept. Much has been written about the violence of feelings during the nonimportation phase of colonial opposition to the Stamp Act, but the words of another British merchant describing conditions in Charleston in his letter home sum the matter up. "It is worth your life," he wrote his father, "to have a piece of English cheese in the house."[22]

Lloyd's disappointment was complete when, after repeal, he tried but was unable to secure the vacant post of collector of the custom.[23] It is one of the challenges of history to speculate on what might have happened had the mild-mannered Caleb Lloyd been appointed Charleston's chief customs official instead of the rapacious Daniel Moore. How much difference does a single individual make? In the largest sense, probably not much. But every difference makes a difference, and the confrontation with Moore certainly helped push conservative Henry Laurens, future president of the Continental Congress, across the chasm between Whig merchant and revolutionary patriot.

On his side of the water, Champion concluded that the Stamp Act was ill-advised, but was not in itself unjust. Champion thought the American agitation of a piece with previous trade grievances, beginning with the giveaway of the captured sugar islands by treaty in 1763.

> They had already borne the loss of their and our most lucrative Trade, the exchanging of manufactures of this Country for Bullion, with great murmurs. The Stamp Act was but a name. Had not the modes of Judging by the Admiralty Courts, had not Grievances been added to Grievances, I have not a doubt but the Stamp Act would have been received without a murmur.[24]

Champion thought the mode of collection the only real problem with the act, and wrote, "I cannot see the injustice of the Stamp Act if it undergoes a proper alteration."[25]

Once established as a merchant in Bristol, Champion found in that city the scope that his political energies required. Bristol, like Charleston, was enjoying a boom that peaked in the second half of the eighteenth century, a period that one author has called "Bristol's Golden Age." Second only to London in size by midcentury, Bristol saw its population approximately treble between 1700 and 1800, a development accompanied by rapid physical and economic growth. Its wealth was based on manufacturing and a great inland trade with its hinterland (the western counties and Wales), but overseas commerce led its economy, with the plantation trade with Virginia and South Carolina far outweighing the northern colonies in importance. The humble "Carolina hat," described in 1702 as "a slight, coarse, mean commodity," illustrates the pull of markets in faraway South Carolina, reaching across the Atlantic, through the Bristol entrepot, to Frampton Cotterell's felt hat factory in Gloucestershire, where a "great number of workers" were employed to make them.

The city's vigorous political life included political clubs such as the Tory Steadfast Society and the Whig Union Club, and the wide franchise meant a large contingent of unorganized freemen whose vote had to be solicited.[26] Merchants, too, had long possessed an organization, the Merchant Venturers Society (SMV), which exerted substantial influence in Parliament through its petitions. Bristol merchants not belonging to the SMV (and many substantial ones did not) were routinely invited to attend the society's meetings that considered issues affecting the port's trade. These unaffiliated merchants also could and did organize and petition on their own.[27] Historians Deborah Olsen and Walter Minchinton both claim that Champion was active in Bristol's agitation to repeal the Stamp Act.[28] He probably joined the Bristol merchants "not of the Hall" in their separate petition to Parliament. It is certain that the society, which Richard did not formally join until 1767, took the crucial first step in the English side of the repeal movement when it wrote to the London merchants suggesting they organize an opposition.[29]

The Bristol initiative, disclosed in the testimony of Barlow Trecothick, chairman of the London Committee before the House of Commons, also reveals the strategy followed by the merchants' lobby.

> We were called on by the Bristol Merchants—this hastened our meeting for all the Merchants trading to North America. They met, chose a committee, they instructed that committee to write circular Letters to the manufacturing Towns requesting their Support in an application to Parliament, and to use their interest with the Members to make the interest of Great Britain the Basis for their application. . . . Many of the manufacturing Towns sent for the form of a petition which we declined particularly at Bristol—we thought it too indecent and desired them to speak for their own feelings and that none should complain but what they were aggrieved. . . . Thirty circular letters sent for petitions to most Towns. In every Answer they were thankful for our Motions and desired copy of [other?] Petitions.[30]

Bristol's SMV Standing Committee dealing with the Stamp Act crisis numbered thirteen, temporarily enlarged to eighteen. Six members traded with or had connections to South Carolina, including William Reeve, the society's master, and Thomas Farr, who had been in South Carolina only the year before.[31] The SMV sent a delegation (Reeve, Farr, and Joseph Farrell) to present their petition to the House of Commons and to oversee Bristol's interests there. Merchants not of the Hall met, drew up a separate petition,

and requested the American merchant Henry Cruger and Common Council-
lor Samuel Sedgely to present it. Once the repeal bill's passage in the Commons seemed certain, the other delegates returned home, but Thomas Farr
remained to represent Bristol's interests, to work with the London committee, and to see repeal through the House of Lords.[32]

A short digression on the subject of Thomas Farr is warranted here, for
the Farr family is as important an example as the Lloyd-Champion connection in catching and spreading a lobby-learned oppositionist's strategy to
South Carolina, but we have far fewer surviving records on them.

The Farrs were a prominent family in the political and commercial
life of Bristol. Richard Farr and Sons traded principally to South Carolina, where they claimed debts of £8000 by the outbreak of the American
Revolution.[33] The firm consisted of Richard Farr and two of his seven sons,
Thomas and Paul. Paul Farr, (with Richard Champion) managed Edmund
Burke's Bristol political organization. Thomas Farr (d. 1791) became a
leader in the Merchants Hall, serving on its Standing Committee from at
least 1757.[34] He was elected master of the society (1771–72), and finally
mayor of Bristol in 1775. Burke, who stayed with Farr at his Blaise Castle
estate during his 1774 Bristol seat election campaign, referred to Farr as his
"particular friend."[35]

Another family member, Thomas Farr Jr. (d. 1788), is known to have
been in South Carolina acting as the firm's agent from the early 1760s.[36] In
1760, Thomas Farr Jr. married Elizabeth Holmes, daughter of South Carolina planter Francis Holmes and Elizabeth Branford and a niece of John
Lloyd's wife. Through his wife, he acquired Hickory Hill, a 280–acre plantation on the Ashley River. He later purchased Savages, a 443–acre plantation
adjacent to it.[37] Through marriage and property, Farr entered the colony's
lesser gentry, and thus became socially eligible for public service.

Farr's political career centered exactly in the critical revolutionary
years. His public career began as deputy clerk of the Commons House of Assembly in the 1765–66 and 1769 sessions. In 1766, he was clerk of the important Committee of Correspondence, which liaised with the colony's agent
Charles Garth during the Stamp Act crisis. Farr won a seat to the House
from St. Andrew's Parish in 1773, and assumed the post of clerk of the
House in 1774.[38] In 1775, the South Carolina Committee of Safety, which became the state's executive branch after the collapse of the royal government, appointed him commissary general, but he served only a few months
before resigning, apparently because he was unable to obtain the services of
a deputy.[39] The next year Farr was elected a member of the Second General
Assembly (1776–78), subsequently representing St. Andrew's Parish in

1779–80, 1784, 1785–86, and 1787–88. He rose to Speaker of the House, the legislature's most powerful position, in 1779–80.[40]

In his business career, Farr was a merchant in partnership with Isaac Dacosta from 1758 to 1763 and with Robert Smyth (another former Bristolian) from 1763 to 1765. He was liked and trusted by Henry Laurens and Peter Manigault, with whom Farr at different times shared the management of several plantations. Manigault described him as "the properest person I can think of" to manage the business affairs of absentee Ralph Izard.[41] Manigault himself was a prominent South Carolina lawyer, planter, and political leader. Representing the parish of St. Thomas and St. Denis from 1757 to 1773, Manigault held the powerful position of Speaker of the House from 1765 to 1772, and, like Laurens, saw continuous service on major House committees.[42] These are the men among whom Farr moved in South Carolina from the mid-1760s on.

Unfortunately, none of the business correspondence of Richard Farr and Sons has come to light. If it did, it would certainly contain detailed political and commercial news, since exchanging such relevant information was a standard business practice of overseas merchant houses. It is therefore certain that Thomas Farr Jr. would have had direct accounts of the strategy by which Bristol's merchant representatives lobbied for the Stamp Act's repeal, especially since his kinsman, Thomas Farr, was among those sent to London by Bristol's Society of Merchant Venturers. As the unaffiliated merchants' delegate and lobbyist, Henry Cruger, described it to his father, "I am every Day with some one Member of Parliament, talking as if it were my own Life. It is surprising how ignorant some of them are of *Trade* and *America.* "[43]

On March 3, 1766, after the repeal bill's success in the House of Commons, and aware that the bill must pass the House of Lords, the Bristol SMV forwarded Farr another petition similar to the one presented to the Commons. Farr's reply on March 5 shows his attention to the committee's business and an understanding of the constant pressure that had the best chance of getting results. "Immediately on receiving your Letter, I went with the petition to the House of Lords, and thro' Mr. Trecothick's [Chairman of the London Committee] means got Lord Dartmouth to deliver it, & it was read immediately after the London Petition." Ever watchful for the interest of the Bristol lobby's constituents, Farr alerted the SMV's Standing Committee that a bill to remove further restrictions on the North American trade would be brought into the House of Commons "next Tuesday, & if the Merchants of Bristol could give any hints on that subject, I believe they would be very readily attended to."[44]

Farr kept the SMV regularly informed of events by letter. On March 17, he wrote, "I have been at the House of Lords this Evening where the Stamp act [repeal] has passt (sic) the 3d Reading without opposition. Tomorrow the King is to come to the House to pass it, & all the No. American Merchants propose going there in a Cavalcade to attend him, amongst whom I am summon'd & believe I shall go in the procession."[45]

The moment the king came out of Parliament on March 18, the date the bill was formally signed, the news was rushed to Plymouth, where London merchants had hired a ship to set sail for America. Farr, too, rushed copies of the repeal bill overland to Bristol to be dispatched immediately on the first American-bound vessel, which beat the London ship to Charleston with the good news.[46]

The other delegates had by this time returned to Bristol, but Farr stayed on, believing that the time was ripe to press for other trade reforms. He attended the House of Commons daily to lobby Bristol members of Parliament (MPs) and others in the merchants' agitation to modify the 1764 Sugar Act in ways that would extend the American trade. The SMV dispatched eight more members to London between December 1765 and June 1766 to press for putting Bristol's suggested alterations into the bill. Bristol's delegation outlasted the more powerful London committee, which disintegrated sometime in April in a clash between the West Indian and North American contingents over the proposed free port feature.[47] This small fact may signal an advance in the Bristol lobby's interest reconciliation ability over that of London, making it a better "school for politics" for South Carolina lobbyists. Bristol had a sizable West Indian trading community, subjecting it to the same internal strains as the London lobby.

Among the list of four changes forwarded to London by the SMV's Standing Committee was a suggestion that South Carolinians could hardly have supported. It proposed to admit foreign indigo duty-free into America and Great Britain, where it would compete on equal footing with the Carolina product for English buyers.[48] Carolinians would naturally fear that the increased supply would drive the price down. Yet Farr, as well as another Carolina trader, Samuel Munckley, joined forces with Abraham Rawlinson of Lancaster to work assiduously for its approval.[49] In another instance, when the SMV initially concurred with the London committee's recommendation to admit foreign white sugars duty-free to North America while retaining the duty on sugar imported into Great Britain (a reversal of the advantage British merchants usually enjoyed courtesy of the Navigation Acts), Rawlinson fired back the following letter:

I would rather see the whole plan upset than to submit to such partiality. Can an English merchant (who with Chearfulness pays All Dutys) see with patience, No. America Import foreign sugars on the most favorable Conditions, & the Merchant in Old England who go to the same foreign market excluded[,] Unless they will Send em to New York or some favored Northern Port. In the Late Administration he was a happy man that was born in Scotland, in this administration, in North America.[50]

The following day, a general meeting of the Hall resolved that the London committee's recommendation was "contrary to the Hall's desire" and advised that Bristol's MPs and Thomas Farr should be advised of the same.[51]

These incidents point up that British merchant lobbies supported American aims, such as the Stamp Act repeal, only so long as it was in their interest to do so. (All the repeal arguments made in their petitions to Parliament were commercial ones [that the trade would not bear the tax], not principled ones).[52] But the point is that political strategies learned in the process of pursuing commercial goals were available for use in subsequent disputes, whose bases were increasingly or in major part political and only whose framework remained commercial.

The political atmosphere immediately following repeal of the Stamp Act and passage of the Declaratory Act favored colonial conciliation, so long as any reforms sought were clearly commercial. A commercial society like South Carolina quickly sensed the opportunity, and a new surge for trade concessions rapidly gathered. Bristol, with its growing force of Carolina merchants in leadership positions, willingly assisted. The lobby continued to operate in its usual aggressive way, in one instance blocking a London merchants' plan to reduce the naval stores' bounty, which had already secured the approval of the Board of Trade and the Treasury. The SMV organized an opposition, instructing agents Charles Garth of South Carolina, Edward Montagu of Virginia, and Henry McCullough of North Carolina to obtain a list of their constituents' "Capital Objections," then successfully petitioned for the bill's defeat.[53]

But in addition to such defensive tactics, the Carolina lobby arranged to introduce legislation that was clearly special interest and of dubious value to the general public. The act to exempt rice from the general import duty during a critical grain shortage in England, even though little rice was consumed in England, is a case in point.

England's ancient corn laws had always protected domestic grain growers from foreign competition, but small shortages between 1758 and 1763 became critical during the poor harvest years of 1763–67. By 1766, rioting and insufficient imports from Europe, to which the merchants had turned first, caused importers to look to America for supplies. When Henry Laurens learned that Garth and a group of Carolina merchants in London believed they saw an opportunity to get the import duty removed from rice, Laurens saw through the scheme at once and dismissed its chances of success:

> Should Parliament be as wise & tender as that one Member [Garth] & the Merchants were after dinner, why then, the Carolina Planter will get an advanced price of all the saving of Duty, upon his Rice, but the English Farmer & Labourer will not get a grain of Rice extraordinary nor one farthing the cheaper, but he will have the satisfaction of paying to America, what otherwise be would have contributed to the Revenue.[54]

Laurens reckoned wrong, however, for a bill brought in to allow free importation of rice on May 5, 1767, made an untroubled passage into law on May 20.[55]

And again, in mid-November 1768, when the SMV noticed that the rice exemption act was about to expire, the Carolina merchant-dominated Standing Committee advised the new master Samuel Munckley to write Bristol's MPs to press for the act's extension for another year. Lord Clare wrote back that the free importation of corn would not be allowed again, and the same principle would likely be applied to rice. He then noted that the legislation might not be having any public benefit, since their (the merchants') accounts of increased rice consumption were inconclusive and unvouched for:

> I must remark that in your comparative Accts of the Consumption of Rice, you do not inform me from whence those Accts are taken, and how they are vouched. The reason given [by you] for the increased Consumption, derived from the low Prices at which the Carolina merchants have been enabled to sell Rice to the Retailers, by the Exemption from Duty, is not absolutely conclusive, if the Fact be true, that the Price to the Consumers is as high if not higher than it was before the Duty was taken off. I am aware that increased Consumption will, upon the same Quantity increase the Price; But the Intention of the Legislation was that the Quantity for home Consumption should be so far increased as to lower the Price to the Consumer; and whether the Profits remain with the Grower, the Merchant or the Retailer, if the Consumer finds no Relief, is to him a matter of mere Indifference, while the Public loses the Revenue arising from the Duty. I throw out these thoughts for further Information. They will occur to others, and I thought to be prepared with Answers.[56]

Clare wrote again on November 22 that conversation with committee members considering the bill revealed them to be unwilling to allow the free importation of corn to continue, and that rice appeared to rest on the same principle. Clare therefore advised the society to petition in favor of continuing the free importation of corn. A petition was promptly sent, which was read before the House of Commons on November 24. On November 29, the committee presented its opinion before the House that the act should be continued. South Carolina's agent Charles Garth presented the bill on December 2, and it became law on December 20.[57]

But the days when the Carolina lobby could engage in an uncomplicated, clearly interest-driven opposition politics were numbered. Using their lobby for a principle contradicted the lobby's traditional supportive role toward government. And as the issues became less obviously commercial and more blatantly political, the more conservative British merchants began to shear away. For the lobby's Carolina members, however, the way to achieve political goals was now plainly marked out, while the distinction between principle and interest had not yet become clear. Indeed, it is doubtful whether ideology and interest are ever completely separable, and in the case of America, they were certainly united.

In the gathering storm, it was Parliament's prerogative to decide whether the struggle was about commercial reform or parliamentary authority. In what was more a shift of perspective than an absolute change of ground, and despite the Declaratory Act, which in theory had settled the matter, Parliament slowly began to interpret America's demands as a challenge to its supremacy.

As the Ministry shifted toward this perspective, the opposition attempted to hold the terms of reference within the commercial sphere, but with declining success. The change moved along as a mixture of both perspectives until 1774, when the government began the sorting-out process in earnest by calling for a general election. The idea was to assemble a Parliament that was willing to interpret America's resistance as opposition not to a commercial or even a political policy, but to the authority of Parliament itself.

For their part, South Carolinians, whose allegiance to parliamentary supremacy was still unquestioned, continued to operate on the premise that parliamentary government went forward by an adjustment of interests as had government by the Board of Trade in the past. Thus, John Lloyd, Thomas Farr, and other South Carolina lobby members, their principles and interests unsevered, could approach the imperial questions of 1774–75 in the same manner and with the same attitudes as they had formerly approached purely commercial issues.

A new factor was added, however, with the 1774 election from Bristol of Edmund Burke to a seat in Parliament. It was a plan conceived and executed almost entirely through the efforts of Richard Champion. Through Burke, the old Bristol-Carolina network expanded to join the Rockingham opposition. Here was the direct link by which Carolina lobbyists' old commercial out-of-doors habits and mental attitudes could absorb and adapt parliamentary opposition tactics to form a new and singular hybrid for future use.

LEARNING OPPOSITION POLITICS IN THE REVOLUTIONARY CRISIS, 1774–1776

Until 1774, Carolina's elites could plausibly claim to have used their lobby only for commercial reforms. Whatever the political implications of the Stamp Act and Townshend Acts nonimportation movements might be, the Carolina lobby in England carefully couched its objections to the legislation in commercial terms only.

Perceptions on the part of the North Ministry, however, were edging the matter closer to a constitutional showdown. Concurrent with this interpretative shift, government moved the forum for discussion and de facto decision-making on colonial affairs from the Board of Trade and the Privy Council into Parliament itself. It was an unfortunate move from the perspective of the American lobbies generally, since colonial lobbies operated with less success in Parliament, where they had to compete with an array of national interests. Although they tried to adapt to these changes, the old networks began to break down.

Carolinians, however, had special connections with the Rockingham party, to whom they now turned for assistance. After his 1774 election to Parliament, Edmund Burke, Lord Rockingham's private secretary, relied more and more on his Bristol constituency and his political manager, Richard Champion, to launch opposition initiatives. Champion, equally enmeshed in the Rockingham Whig party and the Carolina lobby, was an important channel through whom John Lloyd, Thomas Farr, Ralph Izard, Henry Laurens, and other Carolinians could learn the ways and means of a parliamentary opposition politics.

This chapter carries forward a prosopographical focus on Richard Champion and John Lloyd to demonstrate how Carolinians directly participated in the lobby politics of these events. It concludes with a discussion of how, when, and why Carolinians finally despaired of a settlement and opted to follow the other colonies into Independence.

Although he had dabbled in political matters from the mid-1760s, Richard Champion's real plunge into Whig opposition politics can be traced to the Bristol election campaign of 1774. Champion had taken a warm part in the 1769 Instructions movement that was Bristol's response to Parliament's expulsion of Wilkes from his Middlesex seat.[1] But when the arrest of Wilkes's printer, William Bingley, spurred the same group to formulate a protest petition, Champion declined to present it to the city's MPs, Matthew Brickdale and Lord Clare. Since it contained the same arguments (e.g., annual parliaments, a place bill, etc.) as the earlier Letter of Instructions, it seems possible that jealousy of Henry Cruger, his fellow merchant and a delegate in the Stamp Act repeal campaign who had captured the movement's leadership away from Champion, and not just disapproval of the leadership's "visionary radicalism" as Champion claimed, helped cool his willingness to take an active part.[2] But whatever the personal contributing factors, Champion's flirtation with radicalism faded as he found himself temperamentally more and more out of sympathy with its leadership and style, and intellectually out of sympathy with its constitutional aims.

In the years between his split with the Wilkes radicals and his attraction to the Rockingham party, Champion concentrated on his business affairs and several local political and philanthropic issues.[3] Because protecting his trading interests was becoming increasingly difficult as American resistance mobilized, Champion also worked during this interval to expand his correspondence with South Carolina figures close to political events happening there, thus in a sense entering the revolutionary crisis through the colonial door. One correspondent (unnamed), who sat on the colony's important 1769 nonimportation committee of thirty-nine, kept Champion informed of Charleston's politics. On his side, Champion tried to moderate opinion among Charleston's leadership by hinting that South Carolina might need Bristol's support for renewing the rice duty exemption act. Another of his contacts was Peter Timothy, influential editor of the strongly patriot *South-Carolina Gazette.* Any of the several unattributed letters containing inside political news could have been written by Timothy.[4]

Champion was also deeply interested in the news of Russia's bid for supremacy in the war with the Turkish Empire, England's near war with Spain in 1771, and the financial crash of 1772–73.[5] However, the sudden call for a general election in 1774 presented Champion with the opportunity for the plunge into national politics that his ambitions and talents had been waiting for.

By 1774, the division of Bristol Whigs into two distinct types reflected what was happening on the national scene, as the more conservative Rockingham Whigs pulled away from the Chathamites and the Wilkes reformers. The Rockingham Whigs founded their party on an opposition to the Ministry only, with strong emphasis on preservation of the existing political structure. Their assumptions, appeal, and composition were fundamentally elite; they included the great peers, the leading landed gentry, wealthy merchants and manufacturers, and substantial yeomanry. And although they were not above using popular support for their programs, their leadership always assumed that policy came from above.[6]

Bristol's interest in the Townshend Acts controversy had been largely limited to the trading community.[7] But by 1774, "the American question," for which everyone wanted a solution, had reached crisis proportions. When Parliament was unexpectedly dissolved and a general election called, Champion saw an opportunity to cobble together an opposition coalition to challenge Bristol's two incumbents. In Edmund Burke, he saw the perfect candidate—perfect for the time, the place, and his own philosophy, a candidate who was "Indisputably the first literary Character in the Kingdom . . . a perfect master of the Commercial Interest, these Qualities joined to the true knowledge of the constitution."[8]

Champion wrote to Burke, whom he had never met, with an analysis of Bristol's political alignments, and requested permission to place Burke's name in nomination. Champion divided the city into four parties: the Tories and the Whigs of the sort who brought in Clare (what Burke called "Sunshine Whigs of the last reign" and Richard Champion called the Newcastle Party) formed the two major parties. The remaining two were the discontenteds: Whigs who disliked the present system of government, and Tories who disliked Bristol's present members. Upon these last two parties Champion hoped to build his coalition. He hoped to weld to them the Quakers and other religious dissidents angered by their MPs' vote for the Quebec Act, the rebuffed radicals of the Instructions and Protest movements of 1769, merchants and other professionals who wanted more direct representation for their economic interests, plus the small tradesmen, who were uniformly opposed to Brickdale and Clare (or, as dependent voters, might be persuaded to be) to create a formidable third party.[9]

Thus, when a friend of Champion's old rival, Henry Cruger, approached Champion for support of Cruger's candidacy, Champion suggested instead that a regular opposition be formed to defeat both members, and put forward the names of Burke and John Dunning, Bristol's popular town recorder. Cruger was a divisive choice, Champion felt, because he was a young merchant and "only on a par with the other Merchants of the town [which would cause] a great degree of envy."[10]

Cruger, however, solidly in control of the radical faction, declared his intention to stand. When the opposition gathered on October 5, he was unanimously nominated. But Champion still hoped to unseat both incumbents, so Joseph Harford (Champion's business partner) next nominated, and Champion seconded, Edmund Burke. But Cruger's supporters so violently opposed the idea of two candidates that Cruger announced that he would only stand alone. Thus defeated, Harford and Champion had to notify Burke that they had failed. Burke then stood for and was elected to a Yorkshire seat. As expected, the Tory and old corps Whigs put up Brickdale and Clare.

When the first day's polling results on October 7 showed that Clare's former support had seriously diminished, Clare withdrew, reopening a chance to run Burke. Seizing the opportunity, Champion sent immediately to London for Burke to come to Bristol. Then, in a move that was clearly intended to project an outward appearance of harmony among the opposition, Champion asked Mr. Lediard, who had originally nominated Cruger, to propose Burke's name. Champion's appeal to the basic lobbying principle of unity, however, struck no chord with the radical wing of the party. Lediard refused, so Champion proposed Burke himself. Although Brickdale objected that Burke's nomination was illegal, the polling having already begun, Harford insisted on voting for Burke. The sheriffs at last received it and other Burke votes, including that of "John Lloyd, merchant, Charlestown, South Carolina." The polling continued under protest until November 2, and on the following morning, Cruger's and Burke's elections were announced.[11]

It is interesting that John Lloyd was permitted to vote in the Bristol election, as though the port of Charleston was only a little west of Bristol. Lloyd had been back in England for a little more than a year (his arrival date at Falmouth is recorded in Champion's letterbook as September 1, 1773).[12] And although Lloyd's wife accompanied him, there is nothing to suggest that he meant to remain permanently.[13] His letters indicate that he came to England seeking new business opportunities because of deteriorating political and business conditions at home. Although the crash of 1772 did not affect South Carolina as seriously as it did Maryland and Virginia, several Bristol firms, including William Reeve, went bankrupt, necessitating some realignment of business connections.[14]

On the political side, the Tea Act passed by Parliament the previous May (1773), besides reaffirming Parliament's right to tax the colonies, granted the East India Company a virtual monopoly on colonial tea sales. The first shipments of the dutied tea, expected daily, were likely to precipitate another crisis. Indeed, Josiah Quincey had visited Charleston (his first stop on a stump through all the colonial capitals) in March to drum up support for a permanent intercolonial committee of correspondence. A permanent committee would facilitate dealing with the anticipated crisis over tea and be advantageous for organizing coordinated resistance.[15]

Although Quincey got little encouragement in South Carolina, political instability (never good for business) was clearly in the air. Small amounts of the dutied tea arrived in general cargoes and were sold undisturbed, indicating at least an ambivalence on the part of elites toward the issue. The tea, after all, was even cheaper than smuggled Dutch tea. But the arrival on December 1, 1773, of the first exclusively "tea ship" triggered popular resistance.[16]

Resistance in the past had twice turned on a nonimportation, but Charleston's merchants were unwilling to endorse another. They had felt deserted when the other colonies broke through the 1769–70 resolutions, and believed themselves unfairly injured.[17] Indeed, within seven days of the arrival of the first tea ship on December 1, the Charleston merchants founded a Chamber of Commerce expressly to resist rising popular pressure for another nonimportation.[18]

Hoping to head off trouble, John Lloyd left his affairs in the hands of his partners, George and Thomas Inglis, and sailed for England.[19] Indeed, the high prices imported grain enjoyed in England, owing to the lingering scarcity, would alone justify his firm's shift from its former focus on the slave trade to the rice trade, but Lloyd would need to establish different correspondents for that. Thus, a swing through the trading centers of Europe was only good business sense.[20]

It might be too much to credit Lloyd with the foresight that rice exports would win an exemption from the embargo passed by the Continental Congress the following year. Had it remained in force, the exception would have meant a killing for the rice interests. Charleston merchants by 1773 clearly intended to resist any further trade interruptions, and at least some of South Carolina's delegates went to the First Continental Congress determined to fight for rice.[21]

Although we don't know how active Lloyd was in the events leading to Burke's nomination, he was certainly in Bristol by the fall of 1774 and at least voted for him in the election.[22] From that point on, he became more fully drawn into the opposition movement, a vital link in the transatlantic network that interconnected Charleston, Bristol, and London.

While staying in London he supplied Champion with political news from both America and Whitehall.

Writing on June 23, 1775, for example, he passed along the opinions of John Watts, a prominent New York merchant and member of that colony's Council, on colonial resolve. Watts's assessment had been solicited by Massachusett's exiled loyalist Governor Hutchinson, "several Ministerial dependents," and "a Gentleman—a professed friend to America." The latter repeated Watts's remarks verbatim to Lloyd, who passed them on to Champion. As Watts was "a person of consequence & fortune & agent to the Contractors for paying the Army," Lloyd hoped the Ministry would give his report due attention. Lloyd added that he had it on "good authority" that the "Junto have resolved to wait to hear the proceedings of the [Continental] Congress before they determine on any further measures."[23] The letter points out the importance of information networks in both gleaning and shaping opinion on both sides.

Meanwhile, the Charleston contingent of the Carolina network in London was resorting to more proactive lobbying practices in response to the crisis. The previous spring (1774) Henry Laurens, who was also temporarily in England, and Ralph Izard, a permanent absentee, had rounded up all the native South Carolinians and other Americans they could find to sign a "Petition of Native Americans" protesting the Massachusetts Government Bill (one of five acts of Parliament known to Americans as the "Intolerable Acts"). Over half the signers were native South Carolinians, a fact that gave "particular pleasure" and encouragement to the opposition back home, according to Thomas Farr Jr. in a letter to Ralph Izard.[24]

Who coordinated the petition drive? Apart from Laurens and Izard, who organized and led the petition campaign, the Rockinghamites must have supplied crucial moral and logistical support. The meetings were conducted and petitions signed at their particular gathering place, the Thatched Roof Tavern. Had it been a radical-backed drive, it would have been located at the Kings Arms. This detail signals that South Carolinians in London (and a list of these signers is a partial census of the province's political leadership for the next two decades), like those in Bristol, allied themselves with the Rockingham rather than the radical opposition.[25]

We next find John Lloyd in Bristol (and later Southampton, a major port for the Carolina rice trade) writing to John Almon, editor of the Whig publication *The Remembrancer*, about South Carolina's conditions, with the clear purpose of getting the Carolina viewpoint in print.[26] Here we find the first mention of the idea, repeated often thereafter, that American geography made the colonials unbeatable in war, since the maritime towns could be abandoned and the people withdrawn into an endless interior. There are seven letters from Lloyd to Almon between September 1775 and December 1776 (and two from Izard in 1776 and 1777) in the correspondence, all bearing editorial markings indicating Almon published them.[27]

Lloyd's first letter in the correspondence is dated from Bristol on September 21, 1775. Lloyd had gone to Bristol to assist Champion's efforts first to thwart a Tory loyal address to the king, while simultaneously prodding a Whig petition drive from a politically divided and at this point generally supine opposition. Motivating the opposition to act would be difficult. Spirits were still at a low ebb. A London merchants' petition drive instigated by Burke nine months earlier had failed despite careful planning and management. Merchants, and particularly the powerful London merchants, were deemed the most likely to win the Ministry's attention. That earlier effort had been coordinated by the prominent London merchant William Baker. He liaised with Bristol's supporting movement managed by Richard Champion and Paul Farr.[28] Additional support came from Bristol's Society of Merchant Venturers who sent two delegates to work with the London Committee— Thomas Farr, veteran of the Stamp Act repeal campaign, and William Jones, partner of Farr's fellow delegate in the 1766 effort, Joseph Farrell, since deceased. Champion also went to London to assist in the drive. While there, he took Lloyd to dine with Burke, a meeting in which Champion reported Burke to be "much pleased."[29] No doubt Lloyd also rendered what help he could, but despite all efforts (Farr and Jones stayed in London until March), the drive came to nothing. For the Ministry, the terms of the dispute had changed from a commercial to a purely political discourse. It buried both the London and Bristol petitions in the House of Commons "Committee of Oblivion."[30]

This second Bristol campaign therefore, was to be part of a broader and more ambitious "master plan" of Burke's devising to unite the various opposition elements (not merely merchants) throughout the country behind the numerically inferior (in the House of Commons) Rockingham Whigs in order to topple the North Ministry. But because hostilities had broken out in America that spring, it was necessary to launch the assault before Parliament convened in October, when the Ministry would be able to unite the country behind a wartime psychology. Simply put, Burke's strategy was to separate the contract-hunters from the sound London merchants, unite them to the London Corporation (London's municipal government), and join both to the Marquis of Rockingham. A similar strategy would unite these elements in Bristol, Leeds, and the northern counties. The entire network would be linked by secret committees of correspondence. Once the network was in place and strong enough, Burke planned to launch an assault on the North

Ministry backed by a blitz of petitions to the king, pamphlets, and delegations to the king from the City, the outports and manufacturing towns that would sweep the government away.[31]

For the plan to work in Bristol, however, Champion had to outflank Bristol's conservative backlash, which had grown stronger with the outbreak of actual conflict. The outbreak of fighting also triggered desertions among the American merchants lured by the Ministry's talk of wartime contracts and by hopes for profits from privateering. Actually, few Bristolians cared much about the theoretical underpinnings of the dispute, simply wanting the crisis settled in a way that would injure their interests the least.

But the opposition had reason for hope. Thomas Farr, Burke's "particular friend" who was very much a part of the local Burke organization (Burke had stayed with him on his visits to Bristol in 1774 and 1775), would propitiously succeed the Tory mayor Charles Hotchkiss on September 29. Thomas's brother, Paul Farr, occupied the master's chair at the Guildhall, anchoring the Burke forces there. In the city Corporation Burke's strength was sufficient to protect, if not foster, his interest, and the dissenting population was "in general perfectly well disposed."[32]

But in mid-September, while Champion was in London conferring with Burke about the upcoming campaign, the Tories launched a preemptive strike. On September 18, they requested Mayor Hotchkiss to call a meeting of the Corporation for the purpose of preparing a loyal address. Hotchkiss agreed and issued a summons for a meeting on September 21. On the day of the meeting, Lloyd wrote Almon:

> I am told that some Court Sycophants in the Corporation of this City [of Bristol] have enforced a disposition to comply with the Ministerial wish for an address, similar to those from Liverpoole, etc.; but I hope and believe the majority are of different sentiments.[33]

Champion hurried back to Bristol, while sympathetic Corporation members, to buy time, deliberately absented themselves to prevent making a quorum—a favorite tactic of the Rockingham Whigs in Parliament. (Only eleven members appeared, according to Champion.) By the second meeting of the Corporation on the following day, Champion had marshaled enough votes to defeat the proposal 31 to 12. Having failed to obtain an address from Bristol's municipal government, the Tories decided to turn to popular opinion. They advertised a public meeting to consider the address at the Guildhall on the 28th, Hotchkiss's last day in office. This delay of nearly a week gave Champion, Farr, and Lloyd sufficient time to mobilize an opposition.[34]

First, Champion, Samuel Brailsford (a South Carolina merchant and former member of its provincial assembly who had lived many years in Charleston), and John Fisher Weare advertised a Whig meeting for September 27, a day before the Tory-supported public meeting. Fifty people attended, adopted six resolutions, then considered and approved a petition to the king. Although personal jealousies may once again have intruded— John Mallard, Henry Cruger's partner, fought the petition "inch by inch"— the motion finally passed unanimously. The meeting further decided that its chairman, Thomas Hayes, and several others present should attend the Tory-backed public meeting set for the next day to present their resolutions and read their rival petition. More important for our question about radical methods, Champion privately arranged to pack the meeting with sailors from two of his ships then in port, a gang of dockyard workers, a work crew from his china factory, plus as many of the out-of-work as he could recruit to intimidate Tory waverers. For their part, the Tories were actively recruiting country gentlemen and playing on religious fears by posting bills that the Whig petition was a plot by dissenters to subvert the Constitution.[35]

The next day (September 28) the Tory meeting commenced with the lame-duck mayor in the chair. (Richard Champion later claimed that Hotchkiss had not been duly elected to the chair—one of a number of procedural irregularities he would complain of.) The loyal address was read. After the second reading, Thomas Hayes introduced the Whig resolutions and petition, but was told by the chair that because the Whig proceedings had not been interrupted the previous day, their objections would not be heard.

At this point Champion's hecklers pressed forward, demanding to hear the opposition's proposals. Hayes and Champion were allowed to speak, followed by another Whig, Richard Symons. But further debate was squelched and the chair would not permit a vote. Thus, the signing went forward without the loyal address actually receiving formal approval. Paul Farr recorded a pyrrhic victory: "The opposition we gave to the proceedings destroyed the credit of unanimity, & with candid & disinterested Persons, I think will not raise the reputation of our opponents. . . . All matters considered we have not suffered much from this day's fight."[36]

Lloyd wasted no time getting accounts of these meetings off to Almon for publication in *The Remembrancer:*

> The Ministerial Emmissaries in this City, and a Courtly Mayor, being foiled in their attempt to obtain an address from the Corporation, by a majority of 31 out of 43, determined to have one at large; agreeable to a general sum-

mons, a meeting for the purpose was held at the Guildhall yesterday. When a great number of gentlemen assembled to oppose it, but the party who espoused the measure would not hear any arguments against it, or suffer a division, for which reason several respectable freeholders, & freemen, for and in behalf of themselves & others, intend to publish a protest against the proceedings, which were certainly unjustifiable. . . . On the 27th a numerous meeting of [Whig] merchants, traders, and manufacturers was held at the Guildhall when several resolves were made and a petition to the King, unanimously agreed to.[37]

Lloyd was quick to make the point that the Tory meeting had been divided while the Whig assembly was unanimous.[38] Given Lloyd's background in South Carolina commercial lobbying, unanimity (or at least the appearance of it) was an essential point to be made.

Along with his account to Almon of the Bristol meeting, Lloyd enclosed an extract of a letter from Charleston, South Carolina, dated August 5, 1775, which expressed the people's firm resolve there and which Almon printed in full.[39] We may see this act as symbolic of Lloyd's awareness that whether he was acting on behalf of South Carolina's resistance or Bristol's Rockingham Whigs, his opposition politics were one and the same. It was philosophically and tactically an opposition politics that suited South Carolina's elite leaders well. While the rhetoric of popular sovereignty was trotted out, Burke's appeal was not to the general electorate, but to the proprietors of electoral interests, among them the mercantile interest.

In its tactics, the Rockingham opposition was of the older "old corps" stream—intense exploitation of procedural rules, pressing for every advantage, but always within a framework of established forms.[40] Intensely pragmatic, the Rockingham program struck a familiar chord with men who were suspicious and a bit hostile to theory, particularly to a theory demanding radical reform. The Rockingham Whigs contained enough of the rhetoric of country party ideology to resonate with Carolinians' symbolic view of themselves as English country gentlemen politicians. Coincidentally, country rhetoric also lent them a superficial ideological similarity to other colonials who actually sailed far more closely with the radical opposition stream of thought than Carolinians did.

As John Brewer has pointed out, there were actually two distinct oppositions offering two distinct solutions to the constitutional crisis, both of which owed something to but cannot be equated with the country party model. One, the radical opposition represented by the Wilkites, most City radicals, and the Chatham party, was more directly in line with country party thought as it demanded a *structural* change in government to cure its present ills. They called for more frequent parliaments, a place bill, reform in representation to reflect shifts in population (which would, incidentally, bring greater representation to metropolitan interests), even the complete separation of the executive from the legislative branches. In other words, radicals considered that a change of ministers alone was not enough to remove corruption and solve the crisis. Only a change in the structure and organization of government could counter the institutionalized forces that made tyrannical and oligarchic rule possible. This view actually represented a considerable advance on country party thought, as it was more coherent and laid greater emphasis on direct representation of new interests.[41]

The Rockingham opposition, on the other hand, had a more custodial view of government, not unlike the lowcountry elite's view of its own political role at home. And while Carolinians were anxious to see their interests carry greater weight in Parliament, they were uncomfortable with a program that demanded direct representation of persons and could only result in a diminished representation of wealth. They were too aware of their own well-established domination of the lower house at home and the threat such a system would pose from the less wealthy, but far more populous and seriously underrepresented, backcountry.

Besides, Burke had already endorsed an interest representation of the sort Carolinians were comfortable with in his 1769 description of the House of Commons. Burke saw that the House no longer (if it ever had) represented the single order of traditional theory that, with the peers temporal and spiritual, came together to form the state. It was instead divided into the interests that were the product of the state. When he looked around the House of Commons, Burke saw that "a great official, a great professional, a great military and naval interest, all necessarily comprehending many people of the first weight, ability, wealth, and spirit has been gradually forming in the Kingdom. These new interests [he concluded] must be let into a share of representation, else possibly they might be inclined to destroy those institutions of which they are not permitted to partake."[42] Although he does not name them, these new interests inevitably included the great commercial interests of England. If the Rockinghamites made good on Burke's promise when they finally came into office, Carolinians could expect to secure their future prospects by linking their interest in imperial trade matters to mercantile interest groups like Bristol's, where Burke and the Rockingham party sought so much support.

Besides, Carolinians could count and knew that the direct representation that the radicals advocated could not serve their interest, since the numerically small constituency of wealth based on overseas commerce would never command a majority in Parliament. The metropolitan interests that would benefit would be the small shopkeepers, petty tradesmen, and minor manufacturers.[43] Under the radical program carried to its logical conclusion, and within the empire in which they prospered, Carolinians would be likely to do worse rather than better.

Despite the much touted (by historians) £1500 gift made by South Carolina's lower house to Wilkes in 1769, Carolina's elite leadership was never pro-radical. The gift was a grand gesture passed in haste (the last motion on the last day of the session) by a House eager to adjourn for the Christmas holidays and disapproved of by leaders like Laurens, who was not present at its passage.[44]

As for placemen, Carolinians did not oppose the principle so long as in practice the state's honors went to its best, most able men. Looking at their own situation, they resented not so much the present structure of colonial administration as the ministerial policy of appointing outsiders to provincial offices that should have been awarded to native sons for faithful public service. Worse still, some of these outsiders were the Scots and Welsh, whom Carolina's elite considered their social inferiors. The radical New Englander Josiah Quincey ironically noted during his Charleston visit in 1773 that a ministerial change of this policy for one that would tie the elite's interest to British rule (such as creating a colonial aristocracy who would be the natural recipients of Crown offices and patronage) might restore Carolinians to the British fold, but at the cost of the people's political freedom. Quincey, of course, did not wish to see such a change, since he hoped Britain's colonial policy would push South Carolina farther toward intercolonial cooperation.

> The Council, Judges and other great officers are all appointed by mandamus from G[reat] B[ritain] nay the Clerk of the Board and Assembly. Who are and have been thus appointed? Indigent and —— persons, disconnected and obnoxious to the people, I heard several of the planters say, "we none of us, when we grow old, can expect the honours of the State—they are all given away to worthless poor rascals." . . . The planter (like the fox) prides himself in saying the grapes are sour: his fortune inclines and makes him look with contempt on the official grandee. Thus the rights and liberties of the State are in some measure safe—but from an unstable cause.[45]

If South Carolina's elite did not object to the Constitution by which the British ruled the empire, but only to the way it was administered, how are we to explain their concurrence in the decision for Independence in 1776?

Alison Olson has argued that the empire's multiple voluntary interest group networks (mercantile, religious, ethnic communities, etc.) supplied a means of communication and a form of representation for the colonists that had formerly worked very well. There is ample evidence that this informal machinery worked especially well for South Carolina. Until Lord North disabled these networks by moving the center for colonial administration from the Board of Trade and Privy Council to Parliament in the 1760s, interest group activity acted as a "lubricant that helped keep the British government stable and the [colonial] empire running smoothly." Loss of this lubricant, therefore, as Patricia Bonomi notes, might have caused the works to gum up, allowing old abrasions that were never far beneath the surface to reemerge.[46]

Furthermore, as has been pointed out, shifting the location of de facto imperial decision-making away from the Board of Trade and the Privy Council, the point of entry into the system for these informal networks, was like removing an essential connecting gear in the machinery between Westminster and the colonies. Trying to operate the same strategies on the floor of Parliament met with far less success, since in Parliament imperial interests had to compete with many more purely national interests for attention.

In that sense, it was the agencies of the old colonial system that had been the locus of the empire's international vision and expertise, and their workings were never properly replaced at the parliamentary level. If interest groups were the crank by which colonials had turned the machine, and interest group activity had been the lubricant, the Board of Trade and the Privy Council had been the gear that turned Parliament.

Furthermore, the breakdown in transatlantic communication led to misunderstandings and miscalculations about British intentions in the 1770s. This void left most Americans with no means of constructing alternative explanations to counteract resurgent fears about British corruption and tyranny. In that sense, Olson's work nicely supplements ideological interpretations, and even helps explain why America's "latent" revolutionaries remained latent for so long.

But as we have seen, South Carolinians had fewer inherited fears about British corruption. Indeed, the province's whole experience had been that of a favorite child within the empire. This lack of a history of ideological worry, added to its extremely good working relations within the system for so long, made South Carolina's elite leadership about the most reluctant of all the colonial revolutionaries.

Although she does not develop each individual's reasons for it, Julie Flavell documents a spectrum of commitment to the idea of political independence among a core group of patriots in London in the 1770s that ranged from conservative to moderate to extreme. Her work demonstrates that the South Carolinians were at the very conservative end of the scale—indeed, they were barely on it. Although they were quicker than more radical Americans to recognize that the majority of British public opinion did not support the American position, they were the last to give up hope (a hope encouraged by Lord North) for a good-faith reconciliation with the Ministry. After a meeting with Lord North on November 7, 1775, Ralph Izard rather sanguinely concluded that "I think the American prospect, seems more agreeable . . . than it has been, for these last two years."[47]

These Carolinians' nearly impervious brand of optimistic myopia is easily understood. As elitists themselves, South Carolinians knew where the real political power lay—in Whitehall and Westminster, not in the streets—and they approved of the arrangement. As seasoned lobbyists, they were accustomed to using the strategies of polite but persistent persuasion, not the methods of the mob. No doubt their record of success with this politics encouraged both their greater persistence and a stronger faith in the efficacy of a method that had served them so well for so long.

Yet Carolinians did manage to become revolutionaries at last, a fact that needs explaining. A look at the movement for a declaration of independence in the Continental Congress may shed some light on how and why Carolinians at last decided in favor of Independence. One way to approach the question is to analyze the position on Independence held by each South Carolina delegate, especially those the Assembly elected to serve (or recalled) in the critical winter and spring of 1775–76.

Throughout the 1774–76 period, only two men led South Carolina's delegation; first, the conservative John Rutledge, and, after his return to South Carolina, his brother, Edward. Besides Edward, the other delegates who ultimately voted in favor of the resolution for Independence on July 2 were Thomas Heyward Jr., Thomas Lynch Jr., and Arthur Middleton Jr.

On the radical side of the question, the two South Carolinia leaders farthest along the road to Independence were Christopher Gadsden and William Henry Drayton. Both were outspoken for it. Drayton was a member of the colony's Second Provincial Congress, whom the conservative majority voted into the Chair in November 1775, in order "to prevent his agitating on the floor of the Congress [for Independence]." Presumably this elevation would have made him ineligible for service in the Continental Congress.[48] The Assembly elected Gadsden to serve in the First and Second Continental

Congresses, but it called him home in February 1776 to accept an appointment as brigadier general and commander of the state's provincial forces.[49]

It is tempting to see these moves as maneuvers to keep the tone of South Carolina's delegation conservative on Independence, especially when one considers that two of its presumably conservative members unexpectedly resigned that same February because of ill health. Thomas Lynch Sr., "one of the best friends to this country," according to Henry Laurens, suffered a stroke in February and was replaced by his son, Thomas Lynch Jr.[50] In the same month, Henry Middleton, definitely a conservative on the issue, resigned because of "the infirmities of age," to be replaced by his son Arthur Middleton Jr.[51] The younger Lynch's position is not explicitly known, but Arthur Middleton was said to be an early proponent of a total break with Great Britain.[52]

The mixed character of the Assembly's choices indicates that the question of Independence may not have been uppermost in their selection of replacements. Right up to and beyond the time of Middleton's and Lynch's elections (February and March, respectively), Congress continued to equivocate on debating the question of Independence directly, while repeatedly and explicitly renouncing any intention of seeking Independence in its various petitions to Britain. An indication of how confident conservatives and moderates were in the difficulty of securing a majority for Independence is that they allowed the measures their more radical colleagues insisted must be implemented prior to a final declaration to go forward.[53]

Since Thomas Lynch Jr., Arthur Middleton, and Thomas Heyward Jr. all served on the committee to draft South Carolina's new constitution (see below), it seems very likely that it was for their expertise and support on the immediate question of Congress's May resolution authorizing the adoption of such constitutions that they were chosen, and not for their views on Independence.[54]

But these views must have been of some, if not of first order, importance in the selection process. It is certainly suggestive that the Assembly called the radical Gadsden home in the same month (February) that the conservative Middleton resigned for health reasons.[55] In any event, the South Carolina delegation was thus left (on the question of a declaration of independence, at least) with a conservative leadership and only one delegate known to support it.

Another approach to the problem of explaining how South Carolinians became revolutionaries is to look at their position on forming independent state governments. On May 10, 1776, Congress passed a resolve recommending that colonial assemblies and conventions should "adopt such governments as shall, in the opinion of the representatives of the people, best conduce to the happiness and safety of their constituents."[56]

In South Carolina, where royal government had effectively broken down in 1768 and no courts had sat for over a year, the need for a structure of legitimate government just to get the business of governing done was particularly acute. Added to that were worries about defense. In February 1776, copies of captured letters from Crown officers in the South to General Gage revealed a plan to incite the Indians on the frontier.

J. R. Pole has noted that Edward Rutledge's acceptance of Congress's resolution for independent state governments, while in opposition to a declaration, appears at the very least "ambiguous" but could be explained if Rutledge believed that states could act independently of and without committing Congress to Independence. This analysis seems correct, especially when one remembers that it was South Carolina (along with New Hampshire) that had set the machinery for the May resolution in motion some six months earlier (in November 1775) by requesting congressional authorization to establish a frame of government.[57]

The committee appointed to prepare a preamble for the resolution included Edward Rutledge, Richard Henry Lee, and John Adams, but Adams actually wrote the draft. When it was presented to Congress, the preamble's language sounded so much stronger than the resolve it accompanied that conservatives in Congress could not accept it. James Duane called it "a Machine to fabricate Independence."[58]

Why would Edward Rutledge have endorsed such a preamble if he was not yet committed to Independence? The offending phrase in the preamble called for the suppression of "every kind of authority under the British crown."[59] Accepting for the moment that Rutledge believed that the erection of an independent South Carolina government did not commit *Congress* to Independence, how can we accept that Rutledge believed that by erecting an independent South Carolina the state had not committed *itself* to a separate independence?

Rutledge's actions become explicable when we remember that his brother, John, was elected by the legislature to become South Carolina's first executive (called its president) under the new constitution, adopted in March 1776, which the May resolution retrospectively legitimated. To delay the resolution in order to quarrel with the language of the preamble would have cost precious time in establishing a stable form of government for the province. But, more important, the preamble to the constitution itself states that it is a *temporary* frame of government, to operate only until such time as reconciliation with Great Britain could be achieved.[60]

Moderate leaders back home, like President John Rutledge and Henry Laurens (the province's new vice president), still opposed a final Independence. Laurens wrote to his son in late March 1776 that "in the introduction and conclusion of this form of a Constitution, strong desires for Peace & accommodation with Great Britain are expressed & the Act is therefore declared to be a temporary as well as a necessary expedient."[61]

John Rutledge still held out hope for reunion with Great Britain as late as 1778, "an event as desirable now as it ever was," and even proposed as late as 1779 that the state take a neutral stance during the conflict. The historian Duncan Wallace writes that Rutledge did not dismiss hopes for reconciliation and accept the necessity of a permanent independence until June 3, 1780, when General Clinton rescinded the status of prisoner-on-parole promised to American soldiers captured in the recent battle for Charleston.[62]

So, it seems clear that in 1776, and for nearly two years afterward, neither of the Rutledges considered a declaration of independence to be a commitment to revolution or a document that could not be rescinded. This view is supported by the fact that the Declaration was officially received in the South Carolina General Assembly by an act of the legislature, and not ratified by a convention of the people elected for that purpose. Thus it, like the 1776 Constitution, could be repealed at any time as any statute may be repealed, by a subsequent legislative act.

Returning to our story, Carolina delegates' overt reluctance to accept an official break with Great Britain by a declaration for independence resurfaced again in early June. The Virginia legislature passed a resolution for a declaration on May 15. Its extremist (for Independence) leader Richard Henry Lee laid the resolution before Congress on May 27, but a motion to consider was not made until June 8 (a Saturday), owing to the pressure of Congress's other business. When the motion was made, Edward Rutledge (John Rutledge having returned to South Carolina), John Dickinson, James Wilson, and others were against it.

Some scholars maintain that the reason for this group's opposition was a belief that it was premature, since the middle colonies of New York and Pennsylvania had not modified their delegates' instructions to allow them to act on the question. This objection would certainly be consistent with the lobby's primary strategy of unanimity, which Rutledge in particular would think essential.[63]

Certainly John Adams thought South Carolina's delegates were "firm enough" for Independence, but cited South Carolina's erection of a government giving its delegates ample power to decide the question as evidence for his conclusions. We have already seen that this step did not entail a commitment to Independence in the minds of the delegation's leadership.[64]

On the evening of June 8, at the conclusion of the long day's debate, so weary that he could hardly hold his pen, Edward Rutledge wrote John Jay that he could see "no prudence in a Declaration of Independence before the colonies are united with each other," an indication that he favored it but held back on pragmatic grounds. The debate was to resume on Monday, June 10, when, as he advised Jay, he planned to move a delay of "3 Weeks of (sic) a Month." Rutledge did so move, and consideration was postponed until July 1, exactly three weeks.[65]

On July 1, there is further (impressionistic) evidence that Rutledge's reluctance was grounded *primarily* in a conviction that a unanimous vote was vital before he would bring South Carolina in on the question. John Dickinson opened the debate by presenting the opposing arguments. John Adams then rehearsed the arguments in favor of a declaration. After a period of open debate, New Jersey desired that the arguments in favor be summarized before the final question was put. At this point, Rutledge approached Adams and urged him to take the task. "Nobody will speak but you upon this subject, Mr. Adams. You have all the topics so ready that you must satisfy the Gentlemen from New Jersey."[66]

Yet a straw poll following Adams's second speech showed South Carolina still opposed, along with Pennsylvania. Delaware was split with two delegates on hand (the third, Caesar Rodney, who favored independence was absent). New York abstained because its colonial Assembly had not yet granted its delegates sufficient powers to decide the question. At the end of the day's debate, a vote by Congress as a Committee of the Whole still showed the same alignments. Edward Rutledge then moved to postpone a final vote until the following day, when, according to the historian Robert Taylor, "he thought the members of his delegation might vote in favour of the resolution *for the sake of unanimity.*"[67]

But Rutledge's postponement may be seen in another light. Late (10 o'clock) on the previous evening of June 29, Rutledge again wrote John Jay entreating him to put his pressing state Assembly business aside and come help him oppose a declaration of independence. If Rutledge only desired a unanimous vote, he would not have tried to introduce even more opposition to the measure. It seems far more likely, therefore, that Rutledge's postponement was made to give Jay enough time to arrive from New York to help him oppose the vote rather than to sway his delegation in its favor.[68]

By another account, it was at this point that Adams and Richard Henry Lee approached Rutledge and proposed a bargain. If Delaware and Pennsylvania could be brought to support Independence, would he advise South Carolina's delegation to "suppress its misgivings and, for the sake of colonial unity, follow suit"?[69]

The word "misgivings" in the passage and the sequence of events just recounted suggest that the South Carolinian's reluctance was not grounded in simply waiting for colonial unity to be achieved, but in some genuine misgivings about the choice for Independence itself. Yet, according to the historian Page Smith, Rutledge accepted the bargain.[70]

A rider was dispatched to Delaware to summon Caesar Rodney. He arrived, breathless and mud-spattered, on the rainy afternoon of July 2 to break the Delaware delegation's tie. By prior agreement, two of Pennsylvania's four opposing delegates, Robert Morris and John Dickinson, did not formally take their seats, so that South Carolina could see that Thomas Willing, Benjamin Franklin, and James Wilson, who favored it, formed a voting majority. South Carolina then kept its bargain, and on July 2, 1776, the Virginia resolution for Independence was adopted by twelve states favoring, none opposed, New York abstaining.[71]

Even John Adams, who more than anyone midwifed the Declaration into political life, could not claim it happened out of ideological consensus. He reported to his wife, Abigail, only that the resolution passed without a dissenting vote.[72] The biographer of John Adams, Page Smith, summed up the matter in two sentences: "By such a precarious margin, so late in the day, was independence resolved on and the appearance and fact of colonial unity preserved. It had taken much management, but it was done at last."[73]

Although one cannot state it categorically, it appears that Rutledge and South Carolina's other delegates had become convinced that the state's best interests lay in acting with the other colonies, whatever their reservations might be. They clearly were not in the grips of a belief in a dark ministerial plot to subvert their liberties, but they could not ignore the fact that George III had put the colonies out of his protection by declaring them, South Carolina included, in a state of rebellion, news of which arrived in Charleston on March 21. The Royal Proclamation declaring their ships and cargoes lawful prize further dampened the Provincial Congress's resistance to Independence.[74]

Lastly, in the midst of collapsing imperial ties, South Carolina's low-country leaders felt more acutely than ever the state's political isolation and military vulnerability. From its earliest settlement, regular threats of Spanish and French invasion by sea kept colonial appeals for protection flying to London. On land, South Carolina's elites lived literally surrounded and infiltrated by alien cultures and peoples, a West Indian Island planter fragment set down among European peasantry. Lowcountry culture differed markedly from neighboring North Carolina and Georgia, in both peoples and political character.[75] A black majority nourished a growing African American slave culture in its lowcountry parishes. The state's western borders were peopled with Indians whose loyalty had to be bought. The backcountry was filled with a diverse white population that could become violent when its interests were slighted. If Great Britain would not protect them from their enemies, who would?

At least as important, Carolina's delegates also believed that a declaration of independence was, like the state's constitution, a temporary expedient that could be set aside. It was a legal separation, with legal consequences, and as psychologically serious as a judicial separation is in married life, but (to extend the metaphor) it was not an absolute divorce. It was reversible.

Perhaps when Great Britain saw that the colonies had gone ahead with this important step (this official separation, withdrawal, or what one could even call "secession" from the empire) that could lead to an absolute divorce, perhaps then Great Britain would be persuaded to redress America's grievances. From this point of view, Carolinians could consider a declaration of independence as yet another tactic to put pressure on the British for a negotiated outcome rather than as a commitment to a revolution.

And while South Carolina's conservative leadership did at last manage to become full revolutionaries in the ideological sense, the road to revolution was not prescribed for them by old fears about the aggressive nature of power. It was discovered step by step and day by day. They finally needed no theory of tyranny and no evidence beyond immediate events that they themselves were living through. They were at last convinced by the consistent tendency of British actions that the British Ministry, whether by design, rashness, or mistake, was on a path that spelled oppression for South Carolina and for America.

Each South Carolina leader's commitment to revolution came at its own pace. And when it came, it came not as a fulfillment of latent fears, nor a sudden, blinding flash of insight that saw a pattern of calculated tyranny in British policy and practice since the 1760s. When it came, the decision for revolution was a rational, sorrow-laden choice made because no other choice remained.

Describing the Charleston scene upon the reception of the Declaration of Independence on August 5, Henry Laurens wrote to his son, "I say even at this Moment my heart is full of the lively sensations of a dutiful Son, thrust by the hand of violence out of a Father's house into the wide World. What I have often with truth averred in London & Westminster I dare still aver, not a sober Man & scarcely a single Man in America wished for separation from Great Britain."[76]

When General Clinton rescinded prisoner-on-parole status to Americans captured in the reduction of Charleston on June 3, 1780, even John Rutledge dismissed the idea of reconciliation with Great Britain, declaring that the achievement of Independence at the earliest possible moment should be the goal of America.[77] On this matter and so late in the day did this most reluctant of British Americans at last cross over the line between resistance and revolution.

But none of these ideological permutations upset South Carolina's elites' commitment to their view of interests as the structural basis of the state or interest group strategies as the mode of its politics. That perspective, slowly learned through a commercial past and matured by connections to and cooperation with the Rockingham party up to and through the two great petition drives of 1775, survived the revolutionary crisis unchallenged.

Carolinians felt at home with the Rockingham opposition style. In its principles, policy, and tactics, the Rockingham party seemed the political offspring, if not the metaphor, of South Carolina's commercial lobbying past. Its policy was to intensely exploit procedural rules, pressing for every advantage, but always within a framework of accepted forms. Its constituency was among the largely economic interests thrown up by the British commercial state. These techniques, and this mode of perceiving society's divisions, when grafted to the more defensive attitudes and methods of interest group opposition, found a receptive home among South Carolina leaders who, like the Rockingham Whigs, were economic liberals but social and political conservatives. The party's tactics, programs, and view of the British Constitution and the proper basis of political representation helped reinforce the ideas and values that were subliminal to South Carolina's already formed conception of society as adjusted interests.

To conclude the story of the Carolina lobby's political education abroad, we return to October 11, 1775, when the Bristol Whig petition (with 979 signatures) was presented to the king. William Baker presented the London petition about the same time,[78] and while both petitions were "graciously received," they had no effect.[79]

Burke's provincial strategy did not come off. Only in Bristol was there a major engagement. But the lessons of opposition were not lost on South Carolina's participants in the campaign. And although it was not taken as far as South Carolina would one day take it, the Rockingham Whigs led a "secession" movement from Parliament in 1776 as their final and most extreme opposition tactic.[80]

Of course, the Rockingham secession was meant as a demonstration of disapproval only. No threat to permanently withdraw from Parliament was ever implied. Perhaps the fatal difference between Burke's Rockingham Whigs of 1775–83 and the Southern states' interest in the American Congress from 1820 to 1860 led by South Carolina, was that the Rockingham Whig opposition was born and bred indoors.[81] Its roots went deeply and firmly into its parliamentary past, its shape and actions limited by ancient constitutional forms. But South Carolina's oppositionist creed was conceived out-of-doors and shaped in the crucible of commercial lobbying, where tactical stratagems had to substitute for assertible power and where limits were measured only by the loss of a will to persist. One political lesson Carolinians did not learn from their association with the Rockingham opposition was when and how to stop.

PART THREE

THE LESSONS

"INTEREST GOVERNS THE WORLD," 1768–1787

The lobbying experience had profound consequences for South Carolina's state and national politics. Not only the strategies and tactics (the "patterns of behavior") of lobby politics, but the assumptions embedded in those strategies and tactics became the formula by which South Carolina's leadership pursued its political objectives from the late 1760s on. The purpose of this chapter is to demonstrate how these shaped political action and political thinking in five key events: the legislature's reception of the Massachusetts circular letter in 1768; the nonimportation movement of 1769; the Carolina agitation to exempt rice from the Continental Congress's nonexportation in 1774; the constitutional debates in Philadelphia; and the ratification debates in Charleston. The rice exemption agitation and the constitutional debates on a slave importation exception focus on the politics of engagement with an external power. The Massachusetts circular letter, the nonimportation movement, and the constitutional ratification examples highlight lobby politics applied to problems of internal consensus. A detailed analysis of the effect of the lobby metaphor on the internal workings of the legislature itself during the crisis decade of the 1780s follows in chapter 6.

The critical importance of at least the appearance of unanimity to a commercial lobby's chance of success has been analyzed in chapter 2. The same principle holds paramount for a political opposition. Referring to its leaders' felt need to overcome jarring intercolonial divisions in the early days of the First Continental Congress, Jerrilyn Greene Marston has noted that "unity was so essential to a successful opposition, it is not surprising that Whigs insisted that, whatever the previous history of colonial discord, now the colonists *were* united," and to portray that unity as of a "spontaneous, almost a providential origin."[1] While Continental Congress leaders simply denied existing divisions in 1774, Carolina's elite, well versed in lobby political skills by the 1760s, had the know-how to concoct as well as claim internal unity when the situation required it.

The unanimity card was among the first played upon South Carolina's entry into the Townshend Acts controversy in 1768. It came with the legislature's "unanimous" reception of the Massachusetts circular letter, an event orchestrated by Charleston leaders of the Townshend Acts resistance movement in true lobby-like fashion. The Assembly met for only four days (from November 15 to 19, 1768) before Governor Montagu dissolved it, and only twenty-six assemblymen (a bare quorum) voted to recognize the circular letter, "but for all that," Henry Laurens wrote a correspondent on November 22, "some people call it 'the glorius (sic) unanimous Carolina Assembly.'" The "Unanimous Twenty-six" quickly took its place in the numerology of South Carolina Whig rhetoric, along with the "Glorious Forty-five" and the "Ninety-two Anti-rescinders."[2]

As Laurens indicated, the cry of a "unanimous Carolina Assembly" was a deliberate distortion. The organization behind the event extended back to the Assembly elections in early October. Although the elections aroused little interest in the province generally, feelings in Charleston ran high, and the radicals in particular strove to elect sympathetic assemblymen. The Charleston mechanics, whose group consciousness was strong but who still selected leading merchants and planters to represent them in the legislature, held a meeting and chose for their slate Christopher Gadsden, Thomas Smith Sr., Hopkins Price, Benjamin Dart, Thomas Smith "of Broad Street," and Thomas Savage. The mechanics supported not only the reception of the circular letter but also making some official show of support for the controversial John Wilkes. (As events unfolded, the Wilkes issue was delayed until the next assembly.)[3]

To ensure that the reception of the circular letter retained top priority, moderates offered an opposing slate that included John Lloyd,[4] Henry Laurens, Charles Pinckney, and John Ward. Laurens and Pinckney won over the mechanics' opposition, while Gadsden was acceptable to both parties. Thus, circular letter supporters won from both slates. Although not elected from St. Philips, Lloyd, for whom "great diligence has been used in canvassing and interest-making," according to an account in the *South-Carolina Gazette,* won a seat from Charleston's other parish, St. Michaels. Lloyd, along with Laurens, Pinckney, Dart, Gadsden, Savage, and five others, would serve on the key Committee of Correspondence that would implement the intent of the circular letter.[5]

The "unanimous Carolina Assembly" is also misleading because, but for one upcountry representative, all were lowcountry members. The Assembly's swiftness to organize and proceed, which usually took a week or more from the opening date, effectively excluded backcountry representatives, who had to travel much greater distances. Nor was the lowcountry all of one mind. Five elected assemblymen refused to take their seats in protest of the circular letter.[6]

Meeting on November 19, the Committee of Correspondence wrote the colony's agent, Charles Garth, instructing him to cooperate with other colonial agents to obtain a repeal of the Townshend Acts. The House on the same day directed that a petition be drawn up to be sent to the king. Upon reading the journal of the day's proceedings that evening, Governor Montagu dissolved the Assembly. Within days, as noted above, the collective action of the "Unanimous Twenty-Six" had been written into revolutionary mythology.[7]

This example of the transfer of a traditional lobbying stratagem (unanimity) to political issues and purposes is one indication of the extent to which the imperial interest group experience had penetrated the province's elite political culture. Of course, unanimity is always an advantage in presenting a case to an outside power. But in South Carolina, unanimity acquired special significance because it conferred legitimacy on elite rule. If the people's representatives are of one mind, then the people's consent must be seamless as well. South Carolina's wealthy planter, merchant, and lawyer politicians had established nothing like the great planter class that ruled in Virginia, where "a sort of aristocracy" prevailed. Where the gaps between rulers and ruled are narrower, deference cannot be relied on to legitimate power. The South Carolina elite had to rely almost entirely on consent to legitimate their rule. This equating of unanimity with consent became especially critical during the revolutionary crisis, when the authority of government was assumed by revolutionary committees.[8] When decisions were not unanimous in these committees, the vote was "adjusted" for it.[9] This necessity to demonstrate legitimacy transformed what was formerly a wholly pragmatic lobbying practice into a symbolic ratification of elite rule. It was this special condition (the need to legitimate elite rule) that ensured the reception of the unanimity technique here more than elsewhere, and that transformed the solution of a problem into the expression of a republican principle.

The lobbying experience also influenced ideas about the structure of the state and the basis of representation. The committee of thirty-nine appointed to enforce nonimportation consisted of thirteen merchants, thirteen planters, and thirteen mechanics, the three major interests of the lowcountry economy, "as though these classes constituted the three estates of the realm."[10] Here we see another intellectual consequence of lobbying: the notion that the polity is divided into aggregates of interest rather than social orders of individuals. Furthermore, these interests should have a representation in legal and quasi-legal bodies, especially when the weight of policy bears unequally among them.

The legislative character of the nonimportation committee was understood by both sides of the question. A proponent of the movement and member of the committee, John MacKenzie, referred to the thirty-nine as "Your representatives." Speaking from the other side, William Henry Drayton[11] enlarged on the idea, noting that the Association's "resolutions" were rules, and that its coercive powers (social ostracism and commercial boycott) of nonsigners resembled the combined legislative and judicial functions of a representative institution. In South Carolina, the Association, essentially a lobby in motion, had been transformed into a new political structure. Expanding his thesis in a newspaper essay, Drayton wrote:

> That body is, in effect, the legislature, whose rules and laws are put in execution, and required to be obeyed. When other laws are set up, and other rules pretended or enforced, than what the legislative, constituted by society, have enacted, it is plain that the legislative is changed: and, whoever introduces new laws, not being thereunto authorized by the fundamental appointment of the society; or subverts the old, disowns, and overturns the power by which they were made, and so sets up a new legislative.—Thus the great Mr. Locke thought and wrote. It is now my duty to show, that, upon those principles, the signers to the resolutions are, in effect, the legi___t___e [legislature] of the pro___ce [province]; and that the promoters of the last resolution have disowned and overturned the power of the General Assembly.[12]

The balanced representation in the committee also acknowledged that embargoes were essentially anticommercial, and therefore the only protection for merchants lay in an unexceptional compliance. While some merchants may have benefited from nonimportation to clear their inventories, many more clearly suffered.[13] In South Carolina's indigenous and highly socially integrated merchant community, a "soft" coercion through popular and social pressure probably helped the native merchants achieve unity, but only after a period of strong resistance. According to one of Richard Champion's correspondents, it was a newspaper essay written by Christopher Gadsden, which lumped local merchants together with the despised Scots traders who were beginning to flood into Charleston from Virginia, that finally broke the back of local merchants' resistance.[14] They joined "to give a stroke to Gadsden's [letter in the *South-Carolina Gazette* of June 22, 1769] which reflected on all."[15]

This interpretation overlooks the fact that the merchants had themselves been discussing nonimportation schemes, but ones that in their view distributed the burden of the movement more equitably among all interests. "By the engagement lately entered into, a plan of economy is provided that must necessarily increase the landholder's estates. Such articles as the mechanics indispensably want are allowed to be imported. These two parts of the community are provided for, while the third is subjected to infinite hardships and distress."[16]

After a month of this sort of exchange between a merchant elite who understood the principles of interest-balancing and spokesmen for the mechanics who did not, a new form of agreement proposed by a committee of merchants containing concessions to all groups was read and approved at a general meeting of the inhabitants of Charleston. Since the merchants had at their previous meeting appointed a standing committee of thirteen to oversee the agreement that was now adopted by the general meeting, a similar committee of thirteen mechanics and another of thirteen planters were nominated; thus, the general committee of thirty-nine came into being.[17]

This example of enforcing nonimportation by representatives of all segments of the community was in contrast to the northern ports, where the movement's leadership and implementation remained in the hands of importers.[18] Through elite efforts to co-opt participation from all groups rather than one group coercing all others, the concept of a nonimportation was enlarged to a nonconsumption movement. The lobbying principle of broadening a constituency to spread consensus brought nonimportation to its most mature form in South Carolina. And to whatever extent the general community's consensus was there to be found, lobbying became indistinguishable from representation.

In the northern ports, by contrast, where implementation remained the responsibility of importers, entire merchant communities exerted additional pressure on each other to comply. In the port of Baltimore, the merchant community at first vigorously opposed nonimportation schemes advanced by the politicians, but were coerced into acceptance by Pennsylvania's merchants, who had in turn been coerced by New York merchants. (Baltimore was commercially dependent on Pennsylvania.) The ultimate source of the idea was Boston's popular leaders, who imposed it on a reluctant merchant community there.[19]

These contrasting patterns notwithstanding, merchants and politicians alike understood the necessity of unanimous action to enforce a nonimportation. But in South Carolina, where unanimity was underpinned by a broadened participation and a balanced representation of all segments of the community, the structure of consensus-making was undoubtedly better and more explicitly understood than elsewhere.

More important is the fact that lobbying in South Carolina was becoming difficult to distinguish from political representation. William Henry Drayton, who would by 1774 be an ardent patriot and a leader in the postrevolutionary period, recognized that the lobby of 1769 represented a new political structure. It contained a germ of constitutional thought in its arrangement, composition, and practice. It stood in a direct line to the provincial committees that would govern South Carolina during the first phase of revolution. These committees ultimately resolved themselves first into two Provincial Congresses and finally the General Assembly. As such, the nonimportation lobby of 1769 formed a bridge for the values that subsequently found their way into the new state legislature.[20]

Although Drayton published his observations in England, the dual character of South Carolina's actions went unnoticed there. Interested British observers thought they saw a purely interest-based cast of mind in South Carolina leaders' actions that was fundamentally different from the apparently more ideologically motivated behavior of radical politicians in the northern colonies. Some took it literally, mistaking the processes of interest group politics for a simple market mentality. Superficially at least, the behavior of South Carolina's delegates at the First Continental Congress on the issue of exempting rice from the planned nonexportation resembled nothing so much as the Carolina trade lobby of the 1740s-60s, which seemed to confirm this view. In this episode, South Carolina nearly brought down the Continental Congress unless it agreed to exempt rice from the planned nonexportation. Determined to protect the crop on which their state's economy depended, South Carolina's delegates (with the exception of the maverick Christopher Gadsden) adamantly refused to be a party to the third and final colonial Association unless rice was excluded. On this matter, both planting and commercial interests were agreed.

"Enumerating" rice for the Association's nonexportation phase of the embargo must have seemed to the South Carolina delegates a policy very similar to enumeration under the English Navigation Acts. An agitation to exempt rice from confinement to British ports only, or put the other way around, an agitation for direct rice shipment to European ports, had been standard South Carolina policy since 1705, so commercial opposition methods and style came readily to hand. Furthermore, it must have been galling to find the new government, ostensibly established to restore liberty by excising legal abuses, in fact replicating the very infringements that the colony had struggled against so long. South Carolinians included trade grievances among those in need of redress, and were annoyed when Congress concurred with Virginia in looking back no farther than 1763 for complaints.[21]

Delegate John Rutledge argued South Carolina's case before Congress in strictly commercial terms. The northern colonies, he pointed out, maintained themselves by a circuitous trade, especially in flour. The greatest markets for rice were in Germany and Holland. But as an enumerated commodity, rice had to be reexported through a British port. A nonexportation boycott meant that rice could not find a market without violating the law, which associations, as demonstrations of aggrievement, expressly meant to avoid. The northern colonies, which traded in unenumerated products (wheat and flour), would not only not be hurt by a direct nonexportation, but would actually be helped by the exclusion of rice, which would give their products a better vent. Rutledge argued that the northern colonies agreed to the Association not to protest against English policies, but to preserve and improve their own trade.[22] It is also unlikely that Rutledge had forgotten that only a decade earlier, the northern colonies had lobbied to defeat a bill before the House of Commons allowing direct rice shipment to the Madeira, Canary, and West Indian Islands in order to reserve these markets for their wheat trade.[23]

South Carolina's arguments divided Congress so seriously that debate halted business for several days. When South Carolina's case appeared lost and the Association was about to be signed without the exemption, four of the five Carolina delegates walked out. South Carolina appeared willing to destroy Congress rather than yield in a matter that it could only interpret as a dispute over interests rather than principles. Congress finally yielded to South Carolina's demands. Rice was exempted and the Association passed.[24]

Indigo, which was also originally insisted on, was yielded as a bargaining chip by Christopher Gadsden, who stayed behind to negotiate the compromise. Although South Carolina was certainly serious about wishing to exclude indigo from the nonexportation, it was rice that was named as the crop whose loss would ruin the province's economy and over which there could be no compromise. Still, the fact that Gadsden remained behind and that the four delegates who withdrew returned once rice was exempted may indicate that the Carolina walkout was a tactical ploy rather than an absolute decision.

Despite appearances, it is a mistake to assume that South Carolina's attention to its interests did not go hand in hand with a more principled belief in its rights in republican theory. Interest and principle are never completely separable, and in the minds of South Carolina's delegates engaged in the protection of their state's trade, they were certainly united. Two days after the Carolina delegation's lobby stratagems for the rice exemption succeeded, Edward Rutledge wrote Ralph Izard, "I saw no reason why the inhabitants of this [Pennsylvania] and the neighboring colonies, should have full liberty to export their wheat and flour to every part of Europe, and that we should be so much restricted in our trade. . . . *Equality is the basis of public virtue.*"[25]

For radical behavior, the South Carolina delegation could hardly be surpassed. It was behavior that was consistent with the impression that members from the trading colonies had made upon Caesar Rodney upon their first arrival in Philadelphia. Writing to his brother, Thomas, in early September, Rodney noted, "The Bostonians who (we know) have been Condemned by Many for their Violence, are Moderate men, when compared to Virginia, South Carolina, and Rhode Island."[26]

A tendency to employ desperate remedies is consistent with a lobby's temperamental relationship to power. When all final power lies elsewhere, as imperial power had done in Whitehall, there are fewer conventional ways to obtain a desired outcome and no way to ensure it. When others make rules that guarantee defeat, and conventional lobbying tactics fail to get the rules adjusted, the only way to win the game is not to play. What the lobbying experience may have contributed to a recourse to secession in the nineteenth century can only be guessed at, but it is worth remembering that this early "secession" from national councils took place.[27]

Of course a lobby's original raison d'etre was to negotiate better terms within a set of rules determined by someone else. Threatening to withdraw from the negotiating table can be a tactic, but permanent withdrawal defeats a lobby's purpose. We have already seen that the traditional lobby changed from a quasi-governmental agency to a form of opposition politics in the crucible of the revolutionary crisis (chapters 2, 3, and 4). Even so, there is always the option of *accepting* an undesired outcome, especially when one's negotiating position has shifted from out-of-doors to indoors. However, as much as it was a tactic to win concessions from competing powers, for South Carolina the lobby mode of politics was even more a strategy to achieve the greater imperative: internal stability. Tempting as it is to interpret South Carolina's radical political style as an ungovernable streak originating as a natural corollary to the lobby's essential powerlessness, it may more accurately be viewed as a choice made for the greater object: internal harmony. I will return to this point in the conclusions.

Upon returning to South Carolina the delegates had to deal with the divisions of interest that Rutledge had known would be opened up by the measure. Enlarging on his point to Izard (that the embargo violated principles both of commercial common sense and of equal treatment to colonial trading interests), Rutledge came to the real home truth for Carolinians: "to stop the exportation of indigo is still more foolish; [because] it is unequal . . . between the different parts of the [South Carolina's] province."[28] As Rutledge foresaw, indigo (and other) planters felt their interests had been sacrificed to the wealthier rice growers and demanded that the exception be expunged. Upcountry producers, dependent on their provisions export trade to the West Indies, were furious that the Association had ever been agreed at all, and threatened to march an army to Charleston to keep the port open. As Richard Champion described the situation, "these back settlers concern themselves little in Political Disputes and are indifferent by whom they are governed provided they are not debarred from Trafficking with the fruits of their Industry. . . . These circumstances (lead) me to think that except the Carolina Provincial Congress keep the ports open for Export and which they are allowed to do by the Continental Congress the back settlers will not be quiet."[29]

To accommodate all these conflicting interests, the supporters of the exception devised a complicated scheme to compensate not only the coastal growers of indigo, but also the upcountry corn and hemp growers, lumber cutters, producers of pork and butter, and so on. Rice planters were to deliver one-third of their crop to specially appointed parish committees, where it would be exchanged for an equal value (according to a table of valuations) of indigo, hemp, corn, flour, lumber, pork, or butter. The scheme was unworkable, but fortunately never had to be implemented. The Second Congress moved to strike all exceptions, both southern rice and northern cereals, before it was necessary to use it. The point remains, however, that Carolina leaders knew a fragmented position at home would leave the province with little ramming power in Congress. Having devised a working if not a genuine consensus, the five delegates were returned to the ensuing Congress without opposition, "as their proceedings in the former Congress had been confirmed on the whole, it was deemed best that confidence should be evinced by their reelection."[30]

Observing (and misunderstanding) the events at the First Congress, the British merchant Richard Oswald (whose advice ministers had heeded in the past) devised a Southern commercial strategy to effect the withdrawal of South Carolina from the general embargo when the Second Congress gathered on May 10, 1775. Virginia and Maryland would then likely follow, the Confederacy would be broken, and England could deal handily with each province individually.[31]

Oswald pinned his plan on the simple market motivations that he believed lay behind South Carolina's tenacity in defending the rice exemption. From his mercantile experience, Oswald estimated that if the rice exemption was adhered to when the nonexportation went into effect on September 10, "the planters of Carolina must gain for the year 1775 the best part, if not the whole, of £100,000 sterling by the embargo of all other provisions but rice."[32] This windfall would be realized partly from a threefold to fourfold rise in the European price of rice, since other provisions were to be excluded. But the main profits would be made by smuggling rice to the West Indians, which could easily be done by separate orders to the captain, since "there is no possibility of stopping a ship from deviating to that market once he's cleared port and away from the mobs." Since Indian corn was forbidden there by the embargo, rice planters could conservatively expect to get from £10 to 12 per ton instead of the usual £7 to 8. "This I suppose the Carolina Deputies at the Congress had in view, as one reason for their absolutely refusing to join them unless they were allowed to Export their rice."[33]

Acting on his perceptions, Oswald devised a complicated plan to induce South Carolina to withdraw from the Association. The plan penalized the province by repealing the drawback on rice and closing the Portuguese ports, but offered the greater reward of a trade monopoly on the West Indian market, and granting certain duty concessions to rice shipped there. Thus, the whole of the rice trade (as well as timber, staves, and salted provisions) could be diverted to the West Indies, where (as Oswald reminded Lord Dartmouth) it was vital for the subsistence of the slaves that were the "property of His Majesty's Subjects." "The Carolina planters cannot complain—having got a whole New Market reserved for them, and them only, which they never thought of: and a market capable of consuming the whole of the[ir] exports." The Carolina merchants, too, would benefit from the commissions on the great prices that country produce would command.[34] Such a plan would arouse the jealousy of Virginia and the middle colonies for their lost provisions trade to the West Indies as well as the timber and staves trade from the north. If South Carolina rose to the bait and withdrew from the embargo, the Confederacy would be broken. In Oswald's judgment, "To break the Confederacy by internal means (jealousy and interested feelings) is the best thing."[35]

Other British officials shared Oswald's misapprehension of the motives behind South Carolina's politics. They failed to realize that though a pattern of interest group behavior remained, its rationale had deepened and its purposes had broadened from narrow commercial concerns to include and encompass political principles. A note to Lord Dartmouth in the hand of John Pownall, undersecretary of state in the Colonial Department, on the wrapper of a preliminary draft of Oswald's plan reads,

> The enclosed paper [is] set out awkwardly and the style is unpromising—but there is great knowledge of the subject it treats of and a very uncommon precision and acuteness in the reasoning and reflection. . . .
>
> Mr. Oswald is merchant of great Esteem & credit. . . . Your Ldship's Uncle had a great confidence in his Integrity & ability I believe consulted him much in matters of commercial policy.
>
> Will it not be proper to answer his Letter & encourage him to go on in what he has so ably begun?[36]

As Alison Olson has acutely observed, "The assumption of George III's ministers in 1776 that American assemblies stood in relationship to Parliament much like the mercantile . . . institutions of the day was not preposterous, it was just a little out of date."[37]

The South Carolina-keyed strategy was actually Oswald's second and final plan to effect a disunion. One month before he had sent Lord Dartmouth a preliminary "Plan submitted for breaking up the American Confederacy by detaching one of the Southern Provinces" (either Virginia, Maryland, or South Carolina). In this earlier plan he targets Virginia as the key (but, as we shall see, for quite different reasons) to his disunion strategy.[38] His plan begins with a brief background comparison of the social and political cultures of north and south meant to explain why a southern strategy is more likely to succeed in breaking up the American Congress. He then proceeds to a similar comparison of Virginia (and Maryland) with South Carolina to explore which of them best suits his strategy. A look at these thoughts may cast some light on the differences among regional and individual colonial political cultures, and bolster the claim that distinctive factors were already present in the political culture of South Carolina that would have significance for future events.

The northern provinces, according to Oswald, had no great landed class but were peopled largely by yeomen on a footing of equality in property and esteem. The mercantile class was the only exception to this generality, and while generally better mannered, better educated, and certainly very wealthy, as a class they were too diffuse to afford "any one handle by which a turn might be given in this unwieldy machine of combination."[39]

In the South, the heat prevented white men from doing their own field work. They invested their capital in a "self-perpetuating" form of wealth (slaves) that accumulated to their posterity. Thus, a class of great families interconnected by marriage had arisen. Of all three southern provinces, Virginia was the wealthiest and had the greatest families; so much so that in Virginia "a Sort of Aristocracy prevails; by which these Families have a great weight in all the affairs of the Country."[40]

Yet the southern provinces, as in the North, had no political parties, so that "Government has no party. Being left to themselves, they are all of a side. . . . None of the Gentlemen being under any particular attachment to Administration at home." Based on these realities, Oswald's plan called for the Ministry to win Virginia's leading men to the mother country, who would influence their friends in turn. Oswald suggested a "Person of Address" should be sent to Virginia to persuade "the better sort of people."[41]

When one compares Oswald's Virginia plan to his South Carolina plan, one can see that the Virginia plan is based on a deferential society while the Carolina plan assumes a society of several equal commercial interests comprising a commercial oligarchy, centered in Charleston but radiating outward into the entire lowcountry.[42] Perhaps because he had a merchant's mind and believed appealing to interest a better argument than appealing to social pride, or perhaps because he had doubts about great planter resolve, since leading Virginians "I am sorry to say lye by at present, and leave everything to the pleasure of the Inferior Class," Oswald abandoned the Virginia plan for the South Carolina plan.[43]

Whatever his reason for turning to South Carolina, Oswald's decision poses an interesting question. If, as in South Carolina, you cannot rely on the power of deference to cement the social orders, what can you rely on? Both Oswald's elaborate plan and South Carolina's political behavior in this period suggest that accommodation, interest representation, interest-balancing, bargaining, co-option, and occasionally coercion supplied the dynamics of the system. It is a much more flexible system for a society with narrower gaps between the local elite and the masses.[44]

These essentially commercial methods and commercial perceptions should not, however, be equated with modern democratic values. When Edward Rutledge pronounced in 1775 that equality was the basis of public virtue, he was not advocating a social or political equality for all, either then or for the future. A decade later, in one rather extreme example of the assertion of elite prerogative, Edward's brother, John, hauled William Thompson, a tavern owner and supporter of Charleston's radical popular faction, before the House of Representatives for contempt. Rutledge contended that Thompson had insulted his (Rutledge's) slave, and therefore Rutledge himself. A more extreme interpretation of lése majesty is hard to imagine. Possibly Rutledge was demonstrating (rather heavy-handedly) his power to a rival political faction. If so, he chose to demonstrate it with an incident that carried an unmistakable message about social inequality. On the political side, the General Assembly's unrepresentativeness, its jealousy of its privileges, its press restrictions, its high property qualifications for membership, and its monopolization of nearly all the state's institutional power, whatever it is, is not democracy.[45]

The contrasts that the outsider Oswald draws between North and South, Virginia and South Carolina, show that each section—and even each province—had its own distinct political culture. While a fully researched analysis of each colony to form a comparative dimension lies outside the scope of this study, the testimony of many other observers bears out the existence of critical distinctions. Virginian Robert Beverley wrote, "we are an Infant Country, unconnected in Interest, & naturally disunited by inclination." "Our Forms of Government differ egregiously," he continued, "but our religious Tenets still more so. Our modes of Life vary, & our Articles of Commerce interfere prodigiously. . . . Nor are we naturally more disjointed in Situation than in Temper."[46]

Looking specifically at the lower South, Josiah Quincey observed that "in their general sentiments, opinions, and judgments," the peoples of North and South Carolina "may well be considered opposites in character."[47] Richard Champion echoed the opinion that North Carolina was very differently situated politically from South Carolina, and added the observation that being cut off geographically from the rest of the continent by North Carolina further magnified South Carolina's distinctiveness.

South Carolina's lowcountry political character could only have been intensified by being literally surrounded and besieged by alien cultures. North Carolina, from whose political "Character of the Inhabitants there cannot be much dependence" in Champion's opinion, bounded to the north. Georgia suffered from disturbances that seemed in part ethnic. The 1775 burning of Augusta by a body of two hundred Highland Scotsmen, "not without bloodshed," was in retaliation for the tarring and feathering of a fellow Scot. Commercial as well as political rivalry divided Charleston from Savannah, and the stronger strain of loyalism among Georgia's Tories spread across the

Savannah River into the southern coastal counties of Granville and Colleton and along the lower sea islands, threatening the Carolina leadership from the south.[48]

Champion's description of South Carolina's domestic politics, obtained as it was from his Charleston correspondents, would reflect the local view of their situation, which is more important than a factually perfect account. The province itself, he wrote, was divided internally into two distinct parts. The rice-growing lowcountry with large plantations and many blacks (up to ten times the number of whites) dominated the province politically. The backcountry had recently filled with new immigrants who had little reason for allegiance to the government at Charleston, but whose opinions held the state's unity in the balance. They had few slaves, but lived by the Indian trade, farming, and small manufactures, and were apolitical unless "debarred from Trafficking with the fruits of their Industry." These people formally declared themselves opposed to the Provincial Congress at Charleston on account of the Association. (Apparently unknown to the writer, military units had been raised by backcountry leaders, who declared they would march on Charleston if the Association remained in force.) The Indians would fight on the side of whoever paid them.[49]

Surrounded as they were by alien and threatening cultures and competing powers, it is not surprising that Carolina's elite found that the half besieged, half bellicose political posture of a trade lobby resonated with the defensive "circle of covered wagons" reality of South Carolina's entire situation from the early 1770s through the 1780s. Nor is it surprising that the necessity of keeping the ranks closed or a zero-sum resistance should have exercised such a high priority.

This mode of politics was already sufficiently entrenched to be noticeable to outsiders. Commenting in 1770 on the solidarity and daring of South Carolina's political leadership when it proposed to extend the 1769 embargo to the West Indies, Georgia's Royal Governor James Wright wrote, "such a confederacy to destroy liberty was never known till 1766, and now, both times in Charleston. . . . How far may these people go, or where stop?"[50]

By the time of the meeting of the Constitutional Convention in Philadelphia in 1787, these distinctions among the new states' political cultures were still considered crucial in the search for a government that would answer for all. Charles Pinckney, one of South Carolina's five Federalist delegates, approached the problem of social and political divisions by sketching a picture of American society as one with workable, interdependent parts. In keeping with South Carolina modes of thought, he chose primarily to break society down into interest groups rather than ranks by wealth or birth.

> The people of the Union may be classed as follows: Commercial men, who will be of consequence or not, in the political scale, as commerce may be made the object of the attention of government. . . . Another class is professional men, who, from their education and pursuits, must ever have a considerable influence, while your government retains the republican principle, and its affairs are agitated in the assemblies of the people. . . . The third with whom I will connect the mechanical, as generally attached to them, are the landed interest—the owners and cultivators of the soil— the men attached to the truest interest of their country. . . . These classes compose the people of the Union; and, fortunately for their harmony, they may be said in a great measure to be connected with and dependent upon each other.[51]

He then enumerated the climactic, religious, ethnic, and linguistic bases of cultural difference—the Montesquieuian explanation for differences in habits and opinions that was so widely known among Pinckney and his contemporaries as to be nearly rote. Pinckney added that these differences were magnified still further by the variety in their respective state governmental forms and legal codes, "for, as I have already observed, the constitution or laws under which a people live never fail to have a powerful effect upon the manners."[52]

Madison summed the problem up along different lines during the debate over the basis of representation, the issue that, in Pinckney's opinion, nearly broke the convention up. Madison contended that the important differences between the states resulted partly from climate, but "principally from [the effects of] their having or not having slaves. These two causes concurred in forming the great divisions of interests in the U. States."[53]

What is curious is that both Madison, the political philosopher, and Pinckney, the pragmatic politician, agreed. Slavery was the greatest division within the Union.[54] Yet for the South Carolina delegates, it was a nonissue, not even a subject for discussion. The slave trade might feature in discussions about foreign commerce, but slavery itself as a feature of southern society was an exclusively domestic concern and strictly off limits to federal councils. On that matter Carolina leaders had not changed since Thomas Lynch announced at the debates for the Articles of Confederation fifteen years earlier, "If it is debated whether their slaves are their property, there is an end of the confederation."[55]

Carolinians had come to Philadelphia not to discuss slavery, but to restore their foreign commerce to its former prosperity. Five years of legislative interference with private contracts (the installment acts), enacted during the postwar economic crisis, had sunk the state's credit abroad to its lowest point. These acts were passed in violation of Article VI of the 1783 peace treaty with Great Britain. Investing Congress with the power to make treaties would, it was believed, render these laws unconstitutional. It is not necessary to determine here whether it was the planter elite or small upcountry farmers who originally forced the stay laws through the legislature, or whether they could in legal theory be justified. The laws were, according to Speaker John Julius Pringle, a matter of survival for the state and thus required no further justification.[56] They were, however, no longer a vital necessity, and the backcountry's continued clamor for paper money, plus the possibility of further legislative installment acts, compromised long-held hopes for a commercial treaty with Great Britain that would restore South Carolina's lucrative coastal trade with the West Indies.[57]

Charles Pinckney's speech before the South Carolina House of Representatives, meant to introduce the new Constitution sufficiently for that body to determine on holding a ratification convention, begins with a summary of the reasons why a stronger government was thought necessary. At the top of the list is the decay of commerce.[58] At the ratification convention the following May, Pinckney singled out Section 10 of Article I as the "soul of the constitution," a phrase we may construe to indicate the section's paramount importance. The section's main body is like a negative image of the commerce clause, reciting the powers that states may not exercise, having granted them to Congress as part of the power to regulate commerce. In particular, the prohibitions on paper money, ex post facto laws, and laws impairing the obligation of contracts were the "Thou shalt nots" most needed in South Carolina to recoup the confidence of its foreign creditors. Letters from British merchant Isaac King (whose ties to South Carolina extended far back into the past) to his South Carolina correspondents reflect the deep distrust for the legislature felt by the state's oldest commercial connections.

In 1784, for example, upon hearing of the passage of the first installment act (which delayed the payment of debts due creditors and prohibited creditors from suing in court for them), King wrote that it was an "infamous law." "It is a heavy stroke . . . if ye Assembly possessed any principle of honor, they would be ashamed to act so unjustly and directly contrary to treaty." By 1787, King claimed English creditors had completely lost faith in American credit and wished all his South Carolina land sold rather than possess anything under a government that passed "cruel and unjust acts."[59]

Local elite opinion also opposed the legislation. Thomas Farr Jr., although elected to the House for the 1785–86 session, could not attend the opening of the legislature. Hoping to muster support for repeal of the 1784 installment law, he wrote from Newport to warn a fellow member that "to stop the courts of Justice [from hearing suits for debt] is a matter of the utmost danger, it is a precedent unheard of in any Government whatever, and if gone into will, I fear, wholly ruin the Credit of our Country."[60]

Likewise, John Lloyd, now president of the Senate of South Carolina, wrote to his nephew in London the following spring (an opinion that we can rely on for sincerity, as it is stated in a private letter) that South Carolina was in a "distressed state respecting money matters, by reason of an infamous law, which I flattered myself would be repealed at our last sitting, but, to our eternal disgrace, it continues in force . . . . It is a proceeding that must destroy all mutual confidence among ourselves, and forever blast our national character with foreigners."[61]

By 1787, however, upcountry and lowcountry, although differing greatly in their conceptions about a national government, appeared united in their desire for Congress to regulate trade. In March of that year the legislature, in a nearly unanimous vote, passed an act proposing that the Articles of Confederation be altered to give Congress the power to regulate their trade for fifteen years, although significantly, not the trade in slaves.[62]

For white Carolinians of both sections the commerce clause of the proposed Constitution had a fatal flaw. The power to regulate commerce included the power to regulate the foreign slave trade. While Carolinians had no fears about the security of domestic slavery under this document (Congress could never emancipate their slaves),[63] granting away the power to regulate slave importations represented a possible constraint on their ability to support the institution. This constraint would become critical if natural increase could not keep up either current levels owing to high mortality rates or with the increasing demand for labor from the rapidly developing backcountry. However, angling for exceptions to undesirable features of imperial trade regulations was an old and familiar practice for South Carolina's leadership, and must have seemed a safe and natural way to handle even so critical a question.

The state's delegation actually began from a position of considerable strength. The committee of detail, chaired by John Rutledge, reported out a draft Constitution on August 6 that required a two-thirds majority to pass any navigation acts, no taxes on exports, and an absolute and unrestricted suspension of the law's operation in the matter of slave importations.[64] During the debates that followed, a proposed time limit on the life of the exemption gave South Carolina delegates some unease. Yet most of the parliamentary statutes granting exemptions for their rice trade from the absolute control of the Navigation Acts had to be periodically renewed, at intervals of five years. The 1764 bounty act on hemp had not expired for twenty-one years.[65] The substitution of the odd year 1808 (twenty years' life) proposed by C. C. Pinckney to replace 1800, the year originally proposed, clarifies the South Carolina delegates' state of mind. They were thinking in terms of commercial legislation. Questions about the morality of either the slave trade or the institution itself did not enter into the calculations. To South Carolina's delegates this was a bargain founded upon principles of commercial equity, in form and spirit exactly like the trade exceptions formerly worked out with Great Britain.

To strike the bargain, Carolinians conceded the two-thirds for a simple majority to pass navigation laws, and agreed that taxation on their exports was fair. But what appears to be a concession—agreeing to an import tax on Negroes—was, in fact, a strategy. By setting a tax, but limiting it to ten dollars, the way for Congress to effectively stop importations by laying a prohibitive duty was blocked. The South Carolina legislature had itself used this tactic to stop slave importations in colonial times, and delegates would have been alert to the possibility that Congress might use the import tax for a similar purpose.[66]

South Carolina expected that the Eastern [New England] states, which supported the exemption, would continue to do so out of their own interest in the carrying trade. But should "political prejudices" (this was the code phrase Southerners used to distinguish Northern arguments that slavery constituted a potential domestic enemy and was therefore a defense problem from "religious prejudices" or moral arguments) override economic interest, Carolinians expected that population increases by 1808 would favor their section, and slave interests would have the votes to renew the exception.[67]

It is interesting to note that Madison mentions the North's religious as well as political prejudices while Carolinians entirely ignored the former. The argument was simply not in their political vocabulary. They acknowledged the latter objection, that slave majorities might represent a defensive weakness, but counterargued that they could regulate the demographics of slavery with import stoppages, both foreign and across state lines, as they had done several times in the past.[68] Indeed, the state legislature had passed just such a bill that very spring.[69]

Virginia's desertion of South Carolina on the slave trade exemption has often been explained as crass materialism. That state's oversupply would fetch boom prices in the lower South, where natural increase did not fill the demand. Prohibiting foreign slave imports handed Virginia a monopoly on this valuable trade. But it is also possible that Virginia had genuine fears about unlimited importations. Parliament had systematically rejected Virginia's statutes prohibiting foreign slave imports via duty laws during the colonial period, while permitting South Carolina's.[70] Hence, the utility of this method of control was never adequately tested there.

When confronted with the moral argument during the height of the debate, John Rutledge snapped that "Religion & humanity had nothing to do with this question—*Interest alone is the governing principle with Nations*. If the Northern States consult their interest, they will not oppose the increase of Slaves which will increase the commodities of which they will become the carriers." As for the interest of the South, "If the Convention thinks that N.C.; S.C. & Georgia will ever agree to the plan, unless their right to import slaves be untouched, the expectation is vain. The people of those States will never be such fools as to give up so important an interest." He concluded with the lobbyist's trump card: withdrawal. "The true question at present is whether the Southn. States shall or shall not be parties to the Union."[71] The Carolinians were taken seriously. Roger Sherman of Connecticut expressed the convention's general capitulation to their demands, concluding that "it was better to let the S. States import slaves than to part with them, if they make that a sine qua non."[72]

Here we can see that there was a second, older political vocabulary available to Carolinians in addition to that of republican discourse, one that was more compatible with their experience. That vocabulary was the language of interest, formulated in the mid-seventeenth century and surviving in the imperial commercial world that the South Carolina elite inhabited. "Self-interest will govern," wrote Richard Champion, rephrasing the seventeenth-century maxim, "interest will not lie." Although using it as a criticism, Champion demonstrates that the idea still had political potency in the eighteenth century.[73]

Originally the concept of interest as policy applied only to the interest of princes and states, but by the 1650s, it had been domesticated to apply to the many interests thrown up by the English Civil War. A clear distinction was drawn between "interest," or "self-interest," and self-love, deemed dangerous because a it was a "passion." Interest, dispassionately pursued, was the "center of everything's safety" because it was both a sure guide to the proper course to pursue ("interest will not lie"), and it permitted one to predict the behavior of others. As philosophy, it steered a middle ground between virtue and the passions, permitting beneficial results from nonvirtuous motives. The interest of states thus became not some absolute state-truth, but the reconciliation and accommodation of many interior interests. The concept acquired legitimacy, and by the late years of the Protectorate interest had become de rigueur for statesman-like pronouncements. A commonplace in Restoration rhetoric, a regard for interest was deemed inevitable, and some considered it as a positive good for its predictive value.[74]

It is worth recalling that South Carolina was founded and settled by seventeenth-century men, and that its first written constitution was supplied by Anthony Ashley Cooper, first Earl of Shaftesbury. By 1711, his grandson, the third Earl of Shaftesbury, who had been tutored by his grandfather's private secretary and intellectual companion, John Locke, could write "You have heard it, my friend, as a common saying, that interest governs the world." Shaftesbury's treatise, found on more eighteenth-century South Carolina bookshelves than any other work of philosophy, endorsed dispassionate self-interest as ultimately the most serviceable to the public good.[75]

Shaftesbury was among the first to acknowledge self-interest as part of human nature and to consider that a rational regard for interest(s) formed a necessary component of good government.[76]

> Now as to that passion which is esteemed peculiarly interesting, as having for its aim the possession of wealth . . . if the regard towards this be moderate and in a reasonable degree; if it occasions no passionate pursuit, nor raises any ardent desire or appetite; there is nothing in this case which is not compatible with virtue, and even suitable and beneficial to society. The public as well as the private system is advanced by the industry which this affection excites. But if it at length grows into a real passion, the mischief it does the public is not greater than that which it creates to the person himself. . . .
>
> You have heard it, my friend, as a common saying, that interest governs the world. But, I believe, whoever looks narrowly into the affairs of it will find that passion, humour, caprice, zeal, faction, and a thousand other springs, which are counter to self-interest, have as considerable a part in the movements of this machine.[77]

Once satisfied that the new Constitution proposed at Philadelphia would serve the state's commercial needs without subverting its particular interests, South Carolina's delegates returned home to orchestrate its ratification. The movement took place in two locations: the House of Representatives and the convention itself. The South Carolina historian George C. Rogers Jr. has analyzed the process through a prosopographic study of its chief architects: two sets of brothers, John and Edward Rutledge, and

Charles Cotesworth and Governor Thomas Pinckney. Three of these four had been delegates to Philadelphia. To that list I would add another delegate and a Pinckney cousin, Charles Pinckney.[78]

In the House, John Rutledge and Charles Cotesworth Pinckney deflected a routine motion to thank the delegates, arguing that if the document failed to be ratified, there would be no need. The ploy placed their reputations on the line rather than the document itself. They pushed to have the document considered as a whole rather than paragraph by paragraph, and afterwards, in a critical vote (76–75), Charleston (where support was stronger) was selected over Columbia as the site of the convention.

At the convention, which opened on May 12 and sat from May 13 to 23, the Pinckney-Rutledge coalition firmly managed the proceedings. Governor Thomas Pinckney, elected chairman of the convention, appointed his brother, C. C. Pinckney, chair of the rules committee. This appointment placed a number of important procedural questions within Pinckney's discretion. Young Charles Pinckney, the group's most gifted orator, made the opening speeches before the legislature and the convention.[79] Partly political philosophy and partly a commonsense analysis of South Carolina's conditions and needs, the speeches were meant to educate and persuade backcountry listeners in the document's favor, who would, in turn, carry the message back to their constituents.[80] Similarly, opposition arguments raised in the House by Rawlins Lowndes served as rhetorical questions for Charles Cotesworth Pinckney to further explain the Constitution's purposes. At the conclusion of Lowndes's remarks, Colonel Mayson thanked Lowndes on behalf of several gentlemen of the House for his opposition. "It had drawn forth from the other side much valuable information . . . [so that] those gentlemen that lived in the [up] country were now enabled to satisfy their constituents." (Lowndes was so convinced that ratification was a foregone conclusion, that although elected, he did not attend the convention.)[81]

An upcountry motion on May 21 to postpone the vote on ratification to give the opposition more time to organize went down to defeat. (Setting the same apportionment pattern for the convention as prevailed in the House ensured that the lowcountry had the votes in crucial matters.) As a sop to the upcountry sentiment for a bill of rights, Thomas Pinckney appointed a committee to propose amendments, chaired by the master of committee management, Edward Rutledge. Throughout his public career, Rutledge managed much of his program through the committee structure. In 1792, for example, he chaired nineteen committees.[82] And although committee membership was balanced between the upcountry and lowcountry, none of the nine that Pinckney appointed was an active critic of the Constitution,[83] and none of the proposed amendments, reported back the following day, dealt with individual rights. Three were concerned with safeguarding the state's internal government from federal interference, the upcountry's chief worry. The fourth recommended that the word "other" be inserted between "no" and "religious" in Article VI, guaranteeing that "no religious Test shall be required as a qualification to any office or public Trust under the United States." Francis Cummings, a Baptist minister from the more evangelical upcountry, wished to preserved the sacred character of the oath.[84] It was partially a trade for his support (Cummings was the only member of his delegation to vote for ratification), but chiefly an attempt to bring in upcountry religious interests.

Out-of-doors pressure for the Constitution proceeded without let-up, according to Antifederalist Aedanus Burke. Writing to Antifederalist spokesman General John Lamb, Burke complained that South Carolina's opposition to the Constitution was weak and unorganized while "its friends and abettors left no expedient untried to push it forward." The choice of Charleston for the convention site was crucial, since the town and surrounding lowcountry were solidly for ratification. Everyone was for it, "from the British Consul (who is the most violent man I know for it) down to the British scavenger, all are boisterous to drive it down." The commercial men organized press support, Burke alleged; "the printers are, in general, British journeymen, or poor citizens, who are afraid to offend the great men, or merchants, who could work their ruin." Moreover, the taverns kept continuous open house for the backcountry and lowcountry members.[85]

Burke's biographer, John Meleney, contends that press coverage by Charleston newspapers was reasonably balanced, although none of the opposition opinion examples he cites was generated locally.[86] Burke was right, however, in his allegation that the British consul at Charleston, George Miller, attempted to influence individual members in both houses of the legislature.[87] Merchants, too, clearly supported it, doubtless working for it through the Charleston Chamber of Commerce.[88]

On May 23, 1788, the South Carolina convention ratified the new federal Constitution by a majority of seventy-six votes (149–73).[89] Yet in the following fall legislative session, before an act of Congress could set the new government in motion, radical opposition leader Alexander Gillon proposed a new installment bill that passed despite heated debate.[90] This further interference in private contracts presumably embarrassed the Pinckney-Rutledge group, who had made Article I, Section 10 something of a crusade. The following January, the legislature elected Gillon to the lieutenant governor's chair. One correspondent wryly observed to John Rutledge that

Gillon was selected because of the "belief on the part of some persons skillful in political management here, that his *nominal honor* would be less troublesome in the executive than *his real power* in the legislative department. Whether it be owing to accident or system I know not—but it would seem that all those political personages in the legislature of South Carolina who are hostile to the measures of your family and that of the Pinckney's . . . are lately appointed to offices which remove them from the legislature."[91]

These five events demonstrate that interest group strategies had set the pattern for political problem-solving for Carolina's conservative elite leaders by the end of the colonial period. South Carolina's social composition, its political isolation, and a surviving political tradition compatible with the legitimacy of self-interest infused the lobby's strategies and assumptions with a special relevance for its leadership. Having served an apprenticeship in out-of-doors politics in imperial commercial matters, followed by an intense if brief practicum in opposition politics under the Rockingham Whigs, while at the same time learning the imperatives of home rule, Carolina's ruling elite applied its lobby-learned tactics on two fronts in the Confederation and early Republic. As representatives from one of the smaller independent states, Carolina deputies in Congress and at the Constitutional Convention in Philadelphia resorted to pressure, talk of disunion, and, in one instance, a walkout when facing serious threat to its interests. When faced with opposition at home, Carolinians turned to interest-balancing, trade-offs, co-option, and other pacific measures in combination with more traditional parliamentary procedural tactics to create a nominal consensus that masked a working control.

TACIT RULES AND HIDDEN STRUCTURE

THE SOUTH CAROLINA LEGISLATURE, 1783–1794

It has been noted that interest groups and political institutions mature in much the same way.[1] When one compares colonial Chambers of Commerce to councils of safety or provincial Assemblies, one sees similar developmental patterns. A Chamber of Commerce, for example, learns to accommodate diversity in the mercantile community under its organizational umbrella in order to represent the whole (its constituency) before outside powers. A lobby also seeks to broaden its base much like other political groups. In 1785, for example, New York's, Boston's, and Charleston's Chambers of Commerce exchanged circular letters much as colonial Assemblies had done, proposing united action against Britain's ruinous postwar commercial policy.[2]

Where internal structure is concerned, provincial lobbies and Assemblies also passed through the same developmental stages. Developing side by side in a comparatively fluid social and political context, legislatures and lobbies of the colonial period could influence, and be influenced by, each other's forms and procedures more readily than would be possible at any later time.

By contrast, a lobby developing in a formed state such as eighteenth-century England was obliged to fit the contours of established political institutions. The British House of Commons' formal structure, framed upon an entrenched set of rules, was fairly inflexible. Its structure might be augmented but not fundamentally changed by the development of such informal structures as an (indoors) opposition party or an (out-of-doors) lobby.

Because Parliament's majority controlled the rules to its advantage, an opposition party served an important representative role by giving new interests and political minorities an in-house voice. In a formed state such as eighteenth-century England, the addition of the informal structure of an opposition party was the only available internal means for the House to informally spread its constituency by creating a mode of representation for otherwise voiceless groups.

In a developing state like eighteenth-century South Carolina, solving the problems of minority representation and conflict resolution could go forward with more fluidity. Formal legislative rules were still flexible, and lobbies were still experimenting with procedures. Working side by side, composed of the same leaders, and more nearly equal in status in the imperial system after the mid-eighteenth century, these two problem-solving systems, the South Carolina lower house and the indigenous Carolina lobby, could and did cross each other's boundaries to borrow each other's tactics and to influence each other's development.

While this study focuses on the transatlantic lobby after 1763 as a school for the province's political leaders, the process had its beginnings early in the century. Issues like the rice trade, military security, land, and paper money all generated interaction between provincial lobbyists and the Commons House of Assembly, as well as a good deal of transatlantic lobbying throughout the eighteenth century.[3] From the 1760s on, however, a growing backwoods elite would test the legislature's ability to accommodate its interests. This rising planter class had little or no effective representation in the Commons House of Assembly.[4] And since the lower house was forbidden by Parliament to enlarge its membership, the lowcountry could not create new parishes and members without reducing its own. Backcountry demands for courts and schools led to a threatening Regulator Movement in 1767. A critical challenge to the newly independent legislature, therefore, was how to treat new groups like the backcountry planter interest as the political community widened to include them. How might these groups be brought into the system without granting a direct representation that risked politicizing divisions during volatile times?

The old elites eventually settled on the committee system as a point of entry. There are several reasons. Colonial members locked in constitutional struggles with royal governors discovered that the work of committees could be pursued with more secrecy and independence than that of the whole House. This advantage encouraged their development over the period. When backcountry Regulator demands threatened to erupt into domestic violence unless they found a channel into the legislature, it was before the various committees on government and legal affairs that backcountry interests got a hearing. That crisis saw a marked increase in the number of leading backcountry witnesses called to testify, and backcountry assembly-men such as Tacitus Gaillard rose to leadership roles on committees considering frontier problems.[5] The committee's potential as a site for conflict resolution, a locus where new groups could be represented, and a means for the legislature at large to spread its constituency without formally restructuring came increasingly into view.

Formal government came to a near standstill in 1763 when the Commons House and Governor Boone reached a stalemate in the Gadsden election controversy. It ceased altogether after 1769 (except for six bills in six years), with virtually no legislative committee activity occurring after that year.[6]

As the machinery of provincial government ground to a halt, elite leaders shifted the operational locus of their opposition to British policies from the legislature to their transatlantic lobby in London, where they could still get a hearing and might still hope to turn the crank of imperial machinery in their favor. The shift further hastened the lobby's maturation as a strategy, even as it politicized its role. On the home front, radical extralegal committees formed after 1774, with no legal authority to govern (and to whom the home government did not listen), increasingly turned to lobby practices (like interest-balancing and boycotts) to enforce their political will. In a real sense, the committee as a structure moved closer to the lobby model, while the transatlantic lobby itself took on a political role. If the tail of informal politics did not actually wag the dog in this period, it was the only end of the animal that was still in action.

In the swirl of the revolutionary crisis, these two traditions, the developing and still flexible committee procedures of the colonial lower house[7] and the more systematic strategy of the transatlantic lobby, converged to produce a new politics for South Carolina's broadened political community after Independence. The lobby model contributed representation tactics to older legislative committee practices, to give shape and structure to a politics uniquely adapted for conflict resolution. This is not to suggest that the organic *impulse* for political stability originated from the lobby. South Carolina's famous harmony had roots deep in its own social and political past. But the political methods the legislature found to sustain that value by maintaining stable conditions in unstable times suggest that the imperial lobby supplied a crucial tutorial, whose lessons bore first fruits in the unsettled years following Independence.

A comparison of the committee system of the enlarged (in membership and constituency) postwar legislature with that of the provincial Assembly demonstrates that representation for political minorities like the backcountry was accomplished in a different way after Independence. This new politics allowed the legislature to broaden its base while retarding the growth of another political structure that was beginning to appear in other states: the political party. Party politics was the alternative mode of representation for political minorities that South Carolina's elite most wanted to avoid.

In seeking antecedents for the new state legislature's committee system solution to its dilemma, several "schools" besides the Carolina lobby suggest themselves. Closest to home is the old Commons House of Assembly, from which the new legislature drew most of its membership. Another is the British House of Commons, both as ancestor and original model for the colonial lower house, and as the contemporary model for some aspects of the lobby itself. Straddling the two and partaking of them both is the school of the transatlantic lobby.

In the lobby's relation to the colonial house, overlapping memberships ensured that tactics learned in one would be transferable to the other. In relation to the contemporary British House of Commons, that body and several of its parliamentary boards were the immediate arena of political action for members of the transatlantic lobby. Overall, these three "schools" formed three interconnected circles, yet each had separate lessons to offer.

I

While the deepest cleavage remained the sectional split between upcountry and lowcountry, the end of the Revolution brought more immediate problems to the fore. Patriots, particularly upcountry patriots, resented returning loyalists. Native merchants and planters resented British merchants, while debtors and creditors mutually resented and feared each other. The members of the legislature that met in January 1783 shared only one common imperative: to accommodate the numerous highly divisive issues in such a way that social order prevailed.

The ability of the old leadership to do so was partially impaired by some of the changes contained in the 1778 Constitution, which loosened the lowcountry elites' grip on the wheel of power.[8] But the chief difficulty lay in a "democratic" spirit that mushroomed in the lower house, particularly among the upcountry members. "Our Governments tend too much to Democracy," wrote Ralph Izard to Thomas Jefferson. "A Handicraftsman thinks an Apprenticeship necessary to make him acquainted with his business. But our Back Countrymen are of opinion that a Politician may be born as well as a poet."[9]

This spirit threatened to substitute a confrontation politics for the interest recognition and reconciliation politics evolved through hard practice. William Hornby, a Charleston brewer and critic of the planter aristocracy, complained that those who disapproved of factions, parties, or a responsible opposition had missed "the great change in politics, which the revolution must have necessarily produced. . . . In *these* days we are equal citizens of a DEMOCRATIC REPUBLIC, in which *jealousy* and *opposition* must necessarily exist, while there exists a difference in the minds, interests, and sentiments of mankind."[10] This progression from recognition that separate interests rightfully exist, a position South Carolina's leaders themselves took,[11] to approving partisan politics, or worse, endorsing the principle of formal parties was just the sort of thinking that the old leadership wished to avoid. Divisions of interest were to be accommodated, not institutionalized.

The Senate, meanwhile, remained firmly in the hands of lowcountry conservatives schooled in imperial politics. It is not surprising, then, that most of the bills of accommodation in 1783 originated in the Senate. John Lloyd, elected president of the Senate in 1783 and a former South Carolina leader in the Charleston-Bristol lobby of the 1760s and 1770s, was well versed in the techniques of accommodation. The old elite in the House, however, much reduced in numbers, teetered on the edge of loss of leadership. Lloyd, writing to his nephew in London in late 1784 with reference to debtor pressure for stay laws in the next session, noted:

> The Malcontented party having by several publications endeavoured to influence the Electors throughout the State to make a choice of Men to represent them in the General Assembly from the lower class; the gentlemen of property to preserve their necessary consequence in the community and in order to prevent anarchy and confusion, have almost unanimously exerted themselves in opposition to them, and it is with particular pleasure I inform you that they have pretty generally carried their point, especially in this City [Charleston], & that I expect we shall have an exceedingly good representation, and by that means support the honour and credit of the Country.[12]

Lloyd himself was unanimously returned by his constituents in St. Bartholomews parish, but the experience of his kinsman and fellow Charleston-Bristol lobby-schooled politician, Thomas Farr Jr., illustrates the fragile position of the old elite. Farr stood for reelection from St. Andrews parish, where Lloyd believed "he had not the least doubt of being elected, but a party having been formed against him, he was thrown out."[13]

In that first emotion-charged postwar year, and to some degree throughout the half decade that followed, domestic interests were more polarized than ever before. Probably the most divisive issue before the House was the treatment of the loyalists. In the streets of Charleston, former loyalists were "pumped" by mobs. The less violent organized the Marine Anti-Britannic Society to agitate politically against British merchants and returning loyalist exiles. In the backcountry, where partisan warfare had been the most brutal, resentment against returning loyalists was especially strong. All these groups, but especially the latter, could make themselves felt in the legislature. On the other side of the question were many of the state's leading men, mostly from the lowcountry, who were willing to welcome the exiles back.[14]

It was in this atmosphere that the 1783–84 sessions of the House had to decide how to deal with the more than 250 petitions that requested relief from the confiscation and amercement acts passed by the Jacksonborough Assembly the year before.[15] The problem for elites was how to maintain a harsh statutory policy as a vent for popular vengeance while actually practicing a lenient enforcement policy in order to speed social reconciliation on the one hand, while defusing popular animosity toward restoring trade with Great Britain on the other.[16]

In other words, how best could popular and emotional interests be balanced against elite, pragmatic, and economic interests, always remembering that the largest imperative, social order, had to take account of the greater intensity of antiloyalist feeling in the upcountry? Although the House did pass two bills that eased the most oppressive features of the 1782 legislation, the bill that took the most substantial steps toward reconciliation, a process not completed until 1786, originated in the Senate.[17]

Since the old leadership's grip was not so firm in the House, this approach (passing new laws to ameliorate the effects of previous legislation) became the exception rather than the rule. Rather than pass general laws in response to the large number of petitions for relief, the House handled each case individually, assigning a select committee to evaluate and make recommendations. In this way the interest of the individual petitioner could be served without placing the matter before a committee of the whole House, where debate about principles might call existing policy into question—and, worse yet, let the public see disunity at a time when the appearance of accord was so vital.

Debate carried on within the select committee, which kept no records of either debates or divisions, did not carry the same high level of risk.[18] The committee also allowed for more ample and frequent discussion of a question, as the formal rules of debate did not apply. There was no limit to the number of times a member might speak. The long, more didactic than

consultative orations that were common to the floor of the House were considered both inappropriate and unnecessary within committees. Moreover,
once consensus was achieved within the committee, its official report was
usually rubber stamped by a committee of the whole House without further
debate. Thus, the appearance of unanimity, a tacit rule of the lobby, was
maintained.

The precarious balance on which lowcountry leadership rested meant
that committee leadership could not be equally shared. Of the 1,046 committee assignments made in the 1783–84 session (a process controlled by
the Speaker, invariably a member of the old elite), only 261 or just one-quarter went to upcountry representatives (see table 6.1). Thus, the lowcountry
maintained control.

To offset backcountry resentment and to provide proper representation
for the many private petitioners for relief from the confiscation act, the
House had by late January established the practice of selecting committees
composed exclusively of members from the petitioner's own place of residence.[19] This method not only permitted debate on the sensitive issue of
treatment of loyalists to take place behind closed doors, but allowed local
and sectional perspectives to prevail in granting or denying a petitioner's
request.

Among the petitions presented on January 29, 1783, for example, were
requests from former loyalists Patrick Cunningham of Saluda, John Cunningham of Ninety-Six, and Robert Cunningham (petition not found) for relief from the penalties of confiscation of their estates and banishment. These
were "Ordered . . . to the Committee of the Members of the Parishes and Districts in which the said Petitioners respectively reside." The committee
therefore consisted of House members George Ross, Robert Hanna, and
Charles Saxon, all of Little River District near Saluda where the Cunning-
hams lived. This committee recommended that the petitions of Robert and
Patrick Cunningham be denied as they do "from their *own Knowledge* [em-
phasis added] of their Conduct Believe them to be inveterate enemies to the
Independence of America." They denied the petition of John Cunningham because he had always been attached to the British government, even though
he had not acted "in a Violent Manner, [and] hath Supported the character
of an Honest Man among his neighbors."[20] Both Patrick and John Cunningham's petitions appeared with certificates in their behalf from the inhabitants of their respective neighborhoods. This fairly common practice
indicates that the legislature recognized and normally took into account that
local people might have decided views on what loyalty meant, and that a decision of the committee to override local opinion would have to be explained.

Another case required the committee to determine on fine points of motivation. The petition of William H. Gibbes, who also requested relief from the confiscation and banishment acts, was ordered to a committee of the petitioner's own representatives. They concluded that Gibbes was "a Character beneath the attention or notice of this House; his turn for Buffoonery seems to have been a principal inducement for his being taken notice of by the British Officers to whom he was attached no longer than whilst they remained Masters of the Town, and his motive for signing the Address [congratulating General Clinton on the capture of Charleston] was with a view to recommending himself to them. [Therefore] Your Committee are of Opinion that he would not be a dangerous Person, to the Government, if suffered to reside among us. And that he be amerced 12 per Cent on the Value of his Estate."[21]

Taken together, the petitions to the lower house show that through the medium of the committee a locality's interest in its purely parochial views received direct representation. Interest representation is another characteristic of the lobby, whose existence is predicated on advancing some particular interest of the group at large (whether it be economic, religious, or ideas about allegiance), not those of either the individual or some transcendent abstraction called the common interest. These petitions and their disposition show that practices that have become embedded in a political culture can affect not only that polity's political structure, but also its very ideas about representation.

The same attention to geographic interest can be seen in committee assignments for collective petitions on roads, bridges, ferries, and boundary questions. Residents of Camden and Cheraw districts, for example, complained in 1792 that several milldams built on Big Lynches Creek deprived them of valuable fishing. The House ordered the members of Chesterfield, Darlington, Lancaster, and Kershaw Counties, all counties through which Big Lynches Creek flows, to form a committee. As in this case, when the effects of legislation were exclusively local, its disposition was confined to the representatives of those on whom it directly operated.[22]

This question is worth noting from another perspective. In most states, the courts ruled on water rights.[23] Referral of such cases to the legislature indicates that in South Carolina, legislative and judicial roles were not as fully separated into specialized political structures as elsewhere. Contemporary essayists John MacKenzie and William Henry Drayton respectively referred to South Carolina's 1769 Nonimportation Association Committee as "Your Representatives," who passed "resolutions" and practiced enforcment features like boycotts and ostracism (the social equivalent of a boycott). The rhetoric of legislative power combined with a kind of judgment (economic and social ostracism) suggests that associations became quasi-legal bodies that functioned as small assemblies. In their nature and function they stood as transitional bodies between informal bodies like lobbies practicing interest group politics and duly constituted legislatures. The retention of both a legislative and judicial character in the South Carolina legislature is an additional indicator of the pedagogical role of the lobby in South Carolina's politics.[24]

Returning the discussion to the methods of interest representation in the postwar legislature, one may ask what happened when the effects of statewide legislation affected different groups unequally *within* a given geographic area. How could the committee handle local interest conflicts without a change in overall policy? Taking the legislature's revision of the state's court system as an example, one sees that something like the modern referendum was allowed to decide the issue. In this way responsibility for controversial decisions was pushed out through the committee system to the people at large, maintaining equilibrium within the House without surrendering final power.

The county courts established in 1785 had jurisdiction over small debt cases and some criminal cases, as well as authority over local administrative affairs. These courts were established in addition to the circuit courts for the upcountry in 1769, and were meant to make access to the judiciary more convenient, especially in local matters. When in 1789 the circuit courts were given complete, original, and final jurisdiction, the major obstacle of having to travel to Charleston for all writs and processes came to an end. Many backcountrymen then felt that the county courts were no longer necessary. Petitions complained that having both county and circuit courts required too frequent an attendance for jury service or as witnesses from citizens at the loss of much time and money. But the chief complaint was that the convenience of county courts resulted in great numbers of suits for small debt that might otherwise be settled informally (or not at all). Proponents of the courts included creditors who found the courts "by far the most cheap, easy, and convenient way of obtaining Justice."[25]

Petitions opposing the courts came from Fairfield, Lexington, Lincoln, Orange, Clarendon, and Winton Counties. In all but Fairfield, the courts were abolished. Proponents of the court in Fairfield, however, complained that the anticourt petition was neither advertised nor properly circulated and did not truly reflect general opinion. The House apparently agreed, since in rejecting the anticourt petition, it did not comment on the validity of the petitioners' grievances, but stated it could not grant their request because "they are less numerous" than their opponents. Likewise, it postponed action on a petition from Clarendon County because "they find the petition is not Signed by that clear Majority of the Inhabitants which will shew the true sense of the Community."[26] In this way the voice of the people spoke referendum-style through the fundamental instrument of the lobby, the petition.

II

In judging the importance of the lobby experience relative to other models for this politics, one is struck by suggestive parallels between South Carolina's legislative committees and the Board of Trade. The Board of Trade functioned as a clearing house for sorting out colonial petitions.[27] It gathered opinions, advice, and supporting papers from the various relevant ministries (e.g. Treasury, Admiralty, etc.), interviewed expert witnesses, obtained depositions, and collated opposing petitions before submitting the matter with the Board of Trade's recommendations to the Committee of the Privy Council. From there the matter went before the Privy Council itself, whose ruling was issued in the name of the king in council. In practice, the last two stages were purely formal, as the Committee of the Privy Council accepted verbatim the report of the Board of Trade.[28]

In the same way each committee of the lower assembly, either standing or select, acted as a mini Board of Trade, gathering information and supporting evidence for study and debate, then working out a consensus to embody in its report to the whole House. As with Board of Trade recommendations, the committee reports were almost invariably accepted without question. I do not mean to state conclusively that the lobby experience was the exclusive model for South Carolina's postwar way of handling legislation, especially the private bills arising from the petitions that comprised so much of its business, but the close procedural analogy does suggest that it must have contributed to it.

However, the original source in a historical sense where one might seek South Carolina's postrevolutionary legislative committee's model is the British House of Commons. And indeed, an inventory of the holdings of the legislature's library in 1793 lists copies of Hatsell's *Proceedings in Parliament* and *Precedents in the House of Commons* and the older handbook *Lex Parliamentaria*.[29] A comparison of the procedure for select committees for private bills in the South Carolina Commons House of Representatives to that of the British House of Commons for the same period shows, however, that while there are basic similarities, there are also some significant differences. Despite the lower house's self-conscious imitation of the British House of Commons in formal rituals (a visitor to the Commons House of Assembly in 1773, for example, commented that members sat with their hats on, but took them off when they rose to speak),[30] colonial adaptations to formal procedure introduced variations.[31]

In Britain's House of Commons, committees varied in size from eight to over thirty members. Select committeemen were nominated openly by members of the House, but they could be chosen by secret ballot. The historian Sheila Lambert states that exactly how committees were chosen, except when by ballot, is not known, but speculates that the member in charge of the petition may have named the rest of his committee.[32] When the appropriate number had been selected, the Speaker added the names of certain professionals such as merchants or lawyers depending on the nature of the bill, as well as members from geographic areas directly affected by the bill. The committee might be further enlarged by the order that all who attended the committee should have a voice.[33]

In the South Carolina House the Speaker appointed a select committee's members. He usually chose representatives from the petitioner's own district. Rarely were more than three appointed. It is unclear whether a committee chairman was appointed by the Speaker. None of the three is so designated in the record. One member (a de facto chairman) subsequently presented the committee's report, and may have been chosen by the committee itself rather than by the Speaker. In both Britain and South Carolina, the select committee became the natural place for opposition to gather, as minority opinion could find both a voice and perhaps a majority there. In the struggle with Walpole, such committees became informally known as "committees of accusation."[34] The crucial difference for this discussion, however, is the absolute prohibition for a House of Commons committee to either express an opinion or make a recommendation in its report, since that duty belonged exclusively to the House.

> the committee's sole duty was to examine and cross-examine the witnesses called in support of the allegations and to report to the House a faithful *precis* of the evidence, however deficient, absurd, or contradictory . . . but they were not empowered to express any opinion, since it was the function of the House, having before it the petition and committee's report on its allegations, to judge if it would comply with the petition and give leave to bring in a bill.[35]

The routine and presumably the mandate of a South Carolina select committee was just the opposite. In this respect the committee's procedure bore closer resemblance to that of the Board of Trade. And, like the Board of Trade's recommendations, the committee's report was usually accepted by the House without further discussion. That outcome—that is, keeping debate behind closed doors—is consistent with conventional lobby practice.[36]

Lastly, a nearer model for the postwar legislative committee system, and one logically closer to the state's political culture, is that of its own colonial Commons House of Assembly. When the two are compared along structural and procedural lines, it is clear that the colonial body supplied some important antecedents. But there are crucial differences. One common feature of the pre- and postwar legislatures, clearly the legacy of the colonial House and just as clearly a departure from British House of Commons practice, was the committee's deliberate disregard for record-keeping.

South Carolina's colonial legislative committees kept very few official records, although this was done apparently to keep royal governors rather than the public in the dark. The usual paperwork of committees (minutes, roll call votes, minority reports, names of witnesses, etc.) is almost entirely lacking. The House *Journals,* prepared by the Clerk of the House, record only the names of committee members (but even the chairman is never clearly designated) and the text of their final report. Some committee loose papers exist, but these remained in the hands of either the House Clerk or one of his several deputies who acted as secretary to the various committees. These record-keeping practices deliberately obscured much of the legislature's business from royal governors. Some, like Governor James Glen, complained to the Board of Trade that even with laborious study, the elliptical reporting and poor indexing of the *Journals* left him unenlightened. Little wonder that the lower house, bent on increasing its share of colonial government, struggled to acquire and retain power to select its own candidate for the important position of Clerk.[37]

Another important similarity was the tendency of the whole House to accept the recommendations of the committee without debate, a practice once again at odds with British House of Commons procedure.[38] In the case of the work of the standing committee on petitions and accounts, or of the various select committees appointed for special purposes, the reason might logically be efficiency. A committee's work was wasted if the fruits of its investigation were ignored. But the House followed this practice regardless of whether the report centered on routine matters or more controversial issues. The practice is consistent with colonial lawmakers' desire to make decisions with as much independence from the other branches of royal government as possible. In the case of the postwar House, the reason for secrecy had changed but the means for achieving it had largely been worked out in the colonial period.

A crucial departure from colonial practice, however, was in the function and status of the select (or ad hoc) committee. The developmental trend over the colonial period favored the standing committee, where power was increasingly concentrated. Because joint and conference committees were too public, they declined and their powers devolved to the standing committees, where they could function with less check by rival branches of government.

Service on select committees, therefore, carried less prestige in the colonial period than standing committees, and their work, with rare exceptions, was very routine. These committees usually handled an assigned task (like counting the muskets in the armory or making audits), then dissolved when the business was done.[39] Even private petitions and memorials relevant to their work went to a standing committee on petitions and accounts.

The postwar legislature, however, in a complete turnabout, resorted to the select committee for its most controversial and prestigious work. This practice was almost invariable for petitions to reinstate banished loyalists, but it spread to include other issues on which the public might be divided.[40]

This habit of appointing select committees for work that used to go to standing committees resulted from the need to contain each issue in a temporary, short-lived body. Collecting several similar cases in long-lived, standing committees, as would have happened in the colonial legislature, might have gathered sufficient weight to attract the force of policy-making legislation—an outcome the legislature specifically wished to avoid. The select committee, like the single-issue lobby, could generate nothing more durable than a rope of sand to join potentially explosive postrevolutionary combinations.

When one turns to a quantitative comparison of modes of interest representation in pre- and postwar legislative committees, the case for including the lobbying tradition as an important strand of South Carolina's political culture becomes stronger. In the colonial legislature, once certain universal conventions like seniority or special abilities are eliminated, the most important criterion for committee appointment was the opinion of the House Speaker, invariably a member of the lowcountry elite. In the colonial House, the lowcountry elite shared both a common geography and a social status with the Speaker, and consequently received the overwhelming share of committee appointments.

There does seem to have been some attention paid to geographic representation in the broadest sense. For example, Robert Frakes's analysis of membership on four committees (trade, Indian affairs, correspondence, and powder receiver/armory) during the Cherokee War years of the 1750s and 1760s shows that the powder receiver/armory committee, the committee most relevant to defense, had the widest geographic spread. And even though (as in previous decades) the frontier and midcountry were still not well represented numerically, George Gabriel Powell of the Peedee up-country received enough appointments to this committee to give him lead-ership status during several sessions in this period.[41]

A second committee drawing members from most sections was the com-mittee on Indian affairs, another indication of a recognition of the frontier's greater interest in defense. Representation on the committee of correspon-dence with its vital links to the colonial agent in London, and the committee on trade, which focused on ways to improve the colony's export figures, however, remained solidly in the hands of lowcountry commercial planters and merchants. At the same time, a class of lowcountry South Carolinians who were dissatisfied with their economic position in the British mercantile system, the urban artisans, had no representation in the House. They had to rely on one or another of the Charleston gentlemen (principally Christopher Gadsden) to act as their spokesman.[42] Consequently, representation for nonelite interests in the colonial house was spotty at best.

Moreover, even though two other backcountry members besides Powell achieved leadership status in the colonial lower house, they could only serve as spokesmen for backcountry views in committee.[43] With the backcountry holding only five of the forty-eight seats in the lower house after 1768, an assertible voting majority for its interests in the whole House was impossi-ble. And since there was seldom any attempt to balance membership be-tween the two sections within committees, the chances of finding a majority there were, at best, remote.[44]

To put the case in hard figures, an analysis of committee service by sec-tions for the 1765 (January–August) session shows that of the 311 assign-ments made, 310 (99.7%) went to lowcountry members and only one (0.3%) to the single backcountry member from St. Marks. The top ten leaders (all lowcountrymen) held 138 or 44.3% of the available positions. Of the 545 committee assignments made in the 1772–75 period (which included two new backcountry parishes, St. Mathews and St. Davids), 418 (95%) went to lowcountry members while only 27 (4.9%) went to the backcountry. The top ten leaders (once again all lowcountry members) held 282 (48%) of the assignments.[45]

The last source on which the postwar legislature might have modeled its committee representation patterns are the various extralegal committees and the two Provincial Congresses that governed the colony between 1774 and 1776. The first self-conscious move to recognize the wider community's claims to a meaningful representation came when organizers of the 1769 Nonimportation Movement balanced membership on the enforcement committee among the community's principal economic divisions. That committee comprised thirteen planters, thirteen merchants, and thirteen mechanics. The General Committee of ninety-nine, formed in July 1774 to act as a steering committee for the general meetings, once again reflected the province's chief *economic* divisions, although this time patterned on their numerical strength in the province at large.[46]

This conscious provision for a representation for the colony's economic divisions no doubt came more naturally to the commercially oriented low-country elite. A balanced representation for sectional/geographic interests in the various general committees did not happen. This anomaly was especially glaring in the important General Committee of ninety-nine, which acted as the colony's de facto government between July 1774 and July 1775. It claimed a general representation, but in fact only "theoretically" represented all geographic sections.[47]

When the General Committee, acting in its executive capacity, called for a new, larger organization to meet in Charleston on January 11, 1775, the First Provincial Congress came into being. According to Peter Timothy, who was the congressional secretary, both Provincial Congresses used the methods of committee procedure inherited from the old Commons House of Assembly (although committee size tended to be larger). Since the old patterns of frontier discrimination and domination of important committees by lowcountry members persisted, we may believe his account. Of the 269 delegates in both Congresses, only 127 individual members filled the 487 committee assignments on recorded committees. That means that 47 percent of Congress made decisions for the other 53 percent, who were totally inactive as committeemen.[48]

Among this active minority of committeemen, if one arbitrarily chooses 5 or more assignments as a meaningful level of service, of the 203 appointments made, lowcountry members held 138 (67%) while upcountry members held 65 (32%). If corrected for the "colonization" factor (lowcountry residents serving from upcountry districts), the lowcountry held 152 (75%) to the upcountry's 51 (25%) positions.

Looking at the top 9 most active committeemen (3 members tie for 10th place), the upcountry can count 3 leaders in the first and 4 in the second Congress, but 2 of these are lowcountrymen elected to represent upcountry parishes (William Henry Drayton and the Reverend William Tennent, where

Tennent served first from Charleston and then from the District Eastward of the Wateree). This tendency of the lowcountry to politically colonize upcountry seats makes the upcountry's share of 36 of the 97 (37%) committee positions among the core leaders appear more meaningful than it is. The 2 resident upcountry members (John Lewis Gervais and Joseph Kershaw) account for only 22 of the 97 (22%) available positions. Looked at either way, no trend toward sectional/geographic parity within the committee system of the Provincial Congresses comes to light.

The fact that neither the colonial legislature nor the extralegal committees or the Provincial Congresses of the interim period (even though the political community had officially widened) developed an internal system of committee service parity to answer the 1767 Regulator or threats of armed insurrection from backcountry dissidents in 1775,[49] suggests that some other tradition added that essential missing strand to the legislature's development.

III

Having discussed the character and sources of this new politics, it is time to show it in action. A study of committee assignments for each legislative session in the postwar years from 1783 to 1794 reveals that the disproportionately represented lowcountry shared leadership with the upcountry more as the critical period advanced (see table 6.1).[50]

Table 6.1
NUMBER OF COMMITTEE ASSIGNMENTS BY SECTION

YEAR	UPCOUNTRY	LOWCOUNTRY	TOTAL	UPCOUNTRY % OF TOTAL
1783–84	261	785	1,046	24.9
1785–86	400	1,007	1,407	28.4
1787–88	536	977	1,513	35.4
1789–90	255	417	726*	35.1
1791	356	502	865	41.1
1972–94	523	731	1,254	41.7

*One month into the sitting of the Eighth General Assembly (1789–90) on February 17, 1789, the House and Senate agreed to accept no further petitions of a private nature, presumably because of a large backlog.

Source: Michael E. Stevens and Christine M. Allen et al., eds., *Journals of the House of Representatives, 1783–1784, 1785–1786, 1787–1788, 1789–1790, 1791, 1792–94* (Columbia, S.C., 1977–88).

Table 6.2
RATIO OF UPCOUNTRY TO LOWCOUNTRY AMONG THE TOP TEN LEADERS IN COMMITTEE ASSIGNMENTS

	RATIO OF UPCOUNTRY : LOWCOUNTRY	NO. OF ASSIGNMENTS FOR THE TEN	% OF TOTAL
1783–84	2:8	324 of 1,046	30
1785–86	2:8	374 of 1,407	26
1787–88	3:7	354 of 1,513	23
1789–90	4:6	111 of 726	29
1791	5:5	341 of 865	39
1792–94	4:6	423 of 1,254	33

Source: Michael E. Stevens and Christine M. Allen et al., eds., *Journals of the House of Representatives, 1783–1784, 1785–1786, 1787–1788, 1789–1790, 1791, 1792–94* (Columbia, S.C., 1977–88).

One can further refine leadership by isolating a core group of the ten individuals with the most committee service for each legislative year (see table 6.2). These individuals received from 23 percent to 39 percent of the total committee assignments made each year between 1783 and 1794. When one sorts representation from among this group by section, one sees that there is a steady progression toward parity between the sections among the top ten servers. (The loss of parity in 1792–94 is owing to the failure of upcountry leader Alexander Gillon of Saxe Gotha to serve in that session. Gillon came under investigation by the House in that year for irregularities in his accounts with the public.)

The use of the committee to contain and defuse conflict out of public view, to approximate a de facto balanced representation without reapportioning, and to enhance consensus-making by sharing committee leadership was the lowcountry elite's chief stratagem for dealing with internal conflict, whether broadly sectional or related to specific interests. (I have confined this study to the broadly sectional questions, since disputes between specific interests such as debtors and creditors over such questions as a circulating paper or the stay laws would require another volume, and at any rate can nearly always be as meaningfully approached from the sectional perspective.)

Of course, when interests truly curdled, no tactic could prevent an open debate and vote. Comparing the ratio of numbers of roll call votes to numbers of petitions presented to the House in each General Assembly (expressed as a percentage) may give some indication of the tactic's success

Table 6.3
RATIO OF ROLL CALLS TO PETITIONS

YEAR	NO. OF PETITIONS	NO. OF ROLL CALLS	RATIO (%)
1787–88	250+	47	18.8
1789–90	275+	38	13.8
1791	330+	12	3.6
1792–94	385+	18	4.7

Source: Michael E. Stevens and Chrinstine M. Allen et al., eds., *Journals of the House of Repre-sentatives, 1783–1784, 1785–1786, 1787–1788, 1789–1790, 1791, 1792–94* (Columbia, S.C., 1977–88).

over time (see table 6.3). The drop from 13.8 percent in 1789–90 to 3.6 per-cent in 1791 correlates well with the achievement of parity in committee leadership in that same year. Roll call votes were not recorded until 1787.

One might credit the new state constitution adopted in June 1790 for the sharp decline in the legislature's resort to roll call voting to decide issues. Despite some dispute among historians about whether the old elites tri-umphed or were toppled by the new constitution, the fact that delegates to the convention were apportioned on the same basis as the old legislature en-sured that it would be a lowcountry plan.[51]

While the new constitution did improve upcountry representation, it was not nearly so much as is commonly thought. The size of the House was reduced from 208 members to 124. The lowcountry, with only 20 percent of the state's white population, held 70 seats, or 56 percent of the whole body. This change in the lowcountry's share of total membership represented only a 7 percent decline from the 62 percent that it had been entitled to under the old constitution. The lowcountry still commanded a legislative majority when it was necessary to use it.[52]

The only major upcountry victory was in getting the capital moved to Columbia, but it was a significant one. The measure passed by convention delegates with only a one-vote majority and required a two-thirds majority to change it. The rationale for the move was convenience of attendance for all members, but convenience in this case meant power. Moving the capital meant that upcountry attendance improved vis-à-vis the lowcountry mem-bers who did not like the rustic town of Columbia. Indeed, the one-vote suc-cess of the measure was owing to the fact that the convention was located in Columbia. There were twenty-two absentees from the lowcountry on the day the vote was taken, but only eight from the upcountry. Thus, despite the lowcountry's constitutionally guaranteed majority, the upcountry's better attendance record meant that the sections maintained a de facto parity during the two subsequent sessions.[53]

Lowcountry interests, outraged at the loss of the capital to Columbia, had to be conciliated, so the new constitution also made changes in the executive and judicial branches. The new frame of government required that appellate courts sit and major state officials maintain offices in both Columbia and Charleston. The office of the state treasurer was literally split in two, one in Charleston with jurisdiction over the lowcountry and one in Columbia for the upcountry. The governor was required to be in Columbia while the legislature sat, but might have his permanent residence and live anywhere else in the state at other times.[54] In effect, the government was divided in two, with each section getting an identical set of judicial and administrative services—a piece of interest-balancing that cost the upcountry little.

Not surprisingly, it was a compromise worked out in committee after the lowcountry's defeat on the location of the capital. That issue rocked the convention with three days of such violent debate that C. C. Pinckney proposed a select committee be appointed to work out an accommodation behind closed doors. The resolution was defeated, but reproposed and carried the next day. The committee chosen balanced three lowcountry delegates, C. C. Pinckney, Edward Rutledge, and Robert Pringle, with three upcountry members, Andrew Pickens, Robert Anderson, and Alexander Gillon, together with Governor Charles Pinckney. They met the following Sunday, and devised the "dual" government described above in a report that was unanimous.[55]

Although he has probably confused the apportionment issue on which "the lowcountry stood firm and prevented any reapportionment to the last" with this one, Timothy Ford writing four years later in 1794 may be correct when he reports that "a committee taken from all parts of the country . . . deliberated and reported, I have understood, unanimously, in favour of the present system; and their report with little or no debate, was *unanimously adopted in the convention.*"[56]

IV

The theoretical implications of a polity that conceives itself to be primarily divided into interests rather than individuals remain largely unarticulated in the legislative journals analyzed here, but the assumption is deeply embedded in its legislative practice. One petition does, however (as though knowing the mind of its audience), make the case explicit: the general welfare is not some lofty abstraction that transcends a society's interests. It is the collectivity of its interests. In form and language the petition is reminiscent of the colonial petitions to the Board of Trade. It is signed by sundry inhabitants of the District of Orangeburg, who request legislative permission to erect a toll bridge and causeway over the impassable Edisto River Swamp to the Edisto River in order to link the town of Orangeburg to Charleston via the river. They also ask for a tobacco inspection warehouse in the expectation that "it will open to us a new and extensive Source of Commerce." Speaking to the state's various interests, the petitioners are "sensible that the port Merchants will find it more their Interest to purchase their Tobaccos here, and transport them by water Carriage to Charleston, than to purchase them there [in Charleston] when rolled thro' miry roads, and heavy swamps where they must inevitably receive much injury." They can see no opposition from the lawyers; "ample experience of the Inconveniences they have sustained when riding the Circuit is our best security that they will give it their warmest support." The interests of the legal and mercantile professions when added to the primary interest of agriculture must equal "obviously and uncontradictorily the public Good."[57]

The first full articulation of a theory of interest representation came in 1794. In that year, upcountry demands for reapportionment based on its superior numbers, an agitation given new strength by the results of the first federal census, reached new heights. Backcountry delegates had made the same demand for representation based on numbers alone at the 1790 state constitutional convention, but the lowcountry block passed over it in silence. They also rejected a plan based on ongoing assessments of wealth and numbers, devising instead a plan that made no reference to its basis, although it was clearly some combination of wealth and numbers. Most important, the plan contained no provision for revision, thereby fixing the lowcountry's advantage no matter what changes in population or wealth might occur. Jerome Nadelhaft argues that the state was politically divisible into three, not two, sections: the upcountry, Charleston District, and a swing area composed of Georgetown and Beaufort, and that this political division within the lowcountry meant that the backcountry emerged as the most powerful section after the 1790 constitution.[58]

If this is so, upcountry leaders did not see it as clearly or for very long. The push to reapportion began again in the 1793 session by testing the "no revisions" principle of the constitution. James Green Hunt introduced a bill to add just one representative to his election district of Richland County. It was defeated when a strictly sectional vote divided the House at forty-five votes on each side of the question. Charleston Speaker of the House Jacob

Read cast the deciding negative vote. The same bill was offered again in May of the 1794 session and was again defeated.

Frustrated by political defeat, upcountry leaders formed the Representation Reform Association and took the debate to the public forum. Congressman Robert Goodloe Harper, under the pen name Appius, pressed the upcountry's claims for the right to legislative dominance by numbers alone, citing philosophical authorities and theories for legitimation.[59] On this issue, the usual accommodative techniques failed, at last forcing an articulation of tacit, traditional elite values long held inchoate in the legislature's "old *friendly* habits."[60]

Essays expressing the lowcountry's viewpoint appeared in numbers in the *South-Carolina Gazette and City Advertizer* under the authorship of Americanus (Charleston political writer Timothy Ford). These essays were collected in a thirty-six-page pamphlet published under the title *The Constitutionalist or, An Enquiry How Far It Is Proper To Alter The Constitution of South Carolina.*[61] Americanus's essays amount to more than just a denial of upcountry claims. They offer a strong alternative conception of representation based not on "airy theories" but the common sense of South Carolina's social structure and past political experience.

Americanus occupies himself in his first number disputing the theory of an original "state of nature" composed of unassociated men as proposed by Appius (who concludes that individuals should therefore be the sole unit and basis of representation). Americanus asserts that such a state "never existed since the creation of Adam and Eve. . . . Man knew his powers and rights, before the fancy of philosophers ever engendered this ideal state; and felt the relation in which he stood to his fellowmen, by rules superior to those which were metaphysically deduced from it. . . . When he sat down to reflect upon his rights and his duties, he placed himself under the direction of his senses, and deduced his rule of conduct from the real situation in which he found he occupied in the world."[62]

I quote this passage partly as a reminder that the traditional view of South Carolinian's busy merchant and commercial planter politicians was a distrust for and impatience with theories. In its bid for explicit power, however, the upcountry, like most groups without means to enforce a political will, appealed to theory. It is interesting, therefore, that while Americanus cites Rousseau for a congenial theoretical social model, he constructs a countertheory of power consonant with the old elite's experience of interest group behavior.[63]

Americanus argues that in addition to the natural rights of life, liberty, and property possessed by every individual, there are also acquired "interests," which are attributes of and possessed by associating groups, groups that have existed for just as long as man has had a separate existence. Each of these two descriptions of "contracting" parties (individuals and associating groups) must be taken into account when a civil constitution is formed.[64]

> In no country under heaven is the latter [associating groups] better exemplified than in Carolina, being composed of the mercantile, the planting, the farming and the manufacturing interests. Each of these is as much entitled to consideration, in forming a compact, as any of the others; and neither submitted to it upon the principle of holding their particular rights and interests at the courtesy of the others. . . . There is a more general division into which the society we live in may be viewed; I mean, the holders of slaves, and those who have none; or more properly, those who pursue and must pursue their occupations by "slaves" and those who pursue their occupation by themselves. This latter division is, perhaps, the most comprehensive of any that can be made, and forms two interests very distinguishable from each other. . . . A union between two such people can arise from but two sources, conquest or compact.
>
> Compact then is the foundation on which we stand, subsisting as I have already shewn, between each individual of the one part, and the "whole mass" of the other, so far as respects life, liberty and property, and the other natural rights of men; and between each description of interest, and the residue collectively, so far as regards the common interests of each description. . . .
>
> Every citizen then in society, who was of a particular description of interest, may be said to have contracted in a double capacity. If a planter, he stipulated as a man, that his natural rights should be preserved, and as a planter, that the planting interest should not be swallowed up by the other interests in the state. . . . The same may be said of all the other descriptions.
>
> The natural rights, as all men agree in them, are found easy to adjust; the difficulty springs from "contending interests." That in short, which is made no account of in theory, turns out in practice to be the subject most agitated in arranging the social contract. It is morally impossible that the several interests should be composed in equal numbers. Nor is it necessary they should. . . . As in a free constitution, no man is so poor or contemptible, but his natural rights are to be sacredly regarded, so no existing interest is to set at nought or sacrificed, because of its comparative smallness in regard to numbers.[65]

It is clear that the claims for majority rule had to be answered, since the state's various interests were not equal in either absolute numbers or geographic dispersal. Planting, slaveholding, and commerce, which generated the greatest wealth, were concentrated in the lowcountry while farming and manufacturing formed the interests of the upcountry. Modeling the constitution to base representation on population alone would be to "place the wealth of the lowcountry, and its interests and concerns, under the immediate administration of the back country."[66]

Here, then, we see the function of the argument. The challenge by a full-blown theory of representation based on persons only to the accepted scheme of representation, which grew from much older patterns when arrangements for representation were laid down for the General Meetings to reinstitute government in 1775, threatened the security of wealth. In the ensuing conflict between rival philosophies about the *basis* of the state (wealth, persons, or some combination), an interest group-based theory of representation emerged from the crucible of imperial political practices of the past.

It is tempting to call Americanus's argument intellectually incomplete, and by today's standard of constitutional thought, it is. It has been said that interests have no rights beyond the rights of the individuals who compose them, but that is the product of two more centuries of political experience. Nor was the majority principle necessarily the inevitable winner of the dispute. Constitutional thought tends to follow from what is, and the majority principle got there first and in the places where it counted: Massachusetts, Pennsylvania, the United States House of Representatives—America's winners.

The same challenge occurred in 1775 in Massachusetts, where the identical point was made but the other way around. In that state, where a theory of representation prevailed that saw towns as the equal units on which government operated, men of property on the eastern seaboard, great landowners, merchants, and city professionals saw themselves outnumbered in the legislature by the men of the interior towns. A memorial from Essex County formulated the conflict, and demanded that representation be fixed not on the towns, but on an equality based on either numbers or property, or both. As easterners had a clear superiority in both, the claims of one over the other were left unexplored. The legislative act in response to that petition fundamentally changed the composition of the General Court. The men of property allied themselves with city populations, and Boston's representation jumped immediately from four to twelve.

J. R. Pole has described this wholly instrumental discovery of the majority principle in Massachusetts as the men of property opening a "side door" to it. "The debate about the basis of representation was not a high-minded debate about the forms of government. It was the constitutional expression of a vigorous struggle to command effective legislative powers."

Once in place, the majority principle was hard to dislodge.[67] It is worth noting here that the power of American national mythology ignores the fact that at the time of its determination, the majority principle struck no one as a morally superior constitutional arrangement. In its original context it was the choice that served the ends of power.

It was in South Carolina, where superior wealth and numbers did not coincide in the same section, that the logic (and the threat) of the majority principle were most fully worked out. In the discussion that followed the upcountry's challenge to existing arrangements, lowcountry thinkers sought to isolate and name the fundamental building blocks of the state that should command a representation. Yet both Massachusetts' and South Carolina's leaders had a commitment to republican principles of equality which required that these fundamental units be equal.

What, then, in the South Carolina of 1794 was politically equal to what? Americanus asserted that while all men are clearly equal in their natural rights, the concept has been pushed to mean all men should be equal in their conditions. As men are clearly unequal in the natural abilities that produce unequal levels of accumulation, this leveling conception is both false and unnatural. Wealth, the measure of a man's interest, must also be calculated into the basis on which representation is apportioned. Wealth is unequal; therefore, although one man certainly equals another man, one man does not equal one vote.[68]

This analysis of equality, while tacitly present in the existing apportionment arrangements of the South Carolina legislature, was an explicit assumption of interest group thinking. Indeed, it was the only analysis that guaranteed an equal voice among groups with unequal numerical or economic power.

In light of the progression outlined here, one can trace more clearly the experiential/intellectual pedigree of John C. Calhoun's doctrine of the concurrent or "constitutional" majority formulated some fifty years later.[69] The rights of an absolute majority (itself an interest) may not supersede the rights of interests, because interests are seen as equal to one another no matter how many or few political individuals may compose them. Or, put the other way around, a tyrannous majority, either of individuals or an alliance of the most powerful interests, may not invade the rights of a numerical minority.

According to Calhoun, there are two ways to determine the will of the community.

One regards numbers only and considers the whole community as a unit, having but one common interest throughout, and collects the sense of the greatest number of the whole as that of the community. The other, on the contrary, regards interests as well as numbers, considering the community as made up of different and conflicting interests, as far as the actions of government are concerned, and takes the sense of each, through its majority or appropriate organ, and the united sense of all, as the sense of the entire community. The former of these I shall call the numerical or absolute majority; and the latter, the concurrent, or constitutional majority. I call it the constitutional majority, because it is an essential element in every constitutional government,—be its form what it may.[70]

In this method of taking the sense of the whole community, the majority will of the greatest number of constituent interests (the "concurring" majority) must be considered before law, including supreme law or constitutions, is either made or executed. It is essential, therefore, to identify the units that are to be considered interest groups. Calhoun believed that in America the most important divisions of interest were "almost exclusively geographical, resulting mainly from differences in climate, soil, situations, industry, and production."[71] Although one may point to Montesquieu as the source for this notion and not be proven wrong, it is just as plausible that Calhoun looked to his own state's sectional past, so rooted in these very differences. Moreover, he could not have failed to see the analogy between South Carolina's sectional and political history and the developing sectional problems of the nation.

While Americanus and Appius debated the concurrent versus a numerical majority principle in determining legislative apportionment alone, Calhoun merely took the same thinking one step farther to impair the unequal action of the law once made, when applied to dissimilar or opposing interests. Where absolute majority rules alone, the strongest interest(s) oppress all others. In the concurring majority, less numerous and geographically separated interests, the latter being most vulnerable, are protected.[72] From this analysis it seems clear that Calhoun was drawing at least in part on the political ideas flushed out in the debate to reapportion the South Carolina legislature in the 1790s, and thus indirectly on the thinking implicit in the interest group politics of South Carolina's colonial past.

V

The lowcountry managed to stave off reapportionment until 1808, when it agreed to a constitutional amendment that gave over the Senate's majority to the lowcountry and remodeled the lower house in favor of the upcountry. The result was that each house had a veto on the other. John C. Calhoun later described the settlement in terms of theory. "The government instead of being as it was under the Constitution of 1790, the government of the lower section, or becoming subsequently, as it must have become, the government of the upper section, had numbers constituted the only element, was converted into that of the concurrent majority, and made emphatically the government of the entire population—the whole people of South Carolina—and not one portion of its people over another."[73]

William A. Schaper rightly notes that the 1808 settlement formula was not worked out to conform to a political theory (although it may be reduced to one, as Calhoun did). Rachel Klein has demonstrated that it was the rise of an upcountry planter class that shared an interest in protecting the institution of slavery that accounts for the lowcountry's willingness finally to share power.[74] While this is undoubtedly true, the majority principle in a once again socially homogeneous state would have answered as well as a concurrent theory. But the decision to balance sectional interests as a solution, the chosen method, by this time lay too deeply rooted in the state's informal political history and culture to make any other choice acceptable to its traditional leaders. Interest recognition, interest accommodation, unity as the chief strength of a minority, which is by definition an *opposition* power—these steps marked out South Carolina's political path from colonial dependency to statehood. Achieving harmony through accommodative lobbying practices, or fabricating its appearance when interests fractured, welded a historic value to habit and necessity and created a practicing unanimity that became a permanent part of the state's political culture.

Harmony was a habit that had staying power. The official record of the debates of the 1790 state constitutional convention, for example, so acrimonious at one point as to be described as "all violence and confusion," was deliberately destroyed at the convention's conclusion.[75] This mode of thinking did not go unnoticed in the outside world. Upon learning of South Carolina's unanimous adoption of the Ordinance of Secession on December 20, 1860, Edward Bates of Missouri, Lincoln's future attorney general, wrote this passage in his diary:

> The people of South Carolina however widely they may differ in fact, have a politic desire to present an undivided front to outsiders, and to appear before the world as all of one mind. This feature of their character (the desire to keep up appearances whatever the facts may be) is not shewn for the first time, in their present revolutionary struggle. As long ago as 1790, the Convention which framed their Constitution, deliberately burned its records, to conceal from posterity the differencies (sic) of opinion which existed among them.[76]

South Carolina underwent remarkable demographic changes in the postrevolutionary period. Upcountry diversity challenged old lowcountry homogeneity, at times to the breaking point. But the overwhelming necessity for solidarity joined an older legislative tradition for negotiation and a malleable committee system to a strategy adapted from the lobby experience. The end product was a politics that could preserve at least the appearance of the lowcountry's former, much longed for organic harmony in times when its social and economic bases fractured. At those times the lowcountry managed an achieved harmony until cotton culture confirmed the ascendancy of planter class interests and values throughout the state, and a fundamental harmony was once again genuinely shared. In the process, the state's politics was permanently transformed.

In the divisive year of 1783–84, Christopher Gadsden advised South Carolina's leaders that reviving those methods to achieve accord was crucial for the seeds of the state's former peace and prosperity to regrow. "Let us only permit that natural forbearance, good humour, and harmony we were famous for, to keep down rank and poisonous weeds from checking their growth; and there cannot be the *least* doubt but *common* interest, joined with the *revival* of our old *friendly* habits, will soon give all the cultivation necessary to bring them to the fullest maturity."[77]

It is appropriate that Christopher Gadsden, who epitomizes the combination of a wealthy merchant lobbyist and a radical Whig politician, should give speech to the dual nature of South Carolina's most fundamental trait— harmony. Harmony as an impulse had its roots deep in the "common interest" of its organically homogeneous social past. Gadsden's words, echoing a wistful nostalgia for the state's lost harmony, at the same time offer solid advice and a reminder on how to recover it. He suggests a return to "our old friendly habits" to bridge the gap until a new, truly common interest could grow from the changes wrought by the Revolution.

Events proved him right. The "old friendly habits" of harmony, originating in the informal politics of the colonial legislature, when mingled with the lessons learned in the school of the Carolina lobby and under the pressure to resolve jarring new interests in the independent legislature, matured into a systematic strategy for conflict resolution. For postrevolutionary South Carolina's legislative politics, harmony became an achievement, not merely a given. It was South Carolina's unique achievement, so much so that the outside world would take notice that it was "harmony we were famous for."

Over the critical period from 1783 to 1794, underrepresented groups found parity, if not equality, within the legislature. It was an achievement that enabled the old leadership to retain rule until the spread of plantation agriculture and planter class values restored a genuine social consensus. In 1790, and again in 1808, certain constitutional changes and a new basis of representation restored prewar political harmony. This restorative impulse and the political know-how to accomplish it gave South Carolina its durable and distinctive politics.

Seven

A Comparative View

SOUTH CAROLINA IN THE NEW REPUBLIC, 1783–1800

In a 1966 survey of the literature on colonial politics, Jack Greene concluded that "every colony-state displayed a unique combination of characteristics that produced its own configuration of politics." He did, however, attempt to stake out some common ground by turning to the literature of political culture, from which he constructed a typology based on factionalism.[1]

All colonial polities had two common features: they were hierarchical and they displayed some degree of factionalism. Greene subdivided factionalism into three types. For the first, Greene borrowed Bernard Bailyn's term "chaotic factionalism" to describe a politics of ruthless competition for power, dominance, and economic advantage among leaders and groups whose alliances are temporary and formed for specific purposes. The second type, termed "stable factionalism," featured two semipermanent opposing interest groups. They have relatively stable memberships and represent specific regional, economic, professional, religious, or kinship rivalries. In some instances, relatively well-defined sets of opposing beliefs or principles may further distinguish them.

The third form can be described as "domination by a single, unified group." In this polity a dominant elite monopolizes all power, all access to power, and most primary sources of wealth. The elite is bound by common economic, religious, and kinship ties (or some combination of them). All opposition is suppressed or submerged by repression, manipulation, or "corruption" in the "country" sense; that is, by undermining the independence of its leadership. Presumably this type is the same as what is traditionally termed oligarchic.

The fourth and rarest form is almost "faction free with a maximum dispersal of political opportunity within the dominant group." Greene places South Carolina after 1740 in this group, along with Virginia after 1720. The problem with Greene's categories for this study is that they are descriptive rather than explanatory. Nothing in his taxonomy explains how these political cultures got to be the way that they were or what (if anything) these types of factionalism meant in terms of the political process.

On the other hand, "degrees of factionalism" is just another way of talking about degrees of harmony, the feature that has been identified as central to South Carolina's political culture. Thus, Greene's degrees of factionalism typology makes an appropriate framework for drawing meaningful comparisons between South Carolina and the other mainland colonies.

Although a minute analysis of the nature and sources of the political cultures for each of the remaining twelve colonies is beyond the scope of this study, one may ask to what degree they were more or less harmonious, and why.[2] The same question is made difficult for the postrevolutionary period, as too few studies on individual states exist (a problem this study tries to meet). One way forward is to construct a representative background for the entire period by concentrating on available studies of the political cultures of New York, Massachusetts, Pennsylvania, and Virginia. These colonies are chosen because, when their populations are added to that of South Carolina, the sum represents about 58 percent of British North America's total population in 1775,[3] and because they led the way in the political developments of the Revolutionary, Confederation, and Early National periods.

The contrast between South Carolina and the remaining mainland colonies can be further sharpened by drawing the British West Indies into the comparison. South Carolina's first settlers were Barbadian planters and their servants, and they brought much of South Carolina's original law and custom with them. If the British West Indies and South Carolina developed a similar politics (using tactical harmoniousness as the functional point of comparison), South Carolina's disparity from the other American mainland colonies becomes much clearer and simpler. Its beginnings in an Anglo-Caribbean cultural hearth set South Carolina on a different developmental pathway in political culture, a divergence never quite repaired by the common experience of Revolution.

I

To begin the comparison with the mainland colonies, it is perhaps Massachusetts with its town meeting that most closely resembled the political process of the South Carolina legislature, but in microcosm. Michael Zuckerman's penetrating study shows that New England's famous concord was at least in part a creation of the town fathers, achieved by manipulating town meeting procedures to submerge or delay confrontation until conflicting parties could establish a consensus. Such methods as referring items and adjourning meetings were delaying tactics. The secret ballot, the habit of recording neither votes nor opposing candidates' names, dampened all memory of discord. When discord did break out, the committee structure, where individual responsibility could be blurred, contained the matter while a search to establish common feelings went forward.[4]

Yet the engine behind this politics of harmony arose from the town-based character of society itself. The political desire for concord was only a reflection of religious and community standards. The General Court, on the other hand, had no such imperative. The town was its basic unit, and the requirements of actual representation and the habit of instruction tied representatives to a welter of local interests. Court (county seats, market and maritime centers) and country party politics appeared in Massachusetts by midcentury, unharmoniously jousting with each other for legislative supremacy. These "parties" gave way to more ideologically oriented popular and conservative parties after 1764 with the rise of issues that made divisions along imperial lines the most prominent. But whole towns still remained the basic units. There were few two-party towns. The ideological unity that tied the towns to the General Court after 1774 did not, moreover, survive the Revolution.[5]

As just indicated, the practice of instructing representatives could be an important cause of legislative dispute. The device of instructions enabled a community to bind its representative to vote only one way on an issue, whatever his individual judgment and even before he heard arguments from the rest of the colony. Town meetings, county courts, local associations, and even ad hoc caucuses claiming to represent community opinion could vote instructions. Such ties not only encouraged dispute, but also impaired the process of consensus-building. The practice was common, and both Massachusetts and Pennsylvania were instructing by the 1720s. By the 1750s, Virginia's burgesses were debating instructions as if their existence was long established.[6]

In colonial South Carolina, where few local government (or other) institutions existed to fill such a role, the practice never got under way. The issue of instructions did not even arise until after the Revolution, when, in the unstable year of 1784, a "democratic party" emerged in the lowcountry. When a Charleston brewer challenged Christopher Gadsden on the subject of instructions in a series of newspaper essays, the old radical leader of Charleston's mechanics flatly repudiated the idea. Gadsden argued that the system of instructions could be abused by "juntos," and since it was impossible to determine from the distance of government's seat in Charleston just what represented genuine parochial opinion, "it hath *always* been thought better, upon the whole, to leave the members untrammeled."[7] Gadsden's choice of the word "always" indicates that instructing representatives had never been practiced in the colony. It also emphasizes that a traditional value for local political power (apart from an individual elector's vote) had little or no standing in South Carolina's political culture.

Just the opposite attitude prevailed in Massachusetts, a difference that helps account for that state's greater political factiousness as observed by Jack Greene. One example of the strength of local politics in Massachusetts can be seen in the events following the General Court's 1776 call for a provincial constitution. The town meetings submitted so many suggestions about how a constitution should be formulated that the document could not be drawn until 1778, and then it was almost overwhelmingly rejected. Massachusetts did not acquire a constitution until 1780, although much was hammered out in the way of political theory along the way.[8] South Carolina, on the other hand, had produced two constitutions by 1778, both of them written entirely by members of the legislature and neither submitted to the people for ratification.

Massachusettsians' belief in local power was so profound that the Shaysites' resort to county conventions, a tactic of the previous decade, had political implications that shook the eastern political establishment to its roots. Political culture in Massachusetts, rooted in the power of local authority, gave Shays's Rebellion a potential legitimacy far more threatening than the actual disorder that went under that name.[9]

Although opponents of the Shaysite county conventions hotly denied their constitutionality, it was still true that convention delegates were duly elected by town meetings. As such, they symbolized an alternative and competing mode of representation to that set out in the Constitution of 1780. Conventions also corresponded with each other on views, grievances, and remedies. A denouncer charged that conventions drew up and circulated lists of recommended nominees for election to the House and Senate, a tactic characteristic of formed oppositions. And since the governing conception in Massachusetts still condemned party (as was true of South Carolina as well), the challenge to eastern legitimacy symbolized by reasserting the primacy of local authority to choose modes of representation vied with the convention's role as a form of collective protest.

Which of these interpretations spelled the greatest threat to eastern authority? The conventions, an old method resurrected to meet new problems, stood at a definitional cross-roads. The government at Boston chose to view them as a competing political structure to be ruthlessly crushed. They might as easily have been seen as an informal sort of influence not unlike that exercised by the eastern establishment, bound together by the advantages of family, long records of public service, and proximity to the seat of government. Had government taken this view, Massachusetts would have taken a step in the direction that South Carolina followed and avoided a rebellion.

No such difficult intellectual choices lay dormant in South Carolina's political culture. What local authority existed was the creation and creature of the legislature. South Carolina's political culture could not recognize local faction as a competitor for authority, having no history of representative bodies at the local level. The courts were the only alternate avenue for representation of the people's opinion, which could be made through grand jury presentments. But the courts were equally the outlet for legislative policies through judicial charges to the grand juries. Hence, the legislature's interpretative choices for local discontent were limited to accepting it as an expression of grievance or a lawless riot. But no residual local sovereignty challenged its constitutional authority.

As a result, the Shays-like rebellion that emerged in South Carolina in the 1780s had a very different outcome. Economic conditions in South Carolina resembled those in Massachusetts. The problems of little specie and widespread debt, further complicated by two years of crop failures in 1783 and 1784, all delayed the hoped-for recovery. The 1783 emergency installment acts, or stay laws, prohibiting creditors from suing for their post-war debts (an action that would have dispossessed many planters as well as farmers), were due to expire in July 1785, and the court dockets were crowded with cases. A statewide debtor fear erupted into violence in the upcountry, when a reported one thousand rioters closed the Court of Common Pleas in the Camden District. The legislature, though seriously divided in opinion, responded by renewing and expanding the stay laws to meet the emergency.[10]

The vigorous objection on the part of much of the lowcountry elite leadership noted by some historians sprang from the fear that foreign credit would dry up rather than from any perceived political challenge to its authority. Indoors, conservatives saw the problem as one of competing interests rather than principles. There was no fear that the rioters in Camden were motivated by wider political opinions.[11]

South Carolina's tacit perception of the state as a collection of interests intellectually demoted the Camden confrontation from a rebellion to an economic disorder, reduced ideological conflict in the legislature, and, throughout the 1780s, built up a record of successful conflict resolution that defused factiousness around which political parties might have formed.

Massachusetts politics, born and bred to a conception of the state as a collection of towns, each possessing a legitimate and original local authority, could only interpret the Shays's challenge as rebellion. Fortunately for the state's future stability, Massachusetts' political culture also included a history of fairly stable, party-like factional divisions within the legislature. An avenue existed for the transformation of the functions of the conventions, and those of the political networks of the east, into professionally organized parties, a development that took place during the Federalist period. Future social and economic protest could find a channel into the legislature for resolution.

When we turn to New York, the contrast with South Carolina's politics becomes even sharper. New York, where an organically factious politics ultimately found acceptance in organized party politics, is perhaps the antithesis of South Carolina. Patricia Bonomi has traced the emergence of first factions, then parties, beginning with the polarity of power that existed between landed and merchant interests in the early eighteenth century.

Against a backdrop of a legacy of political turmoil from Leisler's Rebellion, the rivalry between interest-based factions slowly transformed (owing to shifts in certain economic patterns) from economic contests to contests for power. These changes took shape during the administrations of Governors Robert Hunter and William Burnet, and crystallized in the conflicts of Governor William Cosby with Lewis Morris.

The rise of the Livingston-landed party in opposition to the DeLancey-merchant majority in the second half of the century worked itself out against a background of Anglican-Dissenter, "upriver" versus "seaboard," and metropolitan versus Albany rivalries. These multiple rivalries, acted out in daily political practice and without the benefit of faction-reducing processes, culminated in a politics of stabilized, legitimated factiousness. Although taking a more ethnocultural approach in his comparative study of political culture in colonial New York and Pennsylvania, Alan Tully draws similar conclusions. Party politics found their first legitimate expression in New York.[12]

It would be wrong to give the impression that South Carolina's legislative politics were conflict-free. Divisions of opinion certainly existed and opened up in periods of crisis; yet stable parties never formed or persisted

on the basis of these divisions. Any tendency toward party (or faction) formation indoors during the politically volatile years from 1783 to 1787 was
actively discouraged by tooling the legislature's committee system to absorb
and resolve conflict. When conflict became too polarized for the committee
to contain, something like a referendum operated through the petition
process to shift responsibility for decision-making onto the public. Select
committees required that petitions on controversial matters contain sufficient signatures to represent community opinion convincingly. This practice
allowed a sort of "majority rule" to operate, but only (and always) at the discretion of the legislature.[13] In public emergencies like the Camden riots, the
legislature acted at once to co-opt the grievance. These techniques helped
defuse grievances of out-of-doors alignments and ensured that they remained issue-specific.

The other technique for channeling political conflict into the system, le-
gitimized political parties, did not appear in South Carolina until 1787, when
the Federalist Party formed in support of the proposed Constitution. But the
stability of South Carolina's Federalist Party and the strength of its ideological allegiance to national Federalism bear closer examination.

Can the South Carolina Federalists (or the Republicans after 1800) be
characterized as a true party? This is an important question if one is to
argue for a distinctive (and persistent) political culture that valued a seamless harmony above all else.

Those who called themselves Federalists in South Carolina emerged,
like Federalists elsewhere, to press for a new constitution with stronger national powers. Yet, as Mark Kaplanoff has argued, their commitment, either
to the national party or to a Federalist ideology, was wholly instrumental.
South Carolina Federalists' only true allegiance remained where it always
had been—with the interests of the state.[14]

The lowcountry elite's motives for a wanting a stronger national government have already been fully discussed.[15] Briefly, the state's foreign
credit was in a parlous condition owing to various installment, valuation,
and paper money acts passed since 1785. South Carolina Federalists believed that the Constitution's clause prohibiting impairment of contracts
would nullify these laws and restore the state's standing with foreign (especially British) creditors, a credit desperately needed to shore up the fragile economic recovery just getting under way. Yet even as they argued
for these (and other) nationalist aspects of the document at Philadelphia,
Carolinians pursued and defended their state's interests with a fervor and
"intransigence" that set them off even from their Southern neighbors.[16]

Once home, Federalists campaigned hard for ratification. They argued that the state's economic recovery depended on revival of its overseas trade. Charles Pinckney singled out the commerce clause as the "soul of the Constitution." Yet on February 2, 1788, at the very next legislative session and despite the newly ratified Constitution, a new installment act passed 60–45, thanks to lowcountry, Federalist support.

Whether constitutional or not, and Charles Pinckney doubted that it was, he voted for the new act, along with another nationalist delegate to the Philadelphia convention, Pierce Butler. So did delegate John Rutledge. Of the forty-three House members who had voted to ratify the Constitution the previous spring, twenty-six voted in favor of relief, while only seventeen opposed (a majority of 3 to 2).[17]

On examination, the vote did not follow an expected party-line pattern of an upcountry/Antifederalist, lowcountry/Federalist split. It was actually the lowcountry parishes around Charleston, strongly Federalist the previous spring, which pushed the legislation through, while a majority of backcountry representatives (hoping for more radical legislation) opposed it. Charleston's city parishes split, but a majority opposed.[18]

On this analysis, Kaplanoff concludes that Carolina Federalism was not "an idealistic commitment to a political idea, but a rational calculation of particular economic interests." A great many lowcountry Federalist planters had heavy debts, and until the expected economic recovery actually came, they were not going to pay them. Even the anti-installment members from Charleston, being creditors, voted their interest, not Federalist principle.[19]

Pro-debtor relief Federalists like Charles Pinckney argued that the new installment law was just another instance of suspending the normal operation of law in a public emergency. Pinckney declared that "no inducement should tempt him to consent to it; but a wish to preserve the tranquility of the people, and the safety of our laws." Butler predicted civil war unless the legislature intervened, and even debtor relief opponents like Charles Cotesworth Pinckney admitted there was a crisis.[20]

But whether one accepts that South Carolina Federalists were voting their narrow economic self-interest, or out of a perceived necessity to avoid bloodshed (the public interest), the fact remains that "when local concerns conflicted with national commitments, Carolinians put local concerns first."[21]

Party labels in South Carolina were only skin deep and had little staying power in the modern sense. Less than fifteen years later, in 1800, the state's Federalist Party collapsed before a Republican onslaught. But it was the strenuous personal efforts of Governor Charles Pinckney, high Federalist turned Republican, and the removal of the state capital to Columbia, not Republican Party loyalties, that secured majorities for eight Republican electors.

Some Republican electors wanted to vote for the Federalist's vice presidential candidate General Charles Cotesworth Pinckney (Governor Pinckney's cousin) to honor the state. Governor Pinckney deterred some by personal persuasion, while he apparently held others in line only by making liberal promises of patronage. South Carolina's desertion of the Federalist Party shocked the nation. "God forbid!" exclaimed one Massachusetts congressman in disbelief when it became known that Federalist South Carolina had unexpectedly made Thomas Jefferson president.[22]

When we turn to Pennsylvania, we find once again that a party politics rather than a tactical harmoniousness developed to process conflict. In Pennsylvania, religion proved the unbridgeable seam along which legislators divided when casting votes, both before and after the Revolution. If we define a "party" as long-lived, well organized, and consistent in policy, the Quaker Party was a true party until the mid-1760s, during which time it dominated over the proprietary party in the legislature through oligarchic rule.[23]

In some respects its methods resembled those of a lobby.[24] A network organized through the meetinghouses controlled the flow of information and could get out the vote. But two changes over which the party had no control brought it down. A massive non-Quaker immigration between 1750 and 1773, plus the creation of new western counties into which Quakers did not move, brought new constituencies into being. The other change happened in the relationship between America and London. The advent of actual conflict, in which Quakers refused to participate, when added to the economic hardships of war, made Quakers the target of popular reproach. Intense party warfare followed a strong radical challenge, after which the Quaker Party's control collapsed, leaving Pennsylvania broken into a variety of religious and ethnic groups competing for political power.[25]

For a brief period (from mid-1774 to the winter of 1775), radicals sought to consolidate their control by mobilizing broad support. Apparently on the advice of one man, Charles Thomson, radical leaders of the revolutionary committees of Philadelphia practiced a self-conscious policy of appointing Quaker, Anglican, and Presbyterian members in balanced ratios. Here was the opportunity to develop a process of tactical harmoniousness. Yet despite the fact that the tactic of a religiously balanced membership proved "remarkably successfull" in overcoming basic religious divisions for a time and at the local committee level, there is no evidence that the practice spread to the provincial level. Moreover, as Quakers in good standing publicly withdrew their support for resistance politics, while increasingly public opinion demanded acceptance of Independence as a prerequisite for continued participation in Pennsylvania politics, the balance broke down.[26] This transience and localism indicates that political harmony, either tactical or organic, was not a prerequisite in Pennsylvania's elite political culture.

Once the competition was on, alignments by religion began to form in the Assembly. In 1778, Quaker assemblymen made common cause with opponents of the constitution of 1776, agreeing to hold a referendum on calling a new constitutional convention as well as on the test acts that were odious to all groups who refused to sign loyalty oaths (which included some Anglicans). Calvinists, including Scots-Irish Presbyterians and Reformed Germans, on the other hand, supported the constitution and harsh test acts. They also voted as a bloc to purge the College of Philadelphia of its Anglican influences, substituting Presbyterian officers instead.

Outside the legislature, the same alignments held and spread to the local level. Membership of the anticonstitutionalist Republican Club was distinctly non-Calvinist. Voting patterns in some counties showed a correlation between religious affiliation and political position. And while these alignments did not yet constitute professional parties, they were an informal means of expressing policy and laid the foundation for the legitimation of party politics that would soon come.[27]

While religion and ethnicity were crucial in Pennsylvania, these factors had almost no importance in South Carolina politics after 1740.[28] The great religious and ethnic diversity of the upcountry after the massive immigrations of 1768 prevented anything like a coalition of these groups. Moreover, the lowcountry's monopoly of political power through representation made these divisions unimportant within the legislature, where an Anglican majority and old world Presbyterians (a declension of the early Huguenot settlers) shared a secular view of religion. Religious groups were interest groups like any other for South Carolina leaders. It is significant that the state's constitutions of 1776 and 1778 forbade ministers of the gospel from holding legislative office, although they could be and were elected to constitutional conventions.[29] This pattern acknowledged religion's importance as a social constituency while denying it the status of an "estate" in making law.

We have already seen how Federalists traded attention to the religious concerns of the Reverend Francis Cummings for his support in the debate over a strong federal executive in the state's ratification convention.[30]

Taking account of religious groups' sensitivities went far toward making the new federal Constitution more acceptable to strongly Antifederalist upcountry voters, who were, on the whole, of a more evangelical religious stripe than the lowcountry.

Nor was this the first time politicians had used ministers and religion to moderate upcountry political discontent. When upcountry disapproval of the 1774 Continental Association threatened to break into civil warfare, the Council of Safety sent two dissenting ministers, Oliver Hart, a Baptist, and William Tennent, a Congregationalist-Presbyterian, but only one politician, William Henry Drayton, to explain the necessity for it.[31] Thus, for the South Carolina backcountry, religious (and ethnic) identity remained unpoliticized, and might even be turned to when lowcountry leaders needed an avenue of appeal for upcountry cooperation.

Virginia is the most difficult state to set in the comparative framework, because the literature on its political culture is still in the developing stages. Moreover, that development has been impeded by generalizations applied to the state by the ideological and materialist schools that are based on evidence gathered in other colonies, without asking whether these categories are appropriate to Virginia. Virginia, like South Carolina, has not been fully studied on its own terms.[32]

Jack Greene's pioneering body of work on Virginia's political culture has portrayed a tobacco-planting gentry so harmonious, self-assured, and fully in control that even the Robinson scandal could not shake its confidence in its ability (or right) to rule, nor the confidence of the voters. This corpus provided the social base for the broadly shared republican values that the ideological school ultimately attributed to it.[33]

Studies of dissenting Baptists and other nongentry groups, however, plus economic surveys of backcountry wheat growers, indigenous merchants, and producers for the West Indian provisions trade suggest a social and economic diversity that undermines the traditional view of Virginia society as a harmonious, aristocratic monolith.[34] And although these divisions of interest do not add up to class distinctions, or describe schisms in the ruling elite, they do help explain where the new nongentry leaders turned up by the Revolution found their support.

Virginia's harmony at the top did not fracture until the Revolution. Unequal and escalating hardships for the poor and middling sorts, who were being urged to even greater sacrifice in the revolutionary cause by gentry rhetoric, deflated the value of gentry authority. Fissures opened up within the legislature, and parties and factions emerged. (Strong and Onuf also suggest that the absence of a strong Tory element deprived the gentry of a common enemy around which to rally the common people's patriotism.) Challenged and belittled by both imperial demands from above and diminished deference from below, gentry legitimacy was compressed to its narrowest base. Leaders like Patrick Henry (who was popular more by rhetoric than by policy) were ready to step into the new open ground and tap into the unclaimed allegiance of gentry-jaded Virginians.[35]

Unable to accommodate their ideology to popular demands, Virginia's gentry leaders lost control of the state legislature to new men. Yet the split did not mean defeat for the old elite, because as wartime fissures widened into postwar factional disputes, the question was not so much about who should rule, but where, and what policies should prevail. On domestic issues like credit, private debt, and repayment of the state's war debt, the Madison-Jefferson leadership took a hard, conservative line. Their reward was a near total eclipse in state politics. Patrick Henry, in the words of Strong and Onuf, "had only to appear on the floor of the House of Delegates and the best-laid plans for forcing virtue down the throats of recalcitrant yeomen were doomed."[36]

But on issues involving Virginia's relations with other states, such as boundary disputes, and those over the western lands, Virginians were quite happy to rely on the greater experience of members of the Madison-Jefferson group serving in Congress. The old leaders found refuge in national politics or abroad.

With rejuvenated reputations earned there, members of the Madison-Jefferson group reentered state politics after 1790 as guardians against the excesses of state politics and as protectors against Hamiltonian Federalism. Their weapon? The old gentry values of independence and public sacrifice. Virginia's political culture was irrevocably transformed—liberalized—from below, but the rationale for its legitimacy was restored and ratified once again from the top.[37]

Virginia's tale of legislative harmony lost and won again did not happen in South Carolina. Elites staved off the postwar popular challenge by fudging its policies to accommodate popular demands. The old leadership relented on debtor-creditor issues, passing a series of stay laws and supporting a paper money scheme (certificates secured by land, which quickly found their way into many hands) even while keeping up a rhetorical opposition to at least the former measure. That stay laws also protected the large planters from losing their land to foreign creditors, and that the land bank scheme certainly benefited the large planters first if not most, should not obscure the fact that these measures were liberal, effective responses to pressing popular needs.[38]

Moreover, South Carolina's leaders never deserted the state forum for the national one. Charles Cotesworth Pinckney, for example, was successively offered posts by President Washington that included the command of the army (1791), associate justice of the Supreme Court (1791), secretary of war (1794), and secretary of state (1795), but declined them all. Edward Rutledge declined an associate judgeship in 1794, and John Rutledge was appointed minister to Holland by the Continental Congress in 1783, but declined it to return home. He resigned his associate judgeship of the U.S. Supreme Court (1789–91) to become the chief justice of South Carolina. During the troubled 1780s, these men held state offices nearly exclusively.[39]

In summary, a comparison of postrevolutionary legislative politics in South Carolina with Massachusetts, New York, Pennsylvania, and Virginia reveals that none had evolved a comparable system to preempt faction formation. The eastern and midatlantic states handled conflict by resorting to some form of party politics. At times, as in Shays's Rebellion, the system failed altogether. The reasons lie partly in stronger local institutions (as in Massachusetts), in more organized religious and ethnic sentiment (as in Pennsylvania), and in a historic and endemic factionalism that evolved its own balance from experience (as in New York). Virginia's harmonious aristocratic politics did not so much fracture as decamp to the national forum, when its ethos could not bend to accommodate popular demands. Only in South Carolina did elites stay on top of conflict with a system for tactical harmony in its legislature. The system acted both preventively, to cut away the ground on which political factions might form, and proactively, by giving representation to competing interests within the committee structure.

II

Turning from the mainland to the West Indies on the question of harmoniousness and the legislative process, one is immediately struck by the dearth of studies of the island Assemblies for this period. The trend in modern West Indian political historiography has been away from British imperial politics and toward black social history. Although Edward Brathwaite makes a beginning, studies focusing on indigenous West Indian politics and political culture in the eighteenth century are yet to be written.[40]

Despite this handicap, by drawing partly on published sources and partly on original sources, and by confining the comparison to the islands of Barbados and Jamaica (with which South Carolina shared a common branch on the British Empire's cultural tree), one is able to discern some interesting social and political similarities. These similarities sharpen South Carolina's distinctiveness from each of the other mainland colonies taken both individually and from the general pattern of mainland American political culture that other scholars have worked out.[41]

The colony of a colony, South Carolina shared a pedigree with Britain's West Indian islands. It is well established that Barbados was the cultural hearth for the plantation-based colonies on the Leeward Islands, Jamaica, and the land-locked "Caribbean" island culture of lowcountry South Carolina. From there, the culture spread into the Cape Fear region of North Carolina, coastal Georgia, and East Florida.[42]

When making specific comparisons, the developmental parallels between Jamaica and South Carolina become particularly striking. Both were settled in the latter half of the seventeenth century (1664 and 1670, respectively) by Barbadians, men already schooled in the political and commercial problems associated with being staple producers in an imperial system. From this common origin, the two colonies' cultural similarities were further intensified during the eighteenth century by growing linkages in commerce, investment, kinship, and marriage.

To strengthen the comparison quantitatively, one can point out that more than half of South Carolina's original settlers in 1670 (both black and white) are estimated to have been Barbadians. Over the next two decades, new settlers and those acquiring land in South Carolina included representatives of about 10.4 percent of Barbados' great sugar-planting families (those holding at least sixty slaves apiece). An even larger percentage of small to middling Barbados planters (holding between twenty and fifty-nine slaves) are known to have settled in or acquired land in South Carolina, along with several merchants. These same patterns—a predominance of Barbadian origins among settlers, as well as an early basis for a diverse social structure—were replicated in the settlement of Jamaica.[43]

In terms of population, Jamaica and South Carolina shared another common feature. Both developed black majorities. This pattern was not unusual for the sugar islands, but it was unique among the mainland colonies. In South Carolina some lowcountry parishes were so heavily black (ratios of more than nine to one, similar to Jamaica and greater than those found in Barbados) that one contemporary traveler found South Carolina "more like a Negro country."[44] With such racial demographics, concern about slave insurrection was an abiding feature of both societies, if not the controlling factor in their politics. South Carolina had only one serious uprising (the 1739 Stono Rebellion) while Jamaica experienced many times more.[45]

Both also faced external threats. Carolinians experienced numerous threats from the Spanish in Florida, the French in Louisiana, and the Indians on their own borders. Jamaica, like the other Caribbean islands, was vulnerable to pirates and smugglers, as well as the French, Dutch, and Spanish who inhabited neighboring islands and roamed the sea. Both external and internal threats would logically encourage its rulers to display as few divisions as possible.

Both societies grew wealthy, and despite Jamaica's higher absenteeism, both societies developed stable white populations composed of large and small planters, merchants, estate managers, artisans, clerks, and shopkeepers. These "committed settlers" of Jamaica built churches, hospitals, and schools, supported an active press, built houses in an emergent vernacular style, and supported a social and political elite who exerted leadership through "dynamic and self-conscious local political institutions." Kingston and Spanish Town, like Charleston, became respectively a thriving port city and a capital, and Jamaica, like South Carolina, developed and sustained a "self-conscious, articulate, cohesive social class of proprietor-administrators" whose energetic leadership continued throughout the eighteenth century.[46]

Historians of the powerful West Indian lobby have created the impression that Jamaica was ruled entirely from London by an absentee leadership. In fact, its island Assembly and politics were vital, active, and committed to local concerns. Individual assemblymen like the settler planter Simon Taylor could become so engrossed with government duties during Assembly sessions that even personal business had to wait. Taylor's apology for not writing a London correspondent in 1795 was that his time was completely taken up by "attending Duty in this town, the Assembly (sic) in Spanish Town, . . . having been the Chairman of the Principle bills that were brought in, . . . [I was] constantly at work from five o'clock in the morning until six at night."[47]

Like South Carolina, Jamaica also had a wealthy and stable merchant class. Owing to its merchants' connections with the Spanish trade, Jamaica did not suffer the sharp economic decline typical of the rest of the West Indies after the American Revolution, and its shipping actually increased in the postwar years, with profits going into local merchants' pockets.[48]

Jamaican merchants, like Charleston merchants, were also political activists, locally and in Assembly politics. While Spanish Town, the seat of government, was planter-dominated, Kingston, Jamaica's principal port, was very much a merchant's town. Merchants dominated Kingston's Vestry-run politics, had their own "Merchant's Pew" in the church, and had their own merchants' association, situated at the Kingston Coffee House and in the

Old South Sea House adjoining the Custom House in Port Royal Street. In other words, Jamaican merchants had the organizational ingredients for an interest group style of politics.

A merging of the two elites, merchant and planter, began well before the period of the American Revolution, but the coalition became increasingly solid in the postrevolutionary years. In 1817, for example, the elaborate Kingston Commercial Rooms sprang to life. Significantly, this latter establishment appealed for membership subscriptions not only to merchants, but also to

> the Landed Proprietor and the Planting Attorney . . . during their occasional visits in Kingston; . . . and to those whose professional pursuits cannot strictly be termed Mercantile, though all, more or less, are connected with Commerce in this island. . . . It is presumed, select company, and a multiplicity of English Publications, embracing every political party, will prove a sufficient inducement for their patronage and support.[49]

The wealthiest merchants still lived in elegant town houses in the heart of the city during the mid-eighteenth century, but many were also moving out of town to become landowners and planters (a pattern similar to that experienced in South Carolina). And while the old-line landowning "gentlemen" could and sometimes did express disdain for merchants as a group, the Commercial Rooms' appeal for subscribers beyond the strictly mercantile occupations, plus the emphasis that its advertising placed on its broad selection of *political* publications, suggests that Kingston at least had developed a supplementary cosmopolitan strata with a merged merchant-planter political elite.

And while it did not amount to the "vast cousinage" that guaranteed a more organically integrated elite in South Carolina, the shared commercial interests of these social alignments, combined with an awareness of lobby politics that no successful West Indian planter or merchant could fail to appreciate, supplied the basis for an interest group approach to problem-solving. An appreciation for unity, the lobby's functional imperative, is suggested in the name of a Kingston merchants' gathering place—"Harmony-Hall."[50]

In governmental terms, all these similarities between South Carolina and Jamaica elites could add up to the basis for a similar politics, and to a limited extent this appears to be the case. Just as the London Carolina trade lobby had its Charleston side, so the powerful London West Indian Merchants and the West Indian Planters Society (separate organizations that merged to form the West India Committee in 1775) each had their local counterpart(s) in Jamaica.[51]

So much scholarly attention has been focused on the powerful West Indian lobby in London that the existence of these local lobby groups has been entirely overlooked. One can infer from their correspondence with the West India Committee that these local lobbies were well established. They kept records of their meetings, and occasionally sent copies of their minutes to the London Committee for information. Such experience provided the basis for a growing sense of confidence and local initiative. On the matter of freight rates, for example, Samuel Vaughn, a Jamaica assemblyman and member of the Spanish Town merchants' lobby, informed the London Committee that he thought freight rates should be decided in Jamaica. These local committees would have functioned as schools for hands-on lessons in lobby politics, much as happened in Charleston.[52]

Evidence that the Jamaica House of Assembly had adopted an interest group model for a tactical harmony similar to that evolving in South Carolina can be found as early as 1751. Assembly politics was historically plagued by factiousness among its strongest leaders. The ability of certain individuals, like Rose Fuller and William Beckford, to invoke their family influence in England with important ministers, like Henry Pelham and the Duke of Bedford, encouraged this pattern even more. Yet Jamaican assemblymen were also locked in constitutional struggles with royal governors that were just as potent as those happening in South Carolina. In these struggles, Jamaica's leaders discovered that success could only be achieved by constructing a working harmony among themselves.

Royal Governor Charles Knowles (1752–65) himself triggered the process of tactical harmony-making with his heavy-handed challenge to Assembly autonomy. The response was a formally constituted legislative opposition calling itself "the Association," whose eleven signers represented a coalition of every major interest on the island. Naturally, Knowles viewed the Association as simply factious, a "party," a "cabal," a "decemvirate," and (reminiscent of Egerton Leigh's label for the Charleston lobby) a "combination." In an effort to destroy the Association, Knowles devised a plan to divide its merchant and planter members.

On February 5, 1754, the idea to move the capital from Spanish Town to Kingston (a suggestion made by Knowles's predecessor, Edward Trelawney) was revived by a merchants' petition to the Board of Trade. At least one associator, planter Rose Fuller, assumed that Knowles had instigated it to cause trouble, although the Kingston merchants needed little encouragement. Knowles certainly vigorously supported it, a move calculated to excite jealousy between the two interests, as indeed it did.[53]

The following autumn, hoping the Association had become too hopelessly divided to oppose him, Knowles tried to issue writs on his own authority erecting two new parishes in order to increase his legislative support. The Assembly responded with several resolutions, asserting that it alone was the sole judge of the election and return of its members, and declared the writs void.[54] On reading the minutes the following day, Knowles dissolved the Assembly, declaring the resolutions to be the work of the same wicked "Association." This remobilization indicates that the harmony tactic as a stratagem had developed some vitality.

A brief description of the Association will help make its transitional nature between a lobby-learned resistance stratagem and a representative politics clearer. Happily, the Association's "constitution" and rules survive. In the year following his dissolution of the Assembly (1755), Knowles published a defense of his actions (and a condemnation of the Assembly's opposition) in a pamphlet entitled *The Jamaica Association Develop'd.*[55] The pamphlet reprints the contents of the Association's constitution together with an "Extraordinary Paper," a letter from the Assembly's Speaker, Charles Price, which sets out how the Association worked. The Association's charter had been originally agreed with former Governor Trelawney in November 1751 as a means of both reconciling the Assembly's internal factiousness and establishing a basis of cooperation between the governor and the Assembly. Trelawney apparently sent Knowles, his chosen successor, a copy.[56]

But the "Extraordinary Paper," drafted some two years after Trelawney's departure and in light of Knowles's challenge in October 1753 to the Assembly's right to appoint its own receiver-general, gave the Association an absolute veto on the governor's power. The paper sets out a system whereby the governor was requested to consult with various members of the Association in all matters relating to island governance before he acted. That the paper was sent to Knowles while the Assembly sat by the Speaker of the House Charles Price indicates that its signers wished it to be received as representing the weight of the Assembly's opinion.

The Association's constitution (which takes the form of a resolution) states in its preamble that good government relies on "Harmony," "not only among the public Orders of the State, or Branches of the Legislature, but also, among the principal private Members of the Community." To promote the "Blessings of Unity," the undersigned agreed to set aside all private quarrels, to consult with one another, and to reach a consensus before "taking any step" or proposing any bill in either house that affected the public.

They further agreed to support the administration of Governor Knowles "as long as it appears to us to have at Heart the public service." Should any of his measures be deemed hurtful to the public, the associators agreed to join in "desiring him to desist." If he refused, the associators agreed to mount an opposition. To enforce this "harmony," the associators agreed that whatever measures obtained a three-fourths majority would be "promoted by the unanimous concurrence of all."[57] How the Association intended to punish nonassociators is not stated, but Knowles, at least, claimed they proscribed members who "offended" them.[58]

The structure of the Association as set out in the "Extraordinary Paper" appointed certain of its members to cover specific areas of responsibility in a system not unlike a modern-day cabinet structure. The areas named included all the functions of government, that is, matters to do with the Assembly (legislative), the courts (prerogative and common law), "External" (foreign) matters, "Internal" (domestic) matters, and island militia (defense).[59]

Governor Knowles recognized, as William Henry Drayton would of South Carolina's nonimportation Association of 1769, that what was being erected was a new political structure. "For by this Resolution . . . the Legislature is completely destroyed, and instead of the three [constitutional] Powers, . . . here is a Body taking upon itself a Fourth Power . . . [that has] set itself above the Constitution." Unlike the South Carolina Associations, whose signers included private citizens, however, the structure was contained entirely within the government, and was intended not to replace it but to produce a working harmony in a body with a history of "violent" factiousness.[60]

Furthermore, Knowles refers to the eleven members as constituting an "Association-Board."[61] His choice of language implicitly compares the Association's claims with such imperial government agencies as the Board of Trade (which effectively exercised colonial rule), as well as acknowledging that the associators represented and acted for a larger constituency.

The historian George Metcalf credits the creation of the Association not to its Assembly members, but to the skill of former Governor Trelawney, achieved by outmaneuvering the Assembly factions in a mutual game of "eighteenth century politics"—"backstairs intrigue and family connection."[62] However, a contemporary Knowles supporter thought it was the work of Assembly politicians, who foresaw trouble should Knowles be appointed governor. The fact that merchants and planters had formed an address in opposition to Trelawney's earlier plan to secure Knowles's appointment as his deputy governor indicates that island factions could cooperate independent of the governor's direction.[63]

And while the background machinations in this episode certainly include liberal use of family influence, Metcalf's construction overlooks the fact that the Association, once created, served a representative function for local interests. It could not be solely a family politics, since the demands of a broader constituency had to be included in the calculations. It also overlooks the fact that the Association endured for several years after Trelawney's departure.

Another indication that the Association originally sprang from its own membership and their knowledge and experience in lobby politics can be found in Knowles's 1754 speech, in which he accuses associators of making lavish donations and presents to favorites and dispensing public jobs worth £90,000 over the "last few years."[64] These practices, characteristic of the networking, constituency-building nature of a lobby, are as much a part of the lobby's character as the pressurizing tactics on which so much of the discussion in this study has centered.

It is hard to sort out the exact character of events subsequent to the capital relocation controversy, since pamphlet accounts are so partisan. It does seem, however, that a core of the original Association (at least three of the original eleven were dead by 1754), and probably shorn of its merchant members, mounted an opposition in the 1755 session that culminated in a walkout or "secession" not unlike that which South Carolina delegates would use in the Continental Congress twenty years later. Knowles describes the event as riotous. The associators claimed their action was perfectly parliamentary and orderly.[65]

That local merchants and planters could cooperate even temporarily in opposition to imperial authority in this particular way indicates that a politics of harmony in the Assembly, combined with a politics of recalcitrance toward outside (in this case Crown) authority, had evolved in Jamaica along much the same lines as in South Carolina. That it was less successful at maintaining that harmony in periods of crisis should not detract from the similarity of that ideal and of the methods devised to achieve it.

It is tempting to dismiss these episodes as typical of the constitutional struggles taking place elsewhere in colonial British America, and so they were. It is also tempting to accept Knowles's judgment that the Assembly was simply "factious." But there is more to it than that. As Metcalf points out, Knowles's predecessor, Edward Trelawney, faced greater difficulties but governed more successfully than Knowles for fourteen years, simply because he informally practiced the consultative type of politics that Price's "Extraordinary Paper" proposed.[66]

The important point here is not the nature of the disputes or the specific issues at stake. Whether it was constitutional principles or partial interests seeking to aggrandize their power that drove the opposition to oppose, the point to consider is the form that the opposition took and the methods by which it pursued its aims. In *form* and *method,* the opposition took the pattern of a lobby. Even the language of its name, "Association" rather than, for example, "Society," suggests a voluntary, interest-based reason for acting together rather than some shared, organic basis for being. That the goal of this Association was a defense of the Jamaican Assembly's autonomy should not obscure the fact that the way in which the associators constituted and maintained themselves as an organization, and even in the naming of themselves, reflects a *process* of opposition-making rooted in a commercial and imperial experience rather than a parliamentary tradition. That its Association-created legislative harmony cracked while South Carolina's stability deepened during the same period may have been due at least in part to the fact that Jamaica had a Charles Knowles for its governor instead of a consultative executive like William Bull. That no similar schism erupted in 1748 when Governor Trelawney first proposed moving the capital to Kingston[67] suggests that the affair was not a spontaneous explosion of endemic factionalism, but arose from Knowles's naked exploitation of internal divisions beyond the power of the original Association to cope.

Another feature common to Jamaica and South Carolina politics during the postrevolutionary period was the lack of grassroots parties in the modern sense. Both certainly had the social makings for parties. Each had a large yeoman class (Jamaica had over 30,000 whites in 1820, of whom only about 1,189 were men of property) whose interests demanded attention. But we have seen how South Carolina's elites defused social divisions (thereby deflecting party formation) by channeling conflict into the committee system. And when postrevolutionary debtor grievances erupted into social disorder, elites quickly closed down courts and passed stay laws (even if contrary to treaty agreements) to meet the emergency. Quick action left little opportunity for a popular opposition party to coalesce around the discontent.

Jamaica's elite maintained a similar social peace and political control largely through Assembly action for the same period. Legislative initiatives in health and education for smallholding and landless whites, and (in the case of its large free colored population) civil reforms, ameliorated the conditions around which a popular political opposition might have formed.[68]

III

Finally, although the habitual practices and ruling "harmony" ethos learned in the lobby experience explains much of South Carolina's and Jamaica's politics, the problem of slavery, so fundamental to both societies, cannot be ignored. On this subject, any real dissension among ruling whites was unlikely.[69] It has been argued that the political ramifications of slavery were further distinguished in the cases of the West Indies and South Carolina by the presence of a black majority. The argument is undoubtedly true for Jamaica, with its very large black majority, its scattered white population, its two maroon wars, and its numerous serious slave insurrections (and with the example of St. Domingo so close at hand). In such an environment, any individual daring a serious social critique was simply excised out of the system.[70]

South Carolina, one the other hand, had a large and growing white population in its backcountry that might be counted on in case of a major slave insurrection. One historian argues that John Drayton implied as much in 1802 when he remarked that the unprecedented immigration of white settlers to the colony during the twenty years prior to the Revolution had "added thousands to her domestic strength." Although black majorities still pertained in the lowcountry, overall South Carolina's racial composition fell from 2 to 1 to near-parity by the mid-1770s.[71]

Even if this was the "critical social fact" that gave South Carolina's leadership the nerve to risk political divisions among its white authority to join the Revolution,[72] it remains a matter of speculation whether a fear of its black population continued to determine political unity in the postrevolutionary period. Certainly John Rutledge argued against that assumption at Philadelphia, when he assured other delegates that talk of the state's slave population as a "defensive weakness" was mistaken. South Carolina was not afraid of slave insurrections, he assured the Convention, and "wd readily exempt the other states from [the obligation to protect the Southern (states) against them]."[73] By the same token, the fact of a black majority since 1708, the Stono Rebellion of 1739, followed by two abortive revolts the next year, and intermittent plots and alarms over the next nine years did nothing to reduce factiousness in the Assembly in the 1740s.[74]

If a black majority in the lowcountry engendered sufficient fear among whites to mandate unity among its leadership, it was slow to develop and not powerful enough to rule in periods of severe economic distress and interest conflict. It was not until the 1760s, with the perfection of its indigenous lobby politics, that South Carolina elites discovered a *method* to achieve the political unity they desired. It was a method that realized, reinforced, and reflected back the harmony that the tacit code of generally accepted ideals, assumptions, and expectations about political conduct evolved by the 1750s underpinned.

How important were these practices in elevating and sustaining South Carolina's value for harmony as a social and political ideal? To the degree that the politics of harmony made observable a configuration of values that might otherwise have remained intellectually unrecognized because inchoate, to the degree that the politics of harmony were the effective side of its social credo, and to the degree that the success of the method played back into the system to strengthen, renew, justify, and reencode it, to that degree the habitual practices absorbed from the lobbying experience created as well as expressed the political culture of South Carolina.

Thus, while the demographic fact of a black majority must be a contributing factor to constructing a politics of harmony, it cannot be construed to be the sole or even the controlling factor in this period. It took more than just divisions of opinion among whites to create a slave revolution. It took black leadership, a factor certainly present in South Carolina, but above all it took a black political consciousness. While modern research has revealed persistent and widespread individual resistance by South Carolina slaves to the conditions of slavery, a black *political* consciousness sufficient to create a *political* rebellion on the order of St. Domingo never emerged.[75] Nor, given the erratic and loose way in which the slave code was enforced, does it appear that white leadership thought that it would.

White elites' imperative for harmony in the postrevolutionary period had the opinions, interests, and concerns of other whites as its primary reference point. Political leaders' chief concern was for legitimacy in the eyes of each other, especially of lesser whites. This was the engine that turned South Carolina's politics.

One does not need a "fear" theory to account for white unity. Both before and after the Revolution, South Carolina's elites discouraged the emergence of any sort of popular consciousness, whether based on section, class, religion, or an ideology, that might have led to permanent divisions in the legislature and around which an institutionalized party system could be built. For the same reasons (political hegemony), the ruling elite would have opposed any glimmer of a radical critique on the question of slavery. As history unfolded, the social basis for such a critique shrank rather than grew during the antebellum period.

The break with Great Britain and the acquisition of political independence, a chaotic economy, and a perception of narrowed gaps between social groupings threw up local men and interests that challenged South Carolina elite's right to rule. Divisions erupted both within South Carolina's social fabric and its legislature in the 1780s that strained the ingenuity and resources of a ruling elite schooled in the politics of stability. But the managed harmony of the conservative leadership never truly ruptured. South Carolina's political culture did open up as a result of a crisis of elite legitimacy. But the 1780s and 1790s challenge represented by a competing political culture in the up-country dissipated as former radicals slowly assimilated to the social and political ethos of the lowcountry elite. By the time that the state's balance of power (as well as much of its leadership) had passed to men of property in the upcountry, they too were fully schooled in the values, the tactics, the internal truck and barter, and the external bluff and bluster that marked a politics of harmony. It was a politics that owed its practicing origins to a commercial lobbying past. Affirmed and intensified by congruent social ideals—tested and refined by Revolution and Independence—these patterns from the past transformed South Carolina's politics and brought its political culture to its fullest maturity.

When the old elites of the mainland's only other major slaveholding state, Virginia, returned from national councils to reclaim state leadership, they did so burdened with a gentry ethos of republican values that stressed liberty and equality. It was a rhetoric that ultimately had to be made good on. New men with new politics came through the door.

The South Carolina elite's promise of stability through accommodation carried a price tag of a different sort. Flexibility in policy softened the hard edges of confrontation, but it also obviated the necessity for hard thinking about political philosophy. But in the expanding new empire, it contributed a kind of politics that got things done with minimum social risk. Its final legacy would not be known for some time to come.

CONCLUSIONS

While colonial South Carolinians by the mid-eighteenth century enjoyed unusual political order, Revolution and Independence created new stresses and widened gaps in the political community. Self-rule forced state leaders to face the claims of competing domestic and national interests. Pre-revolutionary leaders had arrived at satisfactory—though hard-fought—solutions in their struggles with the mother country. Mostly drawn from the same social strata, political leaders in the new Republic naturally tried to recapture the harmony or simple manageability that had prevailed earlier. They sought to minimize domestic divisiveness and outnegotiate their enemies in federal councils. In the process, politics in South Carolina developed a restorative impulse at home and a radical leadership style abroad. Although sustaining their rule in a changed world would require a new politics, South Carolina's elite politicians believed they could and should lead the state as they always had.

Their reasons were not so far-fetched nor their politics so erratic as they may appear in hindsight. South Carolina's politicians really believed that interest underpinned all politics, and they thought that leaders in other colony-states agreed. If South Carolina leaders were correct, and if the colonies were merely conglomerates of striving interest groups, then the new states would have as a feature of their federal political culture a willingness above all to give and take. Interest groups did in fact exist in all the states. But nowhere was the political process so thoroughly adapted to handle them than in South Carolina, where leaders consciously strove to reduce the divisiveness of the state's own internal politics. South Carolina was as potentially conflict-ridden as any other state. At the same time, South Carolina's leaders strove to maximize the state's voice in federal debates, with clout that relied primarily on the appearance if not the actual fact of being of one mind with the people at home.

Arguably, the Revolution changed the American understanding of the adhesives of society—from a monarchial worldview where deference was paid rank, to a republican mental world with deference paid to virtue and "disinterested" public leaders. By the early nineteenth century, however, democratic and commercial forces unleashed by the Revolution destroyed the notion that the elite could be disinterested, so that deference, the republican adhesive, became redundant. It was a shift that most of the old revolutionary leadership could not follow. Toward the end of his life, a disillusioned Thomas Jefferson would write, "All, all dead, and ourselves left alone amidst a new generation whom we know not and who knows not us."[1]

South Carolina's elite could do what others of the old revolutionary leadership in the early Republic by and large could not. They could admit that they were not disinterested. Indeed, the seventeenth-century tradition South Carolina's leaders adhered to, confirmed by the wisdom learned through experience in the school of commercial lobbying, celebrated interest as the best guide to politics, because it was the best predictor of human behavior. Interest, rightly understood, was infinitely preferable to either the grosser passions for gain or a sentimentalized trust in the virtue of disinterested men. Passion and sentiment had an unreliable emotional basis. Interest, on the other hand, steered a rational, dispassionate middle course, allowing beneficial results to emerge from nonvirtuous motives. For South Carolina's leaders in the new Republic, an unabashed pursuit of the state's interest(s) was not only legitimate but a positive good. When Edward Rutledge declared that equality was the basis of public virtue, he was speaking of an equality of interests, and he and other South Carolina leaders meant to pursue that equality relentlessly.

But South Carolina's leaders also wanted to be seen to play fair. When and where was the naked pursuit of interest not legitimate? When John Rutledge proclaimed that "Interest alone is the governing principle with Nations," he was saying that negotiations between states were fundamentally different from those between autonomous individuals within one's own group and one's own community. States are impersonal creations of society. Not that states wish to reflect amorality, but they have no afterlife to consider as individuals do in their dealings with members of their community. An unrestrained pursuit of interest against outside powers, as a politics, does not have the same meaning and cannot work in the same way when practiced among one's own people. John Rutledge's high-handed imitation of the British House of Commons in invoking parliamentary privilege during a private dispute with a "democratik" tavern owner provoked cries against the "NABOB Tribe" from Charleston's common citizens. Rutledge cost elite leaders more than he gained in that dispute because he forgot that conciliation, not confrontation, was the only legitimate way to practice interest politics at home and the only way to promote and build consensus during factious times. Face-to-face relations between republican citizens, especially with one's social inferiors, had a moral rather than a political character. Although they held on to old world, custodial views of government, South Carolina leaders were classical republicans in that they saw themselves as impartial advocates for the interests of fellow South Carolinians, with no special regard for their own.

When confronting outside and superior powers, however, it was legitimate for delegates of a minority power—as South Carolina historically was—to pursue the state's interest(s) to the limit. Going to the wall for the home folks could be an important factor in creating domestic unity. It was, after all, the adhesives at home that South Carolina leaders most wanted to cultivate. On those bonds and on that unity rested popular consent to the elite's right to rule and Carolinians' understanding of themselves as fit to govern. How South Carolina's elite learned to emulate, and at times simulate, an organic unity through strategies learned in the commercial lobby has been the burden of this study.

An important additional lesson that lobbying taught its South Carolina practitioners was that the strategy can fail. The Rockingham secession from Parliament on the American question not only failed; it was highly unpopular with the British public. Why would Carolina leaders think it a tactic worth emulating? Carolina leaders lobbied the Ministry in the revolutionary crisis, and no colony tried harder or longer to bring the British to the table. The strategy nonetheless failed to win a negotiated settlement. Why should Carolinians continue to practice a method that could fail?

The answer lies in the fact that in a political culture where harmony at home has become a primary value, taking a hard line to assert home interests, even if it fails, may be more important than sacrificing home unity. And when one recalls that the leadership's relations with members of its own community had a moral as well as a republican dimension, such behavior would additionally serve an important symbolic function.[2]

The South Carolina elite's claim to nearly exclusive exercise of power required more than mere consent; it required proof of impartiality toward all interests, especially their own. It is worth recalling that in South Carolina during the early Republic, backcountry demands for a proportionate share in power grew more clamorous, while an increasingly vocal artisan class in Charleston questioned the wealthy nabobs' fitness to govern for all. The rhetoric of disinterest sounded suspect in the mouths of the holders of most of the state's wealth and power. South Carolina elites were in an ambiguous position. In rare moments of individual or collective crisis South Carolina leaders' need to demonstrate selflessness could justify acts that now appear reckless.

While it is true that the personal fortunes of the Carolina delegates to the First Continental Congress would have been put at risk by a non-exportation of rice, they correctly saw the nonexportation would certainly ruin the state's economy, and walked out. After some adjustments to accommodate backcountry interests, the legislature resolved its approval of the actions of its five delegates, and returned them to the next Congress. Joining with the other colonies in a revolution certainly put life and fortune at risk, but most South Carolina Whig leaders declared themselves ready for the sacrifice, and many made it. Although the necessity for such drastic demonstrations did not arise often at this early period, the latent impulse was there.

In the day-to-day business of practicing government, however, such extremes of political behavior were unnecessary. Among the most valuable of the lessons of lobbying was a heightened awareness that jarring interests within the home community existed, and that consultation, coordination, and cooperation fostered consensus. In a time when "partial interests" were bad words, South Carolina leaders could accept that other perspectives existed without troubling themselves about the "rightness" of what they espoused.

This pragmatism paid off time and again. During the second nonimportation movement, Carolina politicians balanced representation on the Association's enforcement committee among Charleston's three major economic groups (planters, merchants, and mechanics) to spread nonimportation's negative effects even-handedly. The tactic moderated explosive divisions and made a success of the boycott. After the war, elite leaders reduced legislative faction during the troubled 1780s by retooling the lower house committees as sites of conflict resolution. Selecting committee membership to fairly represent concerned interests gave the backcountry and other underrepresented groups parity if not equality in deciding controversial issues. Requiring sufficient petitioners' signatures to represent public opinion on the most divisive issues diverted to these committees produced a kind of referendum. When economic disputes threatened social disorder, South Carolina's leaders suspended the law's normal operation. For example, when debtor riots threatened, leaders ignored the newly ratified Constitution to enact new stay laws. By remaining unexercised by the age's disapproval of partial interests, and concentrating instead on the reality of their demands, leaders were able to devise flexible solutions to divisions that were as acute and explosive as could be found anywhere.

Other states also understood the dangers of internal divisiveness. Pennsylvania and New York used agreement by debate to reach decisions. Although ultimately leading to our modern view that favors party conflict, in the short run the intense party warfare of the 1776–90 period in Pennsylvania politics shows the near breakdown of the debate method. It bequeathed to that state a politics that one historian has called "A Game Without Rules."[3]

Massachusetts, too, used a debate among the towns method for resolving issues in its Assembly. Yet these politics had no means for channeling internal conflict into the political system when formal debate broke down. Shays's Rebellion in Massachusetts shows the outcome when institutional methods cannot handle an issue.

The ability of the New England town fathers to tolerate conflict while working toward consensus did not extend to the ability to imagine another's perspective. Massachusetts never sanctioned either principled differences among men or the legitimacy of conflict.[4] Reflecting on these matters during the Shays's crisis, a writer to the *State-Gazette of South Carolina* compared the two polities in similar straits. Recalling the 1785 debtor riots in Camden, he noted that "to rescue the country from . . . impending dangers the [South Carolina] legislature interposed." Then, referring directly to Massachusetts and the Shays's crisis, he continued, "the government refused . . . a temporary departure from the maxims of justice . . . [and] exerted its whole strength to enforce the operation of the laws. And the consequence? An armed force . . . is now on its march to the capital and threatens the existence of the government."[5]

South Carolina's interest-informed politics that gave internal divisions a channel into the state's political system served the state well in the crises of the revolutionary and postrevolutionary periods. It permitted the state to weather conflicts that put more "democratic" states in serious disarray in the 1780s and 1790s. And, at least for the early republican period, this politics kept a conservative leadership in power, prevented social divisions from coalescing into formal parties, and outmaneuvered demands for legislative reapportionment.

The commercial lobby experience contributed a politics that persisted because it reflected South Carolinians' ideas about society and government, and because—practically speaking—it succeeded more often than it failed. In those rare moments that required individual or collective acts of sacrifice as proof of selfless leadership, to fail was the only way to win. And while the lobby's aggressive political style did not always lead to disaster, it does explain how the state's leaders got to the brink of it so often. These preconditions and this politics set South Carolina on a fateful trajectory for the nineteenth century.

APPENDIX: STATISTICAL METHODS

Data on comparative committee leadership trends found in chapter 6 were originally compiled for my D.Phil. dissertation (Oxford University, 1989), where a complete listing for tables 6.1 and 6.2 can be found. All data used in constructing tables 6.1, 6.2, and 6.3 were extracted from the six published volumes of the Journals of the South Carolina House for 1783–94. See Michael E. Stevens, Christine M. Allen, and et al., eds., *The State Records of South Carolina: The Journals of the House of Representatives, 1783–1784, 1785–1786, 1787–1788, 1789–1790, 1791, 1792–94* (Columbia, S.C., 1977–88).

To make the sectional comparison, I defined the lowcountry as the area contained in the colony's original coastal parishes, which served as its election districts after 1716. They include All Saints, Christ Church, Prince Frederick (Williamsburg and Liberty, now Marion), Prince George Winyah (Kingston, now Horry), Prince William, St. Andrew, St. Bartholomew, St. George Dorchester, St. Helena, St. James Goose Creek, St. James Santee, St. John Berkeley, St. John Colleton, St. Luke, St. Paul, St. Peter, St. Philips and St. Michaels (Charleston), St. Stephen, and St. Denis and St. Thomas. Geographically, these parishes lie south and east of the state's fall line. The upcountry is defined as the area contained in the counties and districts (with the exception of Williamsburg, Liberty, and Kingston) created or reestablished in 1785—Abbeville, Chester, Chesterfield, Claremont (Sumter), Clarendon, Darlington, Edgefield, Fairfield, Greenville, Kershaw, Lancaster, Laurens, Marlboro, Newberry, Pendleton (Anderson and Pickens), Orange, Richland, Saxe Gotha (Lexington), Spartan, St. Matthew, Union, Winton (Barnwell), and York. Geographically, this area lies to the north and west of the state's fall line.

I calculated each section's share of committee leadership by two methods. In the first method, leadership was determined by a simple count of committee assignments per legislator, whether select or standing, from both sections. As the overwhelming majority of the House's nonroutine business was conducted in select committees that did not appoint chairmen, it was unnecessary to assign additional weight on that basis. These results appear in table 6.1. I further refined leadership trends by isolating a core group of the top ten individuals with the most committee service for each section in each legislative year. These results appear in table 6.2.

For table 6.3, I tallied the numbers of roll call votes per legislative session for 1787–88, 1788–89, 1791, and 1792–94 by counting the number of entries listed in the index of each published volume for the relevant year. Numbers of petitions may be somewhat higher, as clerks' entries in the Journals do not always state how many petitions were read on a given subject. Numbers of petitions can be found in the editor's methods section at the beginning of each published volume.

NOTES

The following abbreviations are used in the notes:

AHR	*American Historical Review*
CO	Colonial Office
EHR	*English Historical Review*
FO	Foreign Office
HB	Hall Book
Hist. Soc.	*Histoire Sociale*
JAH	*Journal of American History*
JAS	*Journal of American Studies*
JC	*Journal of the House of Commons*
JCTP	*The Journals of the Commissioners for Trade and Plantations*
JEH	*Journal of Economic History*
JHI	*Journal of the History of Ideas*
JSH	*Journal of Southern History*
LB	Letterbook
PRO	Public Record Office
SCHM	*South Carolina Historical Magazine*
SMV	[Bristol] Society of Merchant Venturers
T	Treasury Papers
VMHB	*Virginia Magazine of History and Biography*
WMQ	*William and Mary Quarterly*

INTRODUCTION

1. Some of these ideas are suggested in Robert M. Weir, *Colonial South Carolina: A History* (Millwood, N.Y., 1983), pp. 167–68.

2. James M. Banner Jr., "The Problem of South Carolina," in Stanley Elkins and Eric McKitrick, eds., *The Hofstadter Aegis: A Memorial* (New York, 1974), pp. 60–93, summarizes the literature.

3. Lacy K. Ford, *The Origins of Southern Radicalism: The South Carolina Upcountry, 1800–1860* (Oxford, 1988).

4. Mark D. Kaplanoff, "Charles Pinckney and the American Republican Tradition," in Michael O'Brien and David Moltke-Hansen, eds., *Intellectual Life in Antebellum Charleston* (Knoxville, Tenn., 1987); John C. Meleney, *The Public Life of Aedanus Burke: Revolutionary Republican in Post-Revolutionary South Carolina* (Columbia, S.C., 1989).

5. William A. Freeling, *Prelude to Civil War: The Nullification Controversy in South Carolina, 1816–1836* (New York, 1966). J. P. Ochenkowshi challenges Freeling's thesis in "The Origins of Nullification in South Carolina," *SCHM* 83 (1982): 121–53. For John Rutledge on free trade in 1774, see ch. 5, below; for Pierce Butler, see Freeling, *Prelude to Civil War*, p. 94. Don Higginbotham notes that South Carolina's leaders "fervently articulated it [secession] as the final solution to any seemingly insoluble federal problem" well before the nullification crisis. "Fomenters of Revolution: Massachusetts and South Carolina," *Journal of the Early Republic* 14 (1994): 14.

6. An exception is Robert M. Weir, "Slavery and the Structure of the Union," in Michael Gillespie and Michael Lienesch, eds., *Ratifying the Constitution* (Lawrence, Kans., 1989), pp. 201–34.

7. Jerome J. Nadelhaft, *The Disorders of War: The Revolution in South Carolina* (Orono, Maine, 1981); Robert M. Weir, *Colonial South Carolina: A History* (Millwood, N.Y., 1983); Robert M. Weir, *"The Last of American Freemen": Studies in the Political Culture of the American South* (Macon, Ga., 1986); Lacy Ford, *The Origins of Southern Radicalism: The South Carolina Upcountry, 1800–1860* (Oxford, 1988); and Rachel N. Klein, *Unification of a Slave State: The Rise of the Planter Class in the South Carolina Backcountry, 1760–1808* (Chapel Hill, N.C., 1990).

8. The classic statement of this thesis is Robert M. Weir, "'The Harmony We Were Famous For': An Interpretation of Pre-Revolutionary South Carolina Politics," *WMQ*, 3rd ser., 26 (1969): 473–501.

9. The dynamics of transatlantic lobbies in imperial politics are investigated by Alison G. Olson, *Making the Empire Work: London and American Interest-Groups, 1690–1790* (Cambridge, Mass., 1992).

10. The term "out-of-doors" refers to any political activity that takes place literally outside Parliament's chamber doors. As members of the public could approach MPs in the lobby just outside the debating chamber, these activists became known as lobbyists and their politics as lobbying. The term "indoors" refers to the formal politics of law-making practiced on the floor of Parliament.

Chapter One

SOUTH CAROLINA'S ELITE ON THE EVE OF THE REVOLUTION

1. A number of contemporary travelers' accounts of South Carolina's thriving society and economy survive. See [George Milligan], *A Short Description of South Carolina with an account of the air, weather, and Diseases at Charlestown* (London: John Hinton at the King's Arms, 1770); "Charlestown in 1764," letters of Moses Lopez to his brother, Aaron, in Thomas T. Tobias, ed., *SCHM* 67 (1966): 63–74; "Journal of Josiah

Quincey, Jr., 1773," in Mark A. deWolfe Howe, ed., *Massachusetts Historical Society Proceedings* 64 (1916): 438–81; London Public Record Office (PRO), Colonial Office (CO) Papers, 5/394, ff. 5–20d, Lieutenant Governor William Bull's report to Lord Hillsborough, November 30, 1770.

2. Eugene Sirmans, *Colonial South Carolina: A Political History, 1663–1763* (Chapel Hill, N.C., 1966), chs. 5, 6, 7, and 8; David Duncan Wallace, *South Carolina: A Short History, 1520–1948* (Columbia, S.C., 1961), chs. 9, 12, 14, and 17. Peter Coclanis, "Rice Prices in the 1720s and the Evolution of the South Carolina Economy," *JSH* 48 (1982): 531–44.

3. Peter Coclanis, "Bitter Harvest: The South Carolina Low Country in Historical Perspective," *JEH* 45, no. 2 (1985): 255; Peter Coclanis, "Markets and Merchants in Early South Carolina," unpublished conference paper presented in Charleston, S.C., March 4, 1988, p. 6; Alice Hanson Jones, *Wealth of a Nation to Be: The American Colonies on the Eve of the Revolution* (New York, 1980), p. 357.

4. "Josiah Quincey's Journal," p. 455. Thomas J. Wertenbaker, *The Golden Age of Colonial Culture* (New York, 1949; reprint ed., Westport, Conn., 1980), pp. 127–50, esp. p. 128.

5. Mortimer, *The Universal Director* (J. Coote: Paternoster-row, 1763), pt. III, pp. 3–4.

6. See, for example, the commentary on Henry Laurens's advice regarding planters and backcountry trade in "Interests and Disinterestedness in the Making of the Constitution," in Richard Beeman, Stephen Botein, and Edward W. Carter, eds., *Beyond Confederation: Origins of the Constitution and National Identity* (Chapel Hill, N.C., 1984), p. 88, and compare to Laurens's letter in George C. Rogers Jr. et al., eds., *The Papers of Henry Laurens* (Columbia, S.C., 1968–), IV. 337. Laurens refers to retail trade.

7. George Lillo, *The London Merchant: Or, the History of George Barnwell*, 8th ed. (London, 1737), p. 14; "To the play—George Barnwell," diary entry for February 3, 1764, "Extracts from the Journal of Mrs. Ann Manigault," *SCHM* 20 (1919): 206; another production noted in 1786, p. 218.

8. Ibid., pp. 14–15. The play's London merchants show patriotism by persuading the Bank of Genoa through their agents to refuse the king of Spain the loan he needs to mount an invading armada.

9. R. Nicholas Olsberg, ed., "Ship Registers in the South Carolina Archives, 1734–1780," *SCHM* 74 (1973): 272.

10. George C. Rogers Jr., *Charleston in the Age of the Pinckneys* (Columbia, S.C., 1980), pp. 52–53. For a contemporary view of the merchant in nineteenth-century South Carolina, see Ebenezer S. Thomas, *Reminiscences of the Last Sixty-five Years* (Hartford, Conn., 1840). On the local anti-Scots bias, see Robert M. Weir, "The Role of the Newspaper Press in the Southern Colonies: An Interpretation," in Bernard Bailyn and John B. Hinch, eds., *The Press and the American Revolution* (Worcester, Mass., 1980), pp. 183–86.

11. Robert M. Weir, " 'Liberty and Property, and No Stamps': South Carolina in the Stamp Act Crisis" (Ph.D. dissertation, Western Reserve University, 1966), pp. 40–43. Obviously, a critical deterrent to entering planting directly was the requisite high initial investment. Henry Laurens estimated the setting-up costs for a backcountry plantation in 1764 at £1000 sterling minimum, exclusive of the price of

land and essential implements, with no returns for the first two years. *Laurens Papers*, IV. 338, Henry Laurens to Richard Oswald, July 7, 1764. Compare this figure with the £300 required to set up as a merchant in the same period. Peter A. Coclanis, "The Hydra Head of Merchant Capital: Merchants and Markets in Early South Carolina," in David R. Chesnutt and Clyde N. Wilson, eds., *The Meaning of South Carolina History: Essays in Honor of George C. Rogers, Jr.* (Columbia, S.C., 1991), p. 5.

12. Robert M. Weir, "'The Harmony We Were Famous For': An Interpretation of Pre-Revolutionary South Carolina Politics," *WMQ*, 3rd ser., 26 (1969): 473–501; David Morton Knepper, "The Political Structure of Colonial South Carolina, 1743–1776" (Ph.D. dissertation, University of Virginia, 1971), pp. 27–28.

13. John David Altman, "Societies and Organizations in Colonial and Revolutionary Charles Towne, South Carolina," unpublished seminar paper presented at the University of South Carolina, 1985; "Josiah Quincey's Journal," pp. 43–46, quotation from p. 45.

14. The hold the appointive power exercised over ambitious local office seekers is vividly illustrated in Edward Hooker's 1808 description of candidates for sheriffalties crowding Columbia, soliciting members, and waiting at great expense for the hoped-for appointment. "The Diary of Edward Hooker," in J. F. Jameson, ed., *Report of the Historical Manuscripts Commission of the American Historical Association, 1896* (Washington, D.C., 1897), I. 880–81.

15. Data for percentages compiled from Walter B. Edgar et al., eds., *Biographical Directory of the South Carolina House of Representatives*, vol. I, *Session Lists, 1692–1973* (Columbia, S.C., 1974), pp. 118–48, 629–36.

16. Walter N. Edgar and N. Louise Bailey, eds., *Biographical Directory of the South Carolina House of Representatives*, vol. II, *The Commons House of Assembly, 1692–1775* (Columbia, S.C., 1974), p. 525. St. Philips and St. Michaels, separate parishes under royal government, were merged into a single election district in 1775.

17. Sirmans, *Colonial South Carolina*, pp. 247, 312; Richard Waterhouse, "Merchants, Planters, and Lawyers: Political Culture and Leadership in South Carolina, 1721–1775," in Bruce C. Daniels, ed., *Power and Status: Officeholding in Colonial America* (Middletown, Conn., 1986), p. 170 and tab. 16.

18. Sirmans, *Colonial South Carolina*, p. 248; Knepper, "South Carolina Political Structure," pp. 22–26.

19. The discussion in the next three paragraphs is taken from T. H. Breen, *Tobacco Culture: The Mentality of the Great Tidewater Planters on the Eve of the Revolution* (Princeton, N.J., 1985). The Jefferson citation is from p. 206.

20. Bernard Bailyn, *The Ideological Origins of the American Revolution* (Cambridge, Mass., 1967); Gordon S. Wood, *The Creation of the American Republic, 1776–1787* (Chapel Hill, N.C., 1969).

21. Carl Bridenbaugh, *Myths and Realities: Societies in the Colonial South* (Baton Rouge, La., 1952), pp. 69–118.

22. David Duncan Wallace, *The Life of Henry Laurens, with a Sketch of the Life of Lieutenant-Colonel John Laurens* (New York, 1915), p. 31. Bridenbaugh, *Myths and Realities*, pp. 81–82, 87, 89, 92, 94; "Josiah Quincey's Journal," pp. 450, 451. The social season's largest ball was known as "The Assembly," presumably because it was held in the statehouse.

23. Bridenbaugh, *Myths and Realities,* pp. 79–80; Altman, "Societies and Organizations in Colonial and Revolutionary Charles Towne, South Carolina."

24. Bridenbaugh, *Myths and Realities,* p. 77; "Josiah Quincey's Journal," pp. 442–45, 448, 455.

25. "Josiah Quincey's Journal," p. 455; Mark D. Kaplanoff, "Making the South Solid: Politics and Structure of Society in South Carolina, 1790–1815" (Ph.D. dissertation, Cambridge University, 1979), pp. 142–43.

26. "Josiah Quincey's Journal," p. 456.

27. James M. Clifton, *Life and Labor on Argyle Island: Letters and Documents of a Savannah River Rice Plantation, 1833–1867* (Savannah, Ga., 1978), pp. x-xi. The quotation is from the diary of Col. Langdon Carter.

28. John E. Crowley, "Family Relations and Inheritance in Early South Carolina," *Hist. Soc.* 17, no. 33 (1984): 35–57, esp. 51–57; "The Importance of Kinship: Testamentary Evidence from South Carolina," *Journal of Interdisciplinary History* 16 (1986): 559–77, esp. pp. 567–69, 572, 576–77. The strategy also owes something to the high mortality rates that persisted throughout the period.

29. Crowley, "Family Relations," p. 55.

30. Ibid., pp. 51, 55 (and n.).

31. *Laurens Papers,* VI. 91, HL to Ross and Mill, September 2, 1768; II. 19, HL to Devonsheir, Reeve, and Lloyd, April 29, 1755; and also II. 26, HL to William Whitaker, December 6, 1755. Note that it is planters who display a knowledge of interest group strategies.

32. Converse D. Clowse, *Measuring Charleston's Overseas Commerce, 1717–1767: Statistics from the Port's Naval Lists* (Washington, D.C., 1981), tab. B-41, pp. 70–71; Lewis Cecil Gray, *History of Agriculture in the United States to 1860* (Gloucester, Mass., 1958), II. 1024 (appendix 38). Export figures represent the previous year's crop.

33. G. Terry Sharrer, "Indigo in Carolina, 1671–1796," *SCHM* 72 (1971): 95–97.

34. *Observations Concerning Indigo and Cochineal* (London, 1746); *Further Observations Intended for Improving the Culture and Curing of Indigo, etc. in South Carolina* (London, 1747). British demand for the product doubled between 1750 and 1770. See also Lewis Namier, *The Structure of Politics at the Accession of George III,* 2nd ed. (London, 1981), pp. 319–20, and John J. Winberry, "Indigo in South Carolina: A Historical Geography," *Southern Geographer* 19 (1979): 91–102.

35. N.p. [1748]. The copy in the London Public Record Office is endorsed "rec'd from Mr. Crockatt."

36. George Louis Beer, *The Commercial Policy of England Towards the American Colonies* (New York, 1893; reprint ed., 1948), p. 103.

37. *Ill-judged Bounties tend to Beggary on both Sides . . .* (London, 1748).

38. 21 Geo. III c. 30. Parliamentary debates can be found in Leo Francis Stock, ed., *Proceedings and Debates of the British Parliaments Respecting North America* (Washington, D.C., 1924–41), V. 278–86.

39. Rebecca K. Starr, "A Place Called Daufuskie: Island Bridge to Georgia, 1520–1830" (M.A. thesis, University of South Carolina, 1984), pp. 31–32.

Chapter Two

DEVELOPING THE CAROLINA TRADE LOBBY, 1707–1769

1. See the introduction for a discussion of the term "lobby."

2. Douglas R. Lacy, *Dissent and Parliamentary Politics in England, 1661–1689* (New Brunswick, N.J., 1969), pp. 99–120.

3. Material on merchant communities in this and the following two paragraphs is drawn from Thomas M. Doerflinger, *A Vigorous Spirit of Enterprise: Merchants and Economic Development in Revolutionary Philadelphia* (Chapel Hill, N.C., 1986); Thomas M. Doerflinger, "Philadelphia Merchants and the Logic of Moderation, 1760–1775," *WMQ*, 3rd ser., 40 (1983): 210–13; Carl and Jessica Bridenbaugh, *Rebels and Gentlemen: Philadelphia in the Age of Franklin* (New York, 1962), ch. 6; John Austin Stevens, ed., *Colonial Records of the New York Chamber of Commerce, 1768–1784, with Historical and Biographical Sketches* (New York, 1867); Edward M. Cook Jr., *The Fathers of the Towns: Leadership and Community Structure in Eighteenth Century New England* (Baltimore, 1976), esp. ch. 6; Robert Zemsky, *Merchants, Farmers, and River Gods: An Essay on Eighteenth-Century American Politics* (Boston, 1971), pp. 67, 71–72; J. R. Pole, *Political Representation in England and the Origins of the American Republic* (New York, 1966), pp. 38–54, 73–75.

4. Thomas Cooper and David McCord, eds., *The Statutes at Large of South Carolina* (Columbia, S.C., 1837), II. 600.

5. Leo Francis Stock, ed., *Proceedings and Debates of the British Parliaments Respecting North America* (Washington, D.C., 1924–41), III. 171, January 12, 1707–8; London, Public Record Office, PRO, CO 5/465, f. 301, CO 5/1265, f. 11, petitions of July 18 and September 15, 1715.

6. Alison G. Olson, "The London Mercantile Lobby and the Coming of the American Revolution", *JAH* 49 (1982): 23; *Laurens Papers*, I. 2, 71n; IX. 266n.

7. Stock, ed., *Debates and Proceedings*, IV. 241n. February 24, 1734–35; Walter E. Minchinton, "Political Activities of Bristol Merchants," *VMHB* 79 (1971): 176.

8. Robert Pringle to Andrew Pringle, May 30, 1744, in Walter Edgar, ed., *The Letterbook of Robert Pringle* (Columbia, S.C., 1972), II. 700. Suspecting that profits from money at interest were being underreported, the Commons House inserted a clause in the 1744 tax bill requiring all Charleston residents to swear a special oath on the amount of money they had on loan, including bonds and mortgages. This was in addition to the general oath everyone swore attesting that the return was complete. The dispute reflected a power struggle not between planters and merchants as some historians have claimed, since large planters, too, regularly made loans to their smaller planter neighbors, but a constitutional struggle between the lower house and the merchant-dominated Council. Merchant opposition faded after 1745, when the clause proved less obnoxious than expected. See Eugene Sirmans, *Colonial South Carolina: A Political History, 1663–1763* (Chapel Hill, N.C. 1966), pp. 258–62.

9. Robert Pringle to Andrew Pringle, July 20, 1744, in *Letterbook*, II. 728.

10. Ibid., II. 761, November 19, 1744. The idea remained alive. "Agricola" in 1752 suggested planters set up a "club" to finance the costs of lobbying. "Letter from Agricola," *South-Carolina Gazette*, January 1, 1752, cited in Olson, *Making the Empire Work*, p. 112.

11. *S.C. Statutes*, IV. 187–88.

12. *Laurens Papers*, IV. 383, 396, 420, 479, 558. Laurens to Rossel and Gervais, September 4, 1764; to George Appleby, October 18, 1764; to Lloyd and Barton, December 24, 1764. Laurens may have hoped to stimulate a lobbying effort against the act. He wrote his Bristol correspondent, Henry Bright, on September 12, 1764, "I transmit you a copy of the Law with a few notes on the back of it and leave it to your disposal" (420), and sent to John Knight at Liverpool a copy of the act with his remarks pencilled on the back (381–83). The House Committee of Correspondence, however, instructed the colony's agent Charles Garth to resist any effort to repeal it.

13. English bottoms included ships built in the colonies.

14. Charles M. Andrews, *The Colonial Period of American History* (New Haven, Conn., 1934–38), IV. 96.

15. *S.C. Statutes*, II. 601–2.

16. Andrews, *Colonial Period*, IV. 97.

17. South Caroliniana Library, University of South Carolina, Columbia, Samuel Wragg to Lord Townshend, c. 1724.

18. Stock, ed., *Debates and Proceedings*, IV. 57–58, 61. Bristol merchants had no direct interest in the rice trade, as the slave trade dominated their port. They doubtless concluded, however, that an expanded rice trade would stimulate rice culture with a concomitant increase in slave sales; IV. 3 George II, c. 28. In 1735, the exemption was extended to Georgia; IV. 75 and n. 14.

19. Entry for February 26, 1734, *The Egmont Diary*, quoted in Stock, ed., *Debates and Proceedings*, IV. 241n.

20. CO 5/371, ff. 78–79. The governor, Council, and Assembly of South Carolina sent a similar petition to the king. CO 5/371, f. 77.

21. CO 5/371, f. 92, William Wood to Thomas Hill, June 19, 1746.

22. For this agitation, see *JCTP* (London, 1935–36), 1759–63, p. 328; 1764–67, pp. 21, 32.

23. Rhodes House Library, Oxford, "North Papers: transcripts of documents relating to colonial policy chiefly with reference to the West Indies, 1670–1879," pp. 67–71, 132, 161, 170–71, 191, contain arguments mostly favoring retaining the islands; Richard B. Sheridan, *Sugar and Slavery: An Economic History of the British West Indies, 1623–1775* (Barbados, 1974), pp. 452–54; F. W. Pitman, *The Development of the British West Indies, 1700–1763* (New Haven, Conn., 1917), pp. 334–60; Lowell Joseph Ragatz, *The Fall of the Planter Class in the British Caribbean, 1763–1833* (New York, 1928), pp. 54, 112–13.

24. Lewis B. Namier, *England in the Age of the American Revolution* (London, 1930), pp. 317–27, contains an excellent summary of the main arguments from pamphlet literature.

25. Converse D. Clowse, *Measuring Charleston's Overseas Commerce, 1717–1767: Statistics from the Port's Naval Lists* (Washington, D.C., 1981), p. 62. Charleston was the entrepot for most of the rice grown in Georgia and North Carolina, which was brought to the port via inland rivers; *JC* (London), 29 (1761–64): 982; Andrews, *Colonial History*, IV. 353–54.

26. At least some Charleston merchants were well satisfied with the treaty, which opened new opportunities for land speculations in Florida. See, for example, *Laurens Papers*, IV. 40, 456–57, Laurens to James Grant, October 10, 1764.

27. Louis B. Namier, "Charles Garth, South Carolina Agent," *EHR* 54 (1939): 638. Bristol merchants sent a petition and Liverpool apparently supported the measure before the Board of Trade.

28. *JC,* XXIX. 602, 625.

29. For the 1774 Association debate, see ch. 5, below.

30. 4 George III c. 27. The next year (by 5 George III c. 45) the exemption was extended to North Carolina.

31. *JCTP* (1764–67), p. 22.

32. The South Carolina Commons House of Assembly passed a resolution in 1764 thanking Garth for his conduct in winning the latest rice exemption. Namier, "Charles Garth," p. 635.

33. Weir, "The Stamp Act Crisis," p. 95.

34. The Moore episode can be followed in the *Laurens Papers,* vols. V, VI, VII.

35. Columbia, South Carolina Archives, Garth Letterbook, Committee of Correspondence to Charles Garth, November 28 and December 11, 1766; *South-Carolina Gazette,* March 23, 1767; Maurice A. Crouse, ed., "The Letterbook of Peter Manigault, 1763–1770," *SCHM* 70 (1969): 92–93.

36. PRO, T 1/469, ff. 303–5. Recommendatory letter addressed to Charles Garth and signed by twenty-seven Charleston merchants, July 13, 1766.

37. [Henry Laurens, comp.], *A Representation of Facts Relative to the Conduct of Daniel Moore, Esquire; Collector of His Majesty's Customs at Charles-Town, in South Carolina* (Charleston, S.C., 1767), pp. 16, 18, 20. Bounty certificates on hemp and indigo, which stated that the product was grown in the province, enabled the English importer to obtain a bounty granted by Parliament on these goods. The bounty was credited to the planter's (or export merchant's, if he had already paid the planter) account.

38. T 1/461, f. 252. Capt. James Hawker of His Majesty's Ship of War *Sardoine,* who made the seizure, on appeal expressed amazement at the bold legal campaign mounted by the merchants, who saw it as a test case. "No lawyers to the Northward ever attempted it except for the *HummingBird* and that was only for the Nonenumerated part of the Cargoe."

39. *Representation of Facts,* pp. iii-iv, 3, 26. Although called a "Committee of Seven," only six merchants are ever mentioned.

40. Ibid., pp. 7, 34–35. The Act of Parliament 6 George III c. 52 permitted "two known British merchants residing there" (in places remote from a customhouse) to sign the certificate for the discharge of a bond on nonenumerated goods (such as lumber) in place of the collector and comptroller. Laurens's substitution of two magistrates' signatures was an effort to comply with this exception. Note that these cases differed from the *Active* in that the vessels crossed provincial lines.

41. T 1/459, ff. 166–73 (Moore's account); T 1/459, ff. 179–81 (Roupell's account); *Representation of Facts,* pp. 34–35, 37–38 (Laurens's account).

42. *Laurens Papers,* V. 286–88, 331 (editor's notes).

43. "If the Tax to be gather'd by a British Stamp Act was so odious to the Americans, in what light must that Man appear who dares attempt by his own arbitrary power to levy upon one trading Port a Thousand or £1500 Sterling annually, & to hold other Money Legally collected from them in the King's Chest, *in Terrorem* over their heads." *Laurens Papers,* V. 298, Laurens to James Habersham, September 5,

1767. Laurens referred to the fact that Moore had applied to Customs officials to have his legal fees paid out of the American chest composed of sums collected through port duties.

44. *Representation of Facts*, p. iii.

45. Ibid., p. vi.

46. Olson, "London Mercantile Lobby," p. 25. But in the mind of Laurens at least, principle as well as interest was at stake. "Good God! is it possible for freemen to bear this? . . . such Officers are the most likely instruments to affect a disunion between the Mother Country and her American Offspring." *Laurens Papers*, V. 298, Laurens to James Habersham, September 5, 1767.

47. Ibid., V. 490, "Merchants' Letter to Charles Garth," December 4, 1767. Garth was instructed to draw on Bannister, Hammond, and Manning of London. Money was raised locally by subscription to Gabriel Manigault, spokesman for the original Committee of Seven. Maurice A. Crouse, "Gabriel Manigault: Charleston Merchant," *SCHM* 68 (1969): 230.

48. *Representation of Facts*, pp. iv–vii; *Laurens Papers*, V. 669, Laurens to Richard Oswald, April 27, 1768. A careful search for this "census" of the Charleston merchants' lobby among the records of the Treasury and the Board of Trade, and among the Garth correspondence, proved fruitless. Laurens's pamphlet, *A Representation of Facts*, reprinted the letter but without the names appended.

49. T 1/461, f. 253. Hawker to Lords Commissioners of Customs, October 25, 1767.

50. Max Farrand, *The Framing of the Constitution of the United States* (New Haven, Conn., 1913), 126; T 1/461, f. 253, James Hawker to Lords Commissioners of the Customs, October 25, 1767.

51. *Laurens Papers*, V. 471, 481, 496, 501, 502, 745, Laurens to James Penman (St. Augustine), November 21, 1767; to James Habersham (Savannah), November 25, 1767; to Ross and Mill (London), December 7, 1767; to William Freeman (Bristol), December 11, 1767; to William Fisher (Philadelphia), December 12, 1767; to William Cowles & Co. and William Freeman (Bristol), July 13, 1768.

52. *Extracts From the Proceedings of the Court of Vice-Admiralty in Charles-Town, South-Carolina . . .* (Philadelphia, 1768).

53. *Extracts From the Proceedings of the High Court of Vice-Admiralty, in Charlestown, South-Carolina, Upon Six Several Informations . . .* (Charleston, S.C., 1769). Although Laurens is by this time acting as spokesman for the Charleston lobby, he clearly had the merchant community's endorsement.

54. *Laurens Papers*, VI. 187, Laurens to Ross and Mill, October 31, 1769; VI. 87, Laurens to Ross and Mill, September 1, 1768. Laurens still hoped to draw the London lobby into the action.

55. *Laurens Papers*, VI. xiii, 184–85.

56. *Appendix To The Extracts . . . Together With A Full Refutation of Mr. Leigh's Attempts to Vindicate his Judicial Proceedings* (Charleston, S.C., 1769), p. 30.

57. *Extracts*, p. 39; *Laurens Papers*, VI. 363. Manigault and Neufville released John Rutledge to defend Moore in their action against him in order to discountenance Moore's allegation.

58. *Laurens Papers*, VI. 63–65, Laurens to William Fisher, August 11, 1768; IV. 400–401, Laurens to Isaac King, September 6, 1764; Richard Hofstadter, *The Idea of*

a Party System: The Rise of Legitimate Opposition in the United States, 1780–1840 (Berkeley, Calif., 1969), pp. 9–13.

59. Quoted in P. G. Osborn, *A Concise Law Dictionary* (London, 1927; 5th ed., 1964), p. 200. Insight into the local political culture can be gleaned from Leigh's misreading of it. See Robert M. Calhoon and Robert M. Weir, "The Scandalous History of Sir Egerton Leigh," *WMQ*, 3rd ser., 26 (1969): 47–74.

60. Moore, Hawker, and Roupell all presented the cases against them as disguised attacks on ministerial policy. See T 1/459, ff. 166–73, 179–81; T 1/461, f. 252–53.

61. South Carolina Historical Society, Charleston, Charles Garth to Committee of Merchants, August 2, 1769; *Laurens Papers*, VII. 187–88, Laurens to Ross and Mill, October 31, 1769; S.C. Archives, Columbia, *Journal of South Carolina Commons House of Assembly*, XXXVII, pt. 2, (November 3 1767–November 19, 1768), p. 175, Committee Report of July 24, 1766.

62. *Laurens Papers*, V. 492, "The Remonstrance to Mark Robinson," December 4, 1767.

63. CO 5/390, f. 233. Montagu to Lord Shelburne, October 5, 1767.

64. As, for example, the seniority system of the U.S. Senate or the primary system for general elections.

65. Material for the land dispute described in this section is drawn from Robert M. Weir, *Colonial South Carolina: A History* (Millwood, N.Y., 1983), pp. 112–15; George Edward Frakes, *Laboratory for Liberty: The South Carolina Legislative System, 1719–1776* (Lexington, Ky., 1970), pp. 26–27, 58–59; Eugene Sirmans, *Colonial South Carolina: A Political History, 1663–1763* (Chapel Hill, N.C., 1966), pp. 177–82; Walter B. Edgar et al., eds., *Biographical Directory of the South Carolina House of Representatives* (Columbia, S.C., 1977), II, pp. 165–66, 705–6.

Chapter Three

THE CAROLINA LOBBY ABROAD, 1765–1774

1. The Carolina transatlantic network is reconstructed using the following sources (full citations passim): four letterbook copies of Richard Champion's correspondence preserved in the Bristol Record Office, plus a fifth in the New York Public Library; in-letters found in the published Burke correspondence and in the Rockingham and Portland ms. papers in Nottingham University Library and Sheffield Central Library, respectively; a letterbook of Richard Champion's sister, Sarah, who lived in Champion's household (the Bristol Record Office); three small collections of John Lloyd's letters at the South Caroliniana Library, Columbia, and the South Carolina Library Society, Charleston, S.C., and at the Gloucestershire Record Office, Gloucester City, England. I am grateful to the Sheffield Central Library for allowing me access to the Portland papers.

2. Walter B. Edgar and N. Louise Bailey, eds., *Biographical Directory of the South Carolina House of Representatives*, vol. II, *The Commons House of Assembly, 1692–1775* (Columbia, S.C., 1974), pp. 94, 407–8, 641; George C. Rogers Jr. et al., eds., *The*

Papers of Henry Laurens (Columbia, S.C., 1968–), II. 178; III. 33; V. 26, 603, editor's notes.

3. Humphrey Lloyd, *The Quaker Lloyds in the Industrial Revolution* (London, 1975), p. 187; Deborah M. Olsen, "Richard Champion and the Society of Friends," *Transactions of the Bristol and Gloucestershire Archaeological Society* 102 (1984): 181; Alice Harford, ed., *Annals of the Harford Family* (London, 1909), p. 33.

4. Jack P. Greene, *The Quest for Power: The Lower Houses of Assembly in the Southern Royal Colonies, 1689–1776* (Chapel Hill, N.C., 1963), pp. 206, 481; [Henry Laurens, comp.], *A Representation of Facts Relative to the Conduct of Daniel Moore, Esquire; Collector of His Majesty's Customs at Charles-Town, in South Carolina* (Charleston, S.C., 1767), p. 26. For the Moore affair, see ch. 2.

5. Hugh Owen, *Two Centuries of Ceramic Art in Bristol, being a History of the Manufacture of true Porcelain by Richard Champion* (London, 1873), p. 42. Lady Hyndford was a relation of Lloyd's mother.

6. London, British Library, Addn. Ms. 38305, f. 12.

7. Champion's LB, 38083(2), 5, RC to John Lloyd, May 1767; Sarah's LB, 38083(5), 124, SC to M.L. [1767].

8. See especially the work of P. T. Underdown: "Burke's Bristol Friends," *Transactions of the Bristol Historical and Archaeological Society* 77 (1958): 127–50, and his two unpublished theses, "The Parliamentary History of the City of Bristol, 1750–1790" (M.A. thesis, University of Bristol, 1948) and "Edmund Burke as Member of Parliament for Bristol: A Study of His Relations Both with His Colleague Henry Cruger and with His Constituents, and of the Political Situation in the City during the years 1774–1780" (Ph.D. dissertation, University of London, 1954); also W. R. Savadge, "The West Country and the American Mainland Colonies, 1703–1783, with Special Reference to the Merchants of Bristol" (unpublished B. Litt. thesis, Oxford University, 1952). G. H. Guttridge's short biography, which serves as an introduction to his edition of Champion's letters, is useful but too brief to assess Champion's overall political contribution.

9. W. E. Minchinton, "Richard Champion, Nicholas Pocock, and the Carolina Trade," and "Richard Champion, Nicholas Pocock, and the Carolina Trade: A Note," *SCHM* 65 (1964): 87–97 and 70 (1969): 97–103.

10. Owen, *Two Centuries of Ceramic Art in Bristol*, p. 155. Champion kept a warehouse in London at No. 17 Salisbury Court, Fleet Street, for the sale of his porcelain from 1776 to 1782.

11. Sarah's LB 38083(5), 280, SC to E. Fox, February 20, 1770; W. E. Minchinton, "Richard Champion, Nicholas Pocock, and the Carolina Trade," *SCHM* 65 (1964): 87–97; "Richard Champion, Nicholas Pocock, and the Carolina Trade: A Note," *SCHM* 70 (1969): 97–103; Deborah M. Olsen, Introduction, "The Letterbooks of Richard Champion, 1760–1775," BRRAM Series Booklet no. 35, p. 4.

12. Sarah's LB 38083(5), 26, SC to Sukey Rogers, November 12, 1762. Merchants performed many personal tasks for their colonial correspondents, from overseeing the education of their sons in England to acting as their hosts when they came "home."

13. Champion LB, 38083(1), 69, RC to John Lloyd, September 15, 1763. Sarah Izard, daughter of Ralph Izard, married Lord William Campbell, future royal

governor of South Carolina, on April 7, 1763. Allen Johnson et al., eds., *Dictionary of American Biography* (New York, 1928–37), III. 464–65.

14. RC Letterbook, 38083(2), 293, 189–94, RC to Joseph Champion, December 15, 1769; 38083(3), 294, RC to Edward Witt, June 21, 1772; Olsen, "Richard Champion and the Society of Friends," p. 187, has a different view.

15. Addn. Ms. 20,733 (correspondence of John Almon, 1766–1805), f. 119, Joseph Squire to John Wilkes, February 24, 1770. Richard Champion's interests in Plymouth, including his partnership with William Cookworthy, make it probable that he is the "Mr. Champion" Squire refers to in his letter to Wilkes.

16. Sarah's LB, 38083(5), 215, SC to J. and M. Dallaway [May 1769].

17. "Garth Correspondence," *SCHM* 31 (1930): 134, Committee of Correspondence to Messrs. Hankey and Partners, December 9, 1769; *Laurens Papers,* VI. 161. Laurens to Edward Brice, November 15, 1768. The London bill was drawn on Carolina merchant Robert Smyth, a Bristol native and partner of Thomas Farr Jr. Farr was connected by marriage to both Champion and Lloyd.

18. David Duncan Wallace, *South Carolina: A Short History, 1520–1948* (Columbia, S.C., 1961), p. 235; Owen, *Two Centuries of Ceramic Art in Bristol,* p. 16.

19. Champion's LB 38083(1), 134–35, August 27, 1765. Lloyd served as commissioner of Fort Johnson.

20. A letterbook copy in Champion's hand of the letter from the master of the Merchants Hall, William Reeve, to the Marquis of Rockingham, thanking him for his efforts on their behalf, suggests that Champion may have authored it. Champion's LB, 38083(1), 169–71.

21. Champion LB, 38083(1), p. 146, C. Lloyd to RC, August 1, 1766; November 25, 1766, copy of C. Lloyd's acceptance of the position naming Champion and Harford as his securities.

22. Ibid., 1, 157, C. Lloyd to RC, October 11, 1765, and February 3, 1766; Bedford, PRO, Rugeley Papers, X311/53, Rowland Rugeley Jr. to Rowland Rugeley Sr., August 11, 1766.

23. Ibid., 161, C. Lloyd to RC, April 10, 1766.

24. Ibid., 147, RC to Caleb Lloyd, February 15, 1766.

25. Champion LB, 38083(1), 161, RC to C. Lloyd, February 15, 1766. In South Carolina, too, the objections were initially commercial, with the constitutional argument coming late and from the North. Alterations to the law put by the South Carolina Assembly thorough its agent Charles Garth on February 18 and 21 before the Stamp Act Committee all have a commercial character. R. C. Simmons and P. D. G. Thompson, eds., *Proceedings and Debates of the British Parliaments Respecting America, 1754–1783* (Millwood, N.Y., 1982–), II. 28, 29.

26. P. V. McGrath, *The Merchant Venturers of Bristol: A History of the Society of Merchant Venturers of the City of Bristol from Its Origin to the Present Day* (Bristol, 1975), esp. chs. 6 and 8; W. R. Savadge, "The West Country and the American Mainland Colonies," pp. 13–31. The Carolina hat description is found in Samuel Rudder, *A New History of Gloucestershire* (Cirencister [sic], 1779), p. 60, quoted in ibid., p. 29.

27. W. E. Minchinton, ed., *Politics and the Port of Bristol in the Eighteenth Century: The Petitions of the Society of Merchant Venturers, 1698–1803,* Bristol Record Society, 23 (1963); idem, "Political Activities of Bristol Merchants with Respect to the Southern Colonies before the Revolution," *VMHB* 79 (1971): 165.

28. For the basis of Olsen's and Minchinton's claim, see n. 20.

29. W. E. Minchinton, ed., *Politics and the Port of Bristol,* Bristol Record Society, 23 (1963): 214.

30. Quoted by Lucy Sutherland, "Edmund Burke and the First Rockingham Ministry," *EHR* 47 (1932): 64, and Savadge, "The West Country and the American Mainland Colonies," p. 213.

31. Bristol Central Library, Merchants Hall Book of Proceedings (microfilm of originals in the SMV archives at the Merchants Hall), Book II (1762–72), January 6, 1766. Besides Reeve and Farr, the Carolina traders were Isaac Elton, Isaac Elton Jr., James Dalthera, and Joseph Farrell.

32. Merchants HB, January 6 and 10, February 27, 1766; Savadge, "The West Country and the American Mainland Colonies," pp. 220, 224, 238, 240.

33. London, PRO, Chatham Correspondence, Bundle 343, no. 313.

34. Merchants HB, reel 3 (1752–82), April 16, 1757. Farr signed the Standing Committee minute book as Thomas Farr Jr.

35. P. T. Underdown, "Burke's Bristol Friends," pp. 141–46, and "Edmund Burke as a Member of Parliament for Bristol: A Study of His Relations with His Colleague Henry Cruger and with His Constituents, and the Political Situation in Bristol" (Ph.D. dissertation, University of London, 1954), pp. 465, 468; T. W. Copeland et al., eds., *The Correspondence of Edmund Burke, 1744–1782* (Cambridge, Eng., 1958–63), III. 208, Burke to the Marquis of Rockingham, September 14, 1775.

36. London, PRO, CO 5/511, f. 6. Ship's manifests, Smyth and Farr, Charleston, S.C., consignment to Richard Farr and Sons, Bristol, October 18, 1764.

37. Edgar et al., eds, *Biographical Directory of the South Carolina House,* II. 238, 334.

38. Ibid., II. 238–39; Robert M. Weir, ed., *The Letters of Freeman, Etc.: Essays on the Nonimportation Movement in South Carolina,* collected by William Henry Drayton, tricentennial ed. no. 6 (Columbia, S.C., 1977), p. 101n. For the political importance of the Clerk of the House as record keeper, see ch. 6, below.

39. *Collections of the South Carolina Historical Society,* III, 247; *Laurens Papers,* X. 560n.

40. Edgar et al., eds., *Biographical Directory of the South Carolina House,* II. 238–39.

41. *Laurens Papers,* IV. 391, Laurens to Thomas Farr Jr., September 1, 1764; Maurice A. Crouse, ed., "The Letterbook of Peter Manigault, 1763–1773," *SCHM* 70 (1969): 79, 195.

42. Greene, *Quest,* pp. 38, 206, 460.

43. *Commerce of Rhode Island, 1726–1774* (Massachusetts Historical Society, *Collections,* 7th ser., IX), I. 139, February 14, 1766.

44. Bristol, Merchants Hall, SMV Correspondence 1754–1816, bundle 10, item 12, Farr to William Reeve, March 6, 1766.

45. SMV Correspondence, bundle 10, item 18, Thomas Farr to Richard Farr, March 17, 1766.

46. SMV Correspondence, bundle 10, item 25, Thomas Farr to William Reeve, March 18, 1766. Bristol's location on the west coast of England meant that political news from London could sometimes reach America faster if first sent overland to Bristol and then dispatched by the next ship, than if sent directly from London. The

South Carolina legislature's Committee of Correspondence wrote Garth on May 13, 1766, that it received its first notice of the repeal bill's introduction from Bristol, ahead of Garth's letter from London on the subject.

47. Savadge, "The West Country and the American Mainland Colonies," p. 290.

48. SMV Letterbook I (1753–80), March 10, 1766.

49. Bristol Record Office, Aston Court ms., Samuel Munckley Papers, Mu 2(2) a-d.

50. SMV Correspondence, bundle 10, item 16, Abraham Rawlinson to William Reeve, March 14, 1766.

51. SMV Proceedings, March 15, 1766.

52. For the repeal agitation, see Simmons and Thompson, eds., *Proceedings and Debates Respecting America,* II. 57, 95–97, 100–115.

53. "Garth Correspondence," *SCHM* 31 (1930): 233–39; Savadge, "The West Country and the American Mainland Colonies," pp. 308–9; Ella Lonn, *The Colonial Agents of the Southern Colonies* (Chapel Hill, N.C., 1945), pp. 328–29.

54. *Laurens Papers,* V. 233, Laurens to James Grant, February 11, 1767; V. 688, Laurens to George Appleby, May 24, 1768. When news of the duty's removal broke in South Carolina, rice prices advanced by 20 percent, from 50 to 60 per ct. (hundredweight). Those with advance notice, like Laurens, made great profits for their correspondents in speculation.

55. Simmons and Thompson, eds., *Proceedings and Debates,* II. 458, 462, 486.

56. November 18, 1768, quoted in Savadge, "The West Country and the American Mainland Colonies," p. 333.

57. Ibid., p. 332; Simmons and Thompson, eds., *Proceedings and Debates,* III. 17, 28, 29, 43.

Chapter Four

LEARNING OPPOSITION POLITICS IN THE REVOLUTIONARY CRISIS, 1774–1776

1. P. T. Underdown, "The Parliamentary History of the City of Bristol, 1750–1790" (M.A. thesis, University of Bristol, 1948), pp. 406–10.

2. Champion's LB, 38083(2), 301, RC to _____, December 1769. Champion's personality clashes with Cruger are outlined in P. T. Underdown, "Burke's Bristol Friends," *Transactions of the Bristol Historical and Archaeological Society* 67 (1958): 127–50. Champion apparently tried to muster support for a Wilkes candidacy for a Cornwall seat early in 1770. See ch. 3.

3. Champion's LB 38083(2), 307–21; 30803(3), 116, 139, 229, 328. Champion supported the founding of a library society, drew up a plan to expand the city's dockyards, and opposed the licensing of a new theater. His interest in electoral politics obviously continued, but with no greater success than in the past. In 1771, his sister wrote, "my brother returned Saturday night not much pleased with the success of their expedition. The Election, he says, was lost only because V. Morris was incapable of acting in consistant [sic] with rectitude and Honour." Sarah's LB 38083(5), 323, SC to S. Harford, July 23, 1771. V. Morris is Valentine Morris, for whose color-

ful political career, see Ivor Waters, *The Unfortunate Valentine Morris* (Chepstow, Wales, 1964).

4. Champion LB 38083(2), 272, _____ to RC, August 19, 1769; 133, _____ to RC, London, November 1, 1770; 282, RC to _____, November 18, 1769. Champion agreed with colonial objections to the Townshend Acts, but disapproved of non-importation resolutions as injurious to trade.

5. Ibid., 38083(3), 116., RC to _____, September 10, 1770; 208 and 299, RC to John Lloyd, May 20, 1771, and June 29, 1772.

6. G. H. Guttridge, *English Whiggism and the American Revolution* (Berkeley, Calif., 1963), pp. 38, 43.

7. Paul Langford, "The British Business Community and the Later Nonimportation Movements, 1768–1776," in Walter H. Conser Jr., Ronald M. McCarthy, David J. Toscano, and Gene Shays, eds., *Resistance, Politics, and the American Struggle for Independence, 1765–1775* (Boulder, Colo., 1986).

8. Champion's (New York) LB, unpaginated, RC to Edmund Burke, October 1, 1774.

9. Ibid.

10. Ibid., "Proceedings at Election," LB 38083(4), pp. 374–408, April 1775; P. T. Underdown, "Henry Cruger and Edmund Burke: Colleagues and Rivals at the Bristol Election of 1774," *WMQ*, 3rd ser., 15 (1958): 14–34. Underdown credits Burke's election to the exertions of Champion.

11. Brickdale challenged Burke's election, but a parliamentary committee formed to investigate the matter certified Burke's candidacy. A brief account of the disputed election with a transcript of the committee hearing appears in *The Bristol Poll Book: Being a List of the Freeholders and Freemen, who voted at the General Election for Members to Serve in Parliament for the City and County of Bristol* (Bristol: W. Pine, 1774), p. 133.

12. Champion's (NY) LB, John Lloyd to RC, September 2, 1773.

13. Lloyd later claimed that the outbreak of the war and his wife's ill health prevented his immediate return to South Carolina. South Caroliniana Library, Columbia, S.C., John Lloyd Papers, John Lloyd to Abraham Lloyd, January 29, 1796.

14. Champion LB 38083(3), 299, RC to John Lloyd, June 29, 1772. Champion explains the crash in terms of the London-Edinburgh credit circuit, along which bills of exchange were drawn and redrawn. This explains why South Carolina and Bristol, much less tied up in that circuit than Virginia and Maryland and the Scottish ports, felt the crash much less keenly. See also Richard B. Sheridan, "The British Credit Crisis of 1772 and the American Colonies," *JEH* 20 (1960): 161–86.

15. Mark A. deWolfe Howe, ed., "Journal of Josiah Quincey, Jr." Massachusetts Historical Society, *Proceedings* 44 (1916): 451.

16. David Duncan Wallace, *South Carolina: A Short History, 1520–1948* (Columbia, S.C., 1961), p. 251.

17. Research shows their impressions were accurate. See Langford, "British Business Community," *Politics and Resistance*, p. 287.

18. *South-Carolina Gazette*, December 13, 1773.

19. South Caroliniana Library, Columbia, S.C., John Lloyd Papers, John Lloyd to Abraham Lloyd, January 29, 1796.

20. *Laurens Papers,* IX. 2, James Laurens to Henry Laurens, April 20, 1773. There were also war scares (with France and Spain) in March 1773, and prudent merchants were building up their credit balances by remitting as much to their English correspondents as possible. VIII. 608–9, Henry Laurens to James Laurens, March 11, 1773.

21. Wallace, *South Carolina: A Short History,* pp. 251–56; Edward McCrady, *The History of South Carolina under the Royal Government* (New York, 1899), pp. 733–42. Savadge notes that wheat imports to Bristol in 1775 were enormous. Of the fifty-two ships going out to the colonies that year, all but four sailed in ballast to return loaded with wheat. One merchants' petition claimed that over a million bushels of wheat were imported between September 1, 1774, and September 1, 1775. With that trade restrained, rice could expect to replace at least some of it. See W. R. Savadge, "The West Country and the American Mainland Colonies, 1703–1783, with Special Reference to the Merchants of Bristol" (unpublished B. Litt. thesis, Oxford University, 1952), p. 353.

22. Champion's (New York) LB, Richard Burke to RC, November 24, 1774.

23. Champion LB, 38083(3), 356–59, Lloyd to RC, June 23, 1775. Watts reported that the Americans were firm in their resolutions.

24. Anna Deas, ed., *Correspondence of Mr. Ralph Izard of South Carolina, 1774–1804, With a Short Memoir* (New York, 1844), p. 7. Thomas Farr Jr. to Izard, August 8, 1774; p. 29, Izard to Edward Rutledge, November 15, 1774.

25. The several petitions to king, lords, and Commons, with signatures are reprinted in *Laurens Papers,* IX. 368, 372, 376, 448. J. M. Flavell credits William and Arthur Lee of Virginia with leadership of the drive, but there is a better case for Laurens and Izard in that role. Apart from the evidence that the overwhelming majority of signers were South Carolinians (surely there were at least as many Virginians in London who could have been recruited), the Lees were more closely linked to the Wilkites. The South Carolina complexion of the petition's signatories and the venue make the Lees' leadership unlikely. Julie Marie Flavell, 'Americans of Patriotic Sympathies in London and the Colonial Strategy for Opposition, 1774–1775' (Ph.D. dissertation, University of London, 1989), pp. 19–28, 114.

26. London, British Library, Addn. Ms. 20,733 (Correspondence of John Almon, 1766–1805), f. 70.

27. Ibid., ff. 57, 59, 67, 69, 70, 71, 73, 76, 77, 78–79. The last two letters are unsigned but in Lloyd's hand with the remark "The place from whence this letter is dated [Southampton] will be a sufficient signification from whence it comes."

28. Burke introduced Champion and Baker. The two then coordinated the London and Bristol drives. Champion (NY) LB, William Baker to RC, January 1, 4, 5, 7 1775. Carolina traders on the London standing committee of twenty-four members (besides Baker) included at least Edward Bridgen, Thomas Woolridge, William Greenwood, and John Nutt.

29. Champion's LB 38083(4), 17–18, RC to _____, January 31, 1775.

30. Ibid., 38083(4), 7–8, Richard Burke to RC, January 24, 1775.

31. The best summation of his strategy can be found in T. C. Copeland et al., eds., *The Correspondence of Edmund Burke, 1744–1782* (Cambridge, Eng., 1958–63), III. 206, Burke to the Marquis of Rockingham, September 14, 1775; and also III. 219, Burke to the Duke of Richmond, [September 26, 1775].

32. Ibid.

33. Addn. Ms. 20,733 (Almon correspondence), f. 67.

34. University of Nottingham, Third Duke of Portland Collection, RC to Lord Portland, September 27, 1775; Add. Ms. 20377 (Almon correspondence), f. 69, John Lloyd to John Almon, September 29, 1775.

35. John Almon, *The Remembrancer, or Impartial Repository of Public Events* (London, 1775), p. 240; Sheffield Public Library, Marquis of Rockingham Papers, RC to Lord Rockingham, September 28, 1775; Savadge, "The West Country and the American Mainland Colonies," pp. 483–84.

36. Portland Papers, RC to Lord Portland, September 28, 1775; *Burke Correspondence*, III. 222–24, EB to the Marquis of Rockingham [October 1775]; Paul Farr's remark quoted in Savadge, "The West Country and the American Mainland Colonies," p. 483, from a letter to Burke, September 30, 1775, now missing.

37. Addn. Ms. 20733 (Almon correspondence), f. 69; Peter Force, ed., *American Archives*, 4th ser., III. 816, reprints Champion's petition of protest of the meeting's procedures, which he got published, although without names.

38. Almon, *The Remembrancer* (London, 1775), I. 240.

39. Ibid., p. 241.

40. Archibald S. Foord, *His Majesty's Opposition, 1714–1830* (Oxford, 1964).

41. John Brewer, *Party Ideology and Popular Politics at the Accession of George III* (Cambridge, Eng., 1976), pp. 251–56.

42. Quoted in J. R. Pole, *Political Representation in England and the Origins of the American Republic* (New York, 1966), p. 443.

43. John A. Sainsbury, "The Pro-American Movement in London, 1769–1782: Extra-Parliamentary Opposition to the Government's American Policy" (Ph.D. dissertation, McGill University, 1975), 310–45; George F. E. Rude, "The Anti-Wilkite Merchants of 1769," *The Guildhall Miscellany* 2 (1965): 283–304.

44. Columbia, S.C. Department of Archives and History, *Journal of the South Carolina Commons House of Assembly*, XXXVIII. 215, December 8, 1769; *Laurens Papers*, VII. 273n. The following year Lieutenant Governor William Bull wrote the Earl of Hillsborough that "this unfortunate vote has embarrassed many of the moderate members. It was passed . . . in a very hasty manner where there was no time to consider the propriety of the application or the mode of issuing money." Bull's successor Governor Charles Montagu wrote that "scarcely above two members but what in private condemn it, yet from pride find it difficult to recede." K. G. Davies, ed., *Documents of the American Revolution, 1770–1783*, vol. II, *Transcripts, 1770* (Shannon, Ireland), pp. 172–73, Bull to Hillsborough, August 23, 1770; vol. II, *Calendar, 1770–1771*, p. 403, Montagu to Hillsborough, September 26, 1771. Peter Manigault, Speaker of the House when the resolution passed, wrote the following fall, "I hate to hear any Mention of the Bill of Rights & the Money we threw away upon them. It was always against my Opinion and has been attended with very disagreeable consequences." Maurice A. Crouse, ed., "The Letterbook of Peter Manigault, 1763–1773," *SCHM* 70 (1969): 187, Peter Manigault to Daniel Blake, October 19, 1770. See also Jack P. Greene, "Bridge to Revolution: The Wilkes Fund Controversy in South Carolina, 1769–1775," *JSH* 29 (1963): 19–52.

45. "Quincey's Journal," pp. 454–55. On the ethnic bias, see p. 449.

46. Alison Gilbert Olson, *Making the Empire Work: London and American Interest Groups, 1690–1790* (Cambridge, Mass.: Harvard University Press, 1992), p. 11; Patricia Bonomi, review of above, *WMQ* 50 (1993): 621–24 (quotation from p. 623).

47. Julie Marie Flavell, "Americans of Patriotic Sympathies in London and the Colonial Strategy for Opposition, 1774–1775" (Ph.D. dissertation, University of London, 1989), pp. 264–69, 294 (quotation), and ch. 9; Deas, ed., *Izard's Correspondence,* pp. 142–43.

48. Wallace, *South Carolina: A Short History,* p. 268.

49. Richard Walsh, ed., *The Writings of Christopher Gadsden* (Columbia, S.C., 1966), p. xxiii.

50. *Laurens Papers,* XI. 189, HL to Lachlan MacIntosh, March 24, 1776.

51. *Laurens Papers,* XI. 115–16, HL to John Laurens, February 22, 1776.

52. Edgar et al., eds., *Biographical Directory of the South Carolina House,* II. 456, 459. Arthur Middleton used "junior" to distinguish himself from his grandfather of the same name.

53. Jack N. Rackove, *The Beginnings of National Politics: An Interpretative History of the Continental Congress* (Baltimore, 1979), pp. 89–90, 96.

54. Marvin R. Zahniser, *Charles Cotesworth Pinckney: Founding Father* (Chapel Hill, N.C., 1967) p. 43.

55. *Laurens Papers,* XI. 115, HL to John Laurens, February 22, 1776; Edgar et al., eds, *Biographical Directory of the House of Representatives of South Carolina,* III. 261.

56. *Journals of the Continental Congress,* IV. 342, quoted in Lyman Butterfield et al., eds., *The Adams Papers: Adams Family Correspondence* (Cambridge, Mass., 1963), I. 411 n. 2.

57. Rakove, *Beginnings of National Politics,* pp. 81–82; J. R. Pole, *The Decision for Independence* (Philadelphia, 1975), p. 52.

58. Quoted in Butterfield et al., eds., *The Adams Papers,* I. 411 n.

59. Butterfield et al., eds., *The Adams Papers: Diary and Autobiography* (Cambridge, Mass, 1961), pp. 238–41 (quotation from p. 241).

60. Robert A. Taylor et al., eds., *The Adams Papers: Papers of John Adams* (Cambridge, Mass, 1979), IV. 131–32, John Adams to James Warren, April 20, 1776; Wallace, *South Carolina: A Short History,* p. 271.

61. *Laurens Papers,* XI. 194, HL to John Laurens, March 26, 1776.

62. Wallace, *South Carolina: A Short History,* pp. 281 (quotation), 290, 296. Prisoners of war were thus notified that they must return to their allegiance as British subjects, and might be required to fight against their fellow Americans.

63. Taylor et al., eds., *The Adams Papers,* IV. 342 (editor's notes).

64. Ibid., IV. 195, John Adams to James Warren, May 20, 1776.

65. Paul H. Smith, ed., *Letters of Delegates to Congress* (Washington, D.C., 1976–), IV. 174, Edward Rutledge to John Jay, June 8, 1776.

66. Quoted in Page Smith, *John Adams* (New York, 1962), I. 268.

67. Taylor et al., eds., *Papers of John Adams,* IV. 344 (editor's notes); emphasis mine.

68. Smith, ed., *Letters of Delegates to Congress,* IV. 337–38, ER to John Jay, Philadelphia, June 29, 1776. Jay subsequently informed Rutledge that "plots, con-

spiracies, and chimeras dire" kept him in New York, where a new government was being formed (p. 339).

69. Quoted in Smith, *John Adams*, p. 269.

70. Ibid., p. 270.

71. Ibid., pp. 269–70.

72. Butterfield et al., eds, *The Adams Papers*, II. 29, JA to Abigail Adams, July 3, 1776.

73. Smith, *John Adams*, I. 270.

74. Wallace, *South Carolina: A Short History*, p. 272.

75. Details of these contrasts are discussed in ch. 5, below.

76. *Laurens Papers*, XI. 228, HL to John Laurens, August 14, 1776. Laurens's reference to violence concerns the British attack on Sullivan's Island, which began on June 28.

77. Wallace, *South Carolina: A Short History*, p. 296.

78. Both petitions with their signatures are reprinted by Almon in *The Remembrancer*, I. 242–50.

79. Ibid., I. 257, "Edmund Burke's letter to Thomas Hayes, Chairman of the meeting of merchants, etc. at Bristol, 11 October 1775."

80. Foord, *His Majesty's Opposition*, pp. 359–60. The movement was badly managed and unpopular. The Rockinghamites conceded failure by February 1777 and drifted back.

81. Another difference, not fatal but significant, that may have escaped the South Carolinian's lobby-trained perception of politics is that both the Rockinghamite and Chathamites finally had more in common ideologically with the North Ministry than with the Americans. "In taking up the Patriot cause as far as they did, the Rockinghams in 1774–1775 could be accused of acting the usual part of a group in opposition, that is, of attacking the very measures they would themselves take if they came into power." (Flavell, "Americans of Patriotic Sympathies," p. 99, citing Herbert Butterfield, *George III, Lord North and the People, 1779–80* [London, 1949], p. 15. If, however, South Carolinians felt betrayed when Rockingham and Chathamite support stopped short of supporting a revolution, they were remarkably quiet about it.

Chapter Five

"INTEREST GOVERNS THE WORLD," 1768–1787

1. Jerrilyn Greene Marston, *King and Congress: The Transfer of Political Legitimacy, 1774–1776* (Princeton, N.J., 1987), p. 187.

2. *Laurens Papers*, VI. 176, HL to Edward Jones, November 22, 1768. The lower house contained fifty seats.

3. Paragraphs on the October elections drawn from Edward McCrady, *The History of South Carolina under the Royal Government, 1719–1776* (New York, 1899), pp. 608–10, 667; David Duncan Wallace, *South Carolina: A Short History, 1520–1948* (Columbia, S.C., 1961), pp. 239–40.

4. Active in the Charleston merchants' lobby in the Moore affair (ch. 2) and later in the Carolina network in England (ch. 4).

5. *South-Carolina Gazette,* October 3, 1768.

6. *Laurens Papers,* VI. 176, HL To Edward Jones, November 22, 1768.

7. Ibid., VI. 171.

8. Eva B. Poythress, "Revolution by Committee: An Administrative History of the Extralegal Committees in South Carolina, 1774–1776" (Ph.D. dissertation, University of North Carolina, 1975).

9. *Laurens Papers,* X. 27, January 11, 1775. At the opening meeting of the first General Provincial Committee at Pike's Long Room (a tavern), Henry Laurens noted that "C. Pinckney was called to the Chair & Elections adjusted." According to the *Journals of the Provincial Congress,* Charles Pinckney was elected unanimously.

10. Wallace, *South Carolina: A Short History,* p. 241; McCrady, *South Carolina under the Royal Government,* p. 651, lists the committee members.

11. A member of the Royal Council and outspoken supporter of the Crown, Drayton later became one of the colony's most ardent patriots and an early proponent of Independence.

12. *The Letters of Freeman, Etc.: Essays on the Nonimportation Movement in South Carolina, Collected By William Henry Drayton,* ed. with an introduction by Robert M. Weir, tricentennial ed. no. 6 (Columbia, S.C., 1977), pp. xxix, 20, 55, 136n. The first section of the first paragraph is a near verbatim quotation from John Locke's *Two Treatises on Government.*

13. London, PRO, CO 5/394, ff. 21–25d.

14. T. M. Devine, *The Tobacco Lords: A Study of the Tobacco Merchants of Glasgow and Their Trading Activities c. 1740–1790* (Edinburgh, 1975), p. 128.

15. Bristol Record Office, Richard Champion Letterbooks, 38083(2), 272, _____ to Richard Champion, August 19, 1769. Gadsden's essay advocated excluding all merchants from participation in drawing up a nonimportation agreement since the "Importers of European goods" were most of them "strangers, many of them of a very few years standing in the province," whose "natural affection to the province is too plainly, not to be depended on." Quoted in Marston, *King and Congress,* p. 110.

16. "The Merchants of Charlestown," *South-Carolina Gazette,* quoted in McCrady, *South Carolina under the Royal Government,* p. 648.

17. McCrady, *South Carolina under Royal Government,* pp. 380, 649–50.

18. Ronald Hoffman, *A Spirit of Dissension: Economics, Politics, and the Revolution in Maryland* (Baltimore, 1973).

19. Ibid., pp. 61–93.

20. Drayton, *Freeman,* pp. 55–56. See ch. 6, below, for an analysis of the incorporation of lobbying values and practices into the informal legislative structure.

21. McCrady, *South Carolina in the Revolution,* p. 763.

22. Paul H. Smith, ed., *Letters from Delegates to Congress, 1774–1789* (Washington, D.C., 1946–), I. 292–95.

23. *JC,* XXIX. 602, 625; and see ch. 2, above.

24. Smith, ed., *Letters from Delegates,* pp. 292–95.

25. Anna Deas, ed., *The Correspondence of Mr.Ralph Izard, With a Short Memoir* (New York, 1844), Edward Rutledge to Ralph Izard, October 20, 1774; emphasis

mine. For Congress's debate on this issue, see Smith, ed., *Letters from Delegates*, II. 111, 262.

26. Smith, ed., *Letters from Delegates*, I. 57–58, Caesar Rodney to Thomas Rodney, September 9, 1774.

27. For a useful summary of the literature on the question of South Carolina's tendency to desperate remedies, see Lacy K. Ford Jr., *Origins of Southern Radicalism* (Oxford, 1988), pp. 99–145.

28. Deas, ed., *The Correspondence of Ralph Izard*, Rutledge to Izard, October 20, 1774.

29. Bristol, PRO, Richard Champion Letterbooks, 38083(4), 489–91, Richard Champion to Edmund Burke, October 23, 1775; 499–502, Richard Champion to the Marquis of Rockingham, October 26, 1775.

30. McCrady, *South Carolina under the Royal Government*, pp. 763–70; Smith, ed., *Letters from Delegates*, I. 295; II. 283.

31. B. F. Stevens, ed., *B. F. Steven's Facsimiles of Manuscripts in European Archives Relating to America, 1776–1783* (London, 1889–98), XXIV. doc. no. 2035. Richard Oswald to Lord Dartmouth, February 27, 1775.

32. Ibid., doc. no. 2034. "Memorandum with Respect to South Carolina," Richard Oswald to Lord Dartmouth, February 21, 1775, f. 12.

33. Ibid., ff. 2, 3, 11, 12.

34. Ibid., ff. 6–10, 14.

35. Ibid., f. 21.

36. Ibid., doc. no. 2031.

37. Alison Gilbert Olson, "Parliament, the London Lobbies, and Provincial Interests in England and America," *Historical Reflections* 6 (1979): 386.

38. *Stevens's Facsimiles*, doc. no. 2032, February 9, 1775, endorsed "Thoughts on America."

39. Ibid.

40. Ibid.; emphasis mine.

41. Ibid.

42. On deference in eighteenth-century society, see J. R. Pole, "Historians and the Problem of Early American Democracy," *AHR* 67 (1962): 626–46. It is worth noting that patriots intended using the same phenomenon to influence people for the cause of liberty, "which, if properly fanned by the Gentlemen of Influence will, I make no doubt burst out again into flame."

43. *Stevens's Facsimiles*, doc. no. 2032, Richard Oswald to Lord Dartmouth, February 9, 1775.

44. Robert M. Weir, "Who Shall Rule at Home: The American Revolution as a Crisis for Legitimacy for the Colonial Elite," *Journal of Interdisciplinary History* 6 (1976): 679–700.

45. Michael E. Stevens, "Legislative Privilege in Post-Revolutionary South Carolina," *WMQ*, 3rd ser., 46 (1989): 71–91. It should be noted that there was ample precedent in the eighteenth century for the use of legislative privilege as a personal asset. The dispute should not be viewed in terms of a class struggle but as a personal disagreement over whether Thompson actually intended to insult Rutledge through his slave. Thompson denied it.

46. Robert Beverley to John Backhouse, August 10, 1775, quoted in Marston, *King and Congress*, p. 184.

47. Mark A. de Wolfe Howe, ed., "Journal of Josiah Quincey, Jr., 1773," *Massachusetts Historical Society Proceedings* 64 (1916): 462–63.

48. University of Nottingham, Portland Papers, Richard Champion to the Duke of Portland, October 22, 1775; Champion LB, 38083(4), 489–91, Champion to Edmund Burke, October 23, 1775; 499–501, Champion to the Marquis of Rockingham, October 26, 1775. On the competing business and political orbits of Charleston and Savannah, see Rebecca K. Starr, "A Place Called Daufuskie: Island Bridge to Georgia, 1707–1825" (M.A. thesis, University of South Carolina, 1984).

49. Ibid. The quotation is from the Champion to Edmund Burke letter.

50. James Wright to Lord Hillsborough, July 20, 1770, CO 5/660. pp. 116–35d, in K. G. Davies, ed., *Documents of the American Revolution, 1770–1783* (Shannon, Ireland, 1972–), I. 150.

51. Max Farrand, ed., *The Records of the Federal Convention of 1787* (New Haven, Conn., 1937), I. 402–3. Pinckney delivered this speech in a much more detailed form on the opening day of the ratification convention in Charleston. See Jonathan Elliot, ed., *The Debates in the Several State Conventions on the Adoption of the Federal Constitution As Recommended by the General Convention at Philadelphia in 1787* (Washington, D.C., 1854), IV. 321–22.

52. Elliot, ed., *Debates*, IV. 324.

53. Farrand, ed., *Records*, I. 486.

54. Ibid., II. 451.

55. Quotation in Jack N. Rakove, *The Beginnings of National Politics: An Interpretative History of the Continental Congress* (Baltimore, 1983), p. 161. Threatening disunion would become standard in Southern rhetoric in the nineteenth century.

56. Michael E. Stevens and Christine M. Allen, eds., *Journals of the House of Representatives, 1787–1788, The State Records of South Carolina* (Columbia, 1981), p. xiv. Pringle argued that no contract was so sacred that it outweighed the good of society. "The safety of the people is the law paramount, to which every other must yield." See also ch. 7, below.

57. Hints of the Carolina plan to trade its support for a stronger federal Constitution for a commercial treaty with Great Britain granting them free trade are found in London, PRO, Foreign Office Papers, 4/5:717–19, 791–93, George Miller to the Marquis of Carmarthen, July 10 and December 24, 1787, 4/6:243–46, April 15, 1788. Disappointingly, no treaty materialized. In retaliation, the House refused to permit a reading of British Consul Miller's letter to Governor Thomas Pinckney which objected to a further installment act passed after ratification. It was disallowed on the principle that, as there was no commercial treaty between Great Britain and the United States, Miller had no power to make representations.

58. Elliot, ed., *Debates*, IV. 253.

59. Columbia, S.C., South Caroliniana Library, Isaac King Letterbook, 1783–98, King to Joshua Ward, June 8, 1784; King to Robert Smyth, June 8, 1784; King to Joshua Ward, November 15, 1787; March 12, 1788.

60. Columbia, S.C., South Caroliniana Library, Robert Gibbes Autograph Book, p. 18, Thomas Farr to _____, August 27, 1785.

61. Charleston, S.C., Charleston Library Society, John Lloyd Letters, John Lloyd to T. B. Smith, April 15, 1786. Both Lloyd and Farr ultimately turned to ratification of the U.S Constitution to repair South Carolina's foreign credit. See Elliot, ed., *Debates*, IV. 317, 339.

62. Klein, *Unification of a Slave State*, pp. 165–66.

63. Farrand, *Records*, III. 334.

64. Ibid., II. 183.

65. R. C. Simmons and P. D. G. Thompson, eds., *Proceedings and Debates of the British Parliaments Respecting America, 1754–1783* (Millwood, N.Y., 1982–), I. 333–34, 517; II. 502; III. 161, 254.

66. Farrand, ed., *Records*, II. 400, 415, 449–53.

67. Drew R. McCoy, "James Madison and Visions of American Nationality in the Confederation Period: A Regional Perspective," in Richard Beeman, Stephen Botein, and Edward W. Carter, eds., *Beyond Confederation: Origins of the Constitution and American National Identity* (Chapel Hill, N.C., 1984), pp. 230–33.

68. Foreign importations of slaves were stopped the 1740s and the 1760s for a three-year period in each instance by laying on a prohibitive duty. Thomas Cooper and David J. McCord, eds., *The Statutes at Large of South Carolina* (Columbia, S.C., 1836–41), III (1837). act. no. 669, April 5, 1740; IV (1838). 187, act. no. 933, August 25, 1764.

69. *The State Records of South Carolina: Journals of the House of Representatives, 1787–1788* (Columbia, S.C., 1981), p. 304.

70. Farrand, *Records*, II.371. Parliament's inconsistent policy on this issue indicates South Carolina's home lobby wielded greater influence with London merchants in the slave trade.

71. Ibid., II. 364 (emphasis mine), 373.

72. Ibid., II. 374.

73. G. H. Guttridge, ed., *The American Correspondence of a Bristol Merchant, 1766–1776: The Letters of Richard Champion* (Berkeley, Calif., 1943), p. 50, RC to Messrs. Willing Morris & Co., March 6, 1775.

74. J. A. W. Gunn, "'Interest Will Not Lie': A Seventeenth-century Political Maxim," *JHI* XXIX (1968): 551–64; idem, *Politics and the Public Interest in the Seventeenth Century* (London, 1969), pp. 25–33, 40–52; Albert O. Hirschman, *The Passions and the Interests: Political Arguments for Capitalism before Its Triumph* (Princeton, N.J., 1977), pp. 32–43, 64.

75. Walter Bellingrath Edgar, "The Libraries of Colonial South Carolina" (Ph.D. dissertation, University of South Carolina, 1969), appendix II, p. 228. For Shaftesbury on enlightened interest, see Anthony Ashley Cooper, *Characteristics of Men, Manners, Opinions, Times, etc.*, ed. by John M. Robertson, (London, 1711; reprint ed., 1900), I. 326. Interest as political philosophy probably penetrated South Carolina leaders' thought more through maxim than reading, since the actual numbers of copies of Shaftsbury's tract is quite low.

76. Thomas Fowler, *Shaftesbury and Hutcheson* (London, 1882), pp. 74–75, 138–42, 163.

77. Cooper, *Characteristics*, I. 77, 326.

78. I am grateful to Dr. Rogers, who allowed me to read his paper, "The Ratification Process in South Carolina," presented at the annual meeting of the South

Carolina Historical Society, March 9, 1988, prior to publication. The argument of this paper forms the basis of the following three paragraphs.

79. On Charles Pinckney as a public speaker, see William Pierce's character sketches in Farrand, ed., *Records,* III. 96.

80. According to House member David Ramsay, "Our Assembly is now sitting and the federal constitution has been discussed before them for the sake of informing the country members." Robert L. Brunhouse, ed., "David Ramsay, 1749–1815: Selections from His Writings," in *Transactions of the American Philosophical Society* (Philadelphia, 1965), 55, pt. 4, p. 118, Ramsay to John Eliot, January 19, 1788.

81. Elliot, ed., *Debates,* IV. 287, 316. It seems clear from the record that Lowndes's opposition was sincere.

82. Walter B. Edgar and N. Louise Bailey, eds., *Biographical Directory of the South Carolina House of Representatives,* vol. II, *The Commons House of Assembly, 1692–1775* (Columbia, S.C., 1977), p. 575.

83. Committee members' names can be found in John C. Meleney, *The Public Life of Aedanus Burke: Revolutionary Republican in Post-Revolutionary South Carolina* (Columbia, S.C., 1989), p. 143n.

84. Ibid., p. 144.

85. *South-Carolina State Gazette,* June 26, 1788, quoted in Meleney, *Burke,* p. 146. Lamb was a leader of the coordinated New York and Virginia Antifederalist movement.

86. Ibid., p. 148.

87. PRO, FO 4/6:243–46, Miller to the Marquis of Carmarthen, April 15, 1788.

88. See, for example, Harry Grant to Christopher Champlin, January 23, 1788, in *Commerce of Rhode Island, 1726–1774* (Massachusetts Historical Society, *Collections,* 7th ser., IX), II. 349. On the Chamber of Commerce position for congressional regulation of commerce, see George C. Rogers Jr., *Evolution of a Federalist: William Loughton Smith of Charleston (1758–1812)* (Columbia, S.C., 1962), pp. 137, 152.

89. Elliot, ed., *Debates,* IV. 338–40.

90. Brunhouse, ed., "David Ramsay's Writings," p. 20.; PRO, FO 4/6:693–99, George Miller to the Marquis of Carmarthen, November 30, 1788.

91. Merrill Jensen and Robert A. Becker, eds., *The Documentary History of the First Federal Elections, 1788–1790* (Madison, Wis., 1976), I. 213–14, John Brown Cutting to John Rutledge, February 21, 1789. Since John Rutledge voted for the installment bill, it was Gillon's challenge to the Pinckney-Rutledge leadership in the House, not the installment issue, which lay behind Gillon's elevation to the lieutenant governor's chair.

Chapter Six

TACIT RULES AND HIDDEN STRUCTURE

1. Alison Olson, "Parliament, the London Lobbies, and Provincial Interests in England and America," *Historical Reflections* 6 (1979): 383, 390.

2. George C. Rogers Jr., *Evolution of a Federalist: William Loughton Smith of Charleston (1758–1812)* (Columbia, S.C., 1962), p. 137.

3. See, for example, Robert M. Weir, *Colonial South Carolina: A History* (Millwood, N.Y., 1983), pp. 108–15.

4. The best study here is Rachel N. Klein, *Unification of a Slave State: The Rise of the Planter Class in the South Carolina Backcountry, 1760–1808* (Chapel Hill, N.C., 1990).

5. George Edward Frakes, *Laboratory for Liberty: The South Carolina Legislative Committee System, 1716–1776* (Lexington, Ky., 1970), p. 104.

6. Ibid., pp. 98, 101–2, 114.

7. Ibid., pp. 34–35.

8. David Duncan Wallace, *South Carolina: A Short History, 1520–1948* (Columbia, S.C., 1961), pp. 279–81.

9. Julian P. Boyd, ed., *The Papers of Thomas Jefferson* (Princeton, N.J., 1953), VIII. 196. Ralph Izard to Thomas Jefferson, June 10, 1785.

10. Charleston, *Gazette of the State of South Carolina,* quoted in Gordon S. Wood, *The Creation of the American Republic, 1776–1787* (Chapel Hill, N.C., 1969), p. 608.

11. See, for example, the elaborate trade-off scheme to balance the interests of indigo, hemp, and other producers with that of rice planters, whose crop won an exemption from the planned Continental Congress embargo of 1775 described in ch. 5, above.

12. Charleston, South Carolina Library Society, John Lloyd and Thomas Farr Letters, John Lloyd to T. B. Smith, December 7, 1784.

13. Ibid. Thomas Farr was subsequently chosen to replace Benjamin Elliot, who declined to serve, and qualified on February 15, 1785. Lark Emerson Adams and Rosa Stoney Lumpkin, eds., *The State Records of South Carolina: Journals of the House of Representatives, 1785–1786* (Columbia, S.C., 1979), p. 604 and n.

14. Rogers, *Evolution of a Federalist,* pp. 104–5; Jerome Nedalhaft, *The Disorders of War: The Revolution in South Carolina* (Orono, Maine, 1981), pp. 97–98. The legislature diverted the site of conflict with Charleston radicals by incorporating the city in the summer of 1783.

15. Thomas Cooper and David J. McCord, eds., *The Statutes at Large of South Carolina* (Columbia, S.C., 1836–41), IV. 516–25. In all, 571 petitions were received in 1783–84, the largest number for the decade, or for any previous year.

16. Robert M. Weir, "'The Violent Spirit': The Reestablishment of Order, and the Continuity of Leadership in Post-revolutionary South Carolina," in Ronald Hoffman, Peter J. Albert, and Thad W. Tate, eds., *An Uncivil War: The Southern Backcountry during the American Revolution* (Charlottesville, Va., 1985), pp. 70–98.

17. Michael E. Stevens, Christine M. Allen, and et al., eds., *Journals of the House, 1783–1784* (Columbia, S.C., 1977), pp. x-xi.

18. One occasionally finds notes filed with committee reports, but only the committee's final report was read before the House.

19. The old Commons House of Assembly usually granted local interests a representation on pertinent committees, but not a sole and exclusive one.

20. *Journals of the House, 1783–84,* January 29, 1783, pp. 58 and n., 59 and n., 209.

21. Ibid., pp. 22, 27 and n., 219.

22. *Journals of the House, 1792–1794,* December 4, 1792, p. 66.

23. Morton J. Horwitz discusses water rights cases at length in his *Transformation of the American Law, 1780–1860* (Cambridge, Mass., 1977), pp. 34–46, all of which were argued in courts.

24. On the 1769 association as a prelegislative body, see ch. 5, above. By contrast, the trend in colonial Massachusetts, Pennsylvania, and Virginia, was toward a greater separation of legislative and judicial powers. Alison G. Olson, "Eighteenth-Century Colonial Legislatures and Their Constituents," *JAH* 79 (1992): 547, 562–67.

25. *Journals of the House, 1791,* January 21, 1791, pp. 93–94.

26. Ibid., pp. xi-xii, xxiii, December 10 and 15, 1791, pp. 366, 401.

27. Alison G. Olson, "The Board of Trade and London-American Interest Groups in the Eighteenth Century," *Journal of Imperial and Commonwealth History* 8 (1980): 33–50.

28. Gwenda Morgan, "'The Privilege of Making Laws'": The Board of Trade, the Virginia Assembly and Legislative Review, 1748–1754," *JAS* 10 (1976): 3.

29. *Journals of the House, 1792–1794,* 435n., December 19, 1793.

30. "Journal of Josiah Quincey," p. 452. Taking off one's hat indicated a formal debate, during which specific speaking rules applied.

31. Steven A. Watson, "Parliamentary Procedure as a Key to the Understanding of Eighteenth Century Politics," *The Burke Newsletter,* III. 108–28.

32. Sheila Lambert, *Bills and Acts: Legislative Procedure in Eighteenth-Century England* (Cambridge, Eng., 1971), p. 96.

33. O. Cyprian Williams, *The Historical Development of Private Bill Procedure and Standing Orders in the House of Commons* (London, 1948), I. 23–35.

34. P. D. T. Thomas, *The House of Commons in the Eighteenth Century* (Oxford, 1971), p. 265; Foord, *His Majesty's Opposition,* pp. 191, 211.

35. Williams, *Historical Development of Private Bills,* I. 31.

36. See, for example, the disposition of the petition of Susannah Smyth, *Journals of the House, 1783–84,* pp. 535–36, 545, March 9, 11, 1784.

37. Frakes, *Laboratory for Liberty,* pp. 34–37, 59–61.

38. Ibid., p. 62.

39. Ibid., pp. 22, 34, 61, 84, 97.

40. See, for example, the county courts controversy, above.

41. Frakes, *Laboratory for Liberty,* p. 88; Jack P. Greene, *The Quest for Power: The Lower Houses of Assembly in the Southern Royal Colonies, 1689–1776* (Chapel Hill, N.C., 1963), p. 484.

42. Frakes, *Laboratory for Liberty,* pp. 89–91, 107, 110.

43. They were Joseph Kershaw and Tacitus Gaillard of St. Marks and St. Matthews parishes, respectively. Greene, *Quest for Power,* pp. 479, 481; Frakes, *Laboratory for Liberty,* pp. 104, 106–7.

44. Weir, *Colonial South Carolina,* p. 315.

45. Frakes, *Laboratory for Liberty,* pp. 157–61, 163–69.

46. Weir, *Colonial South Carolina,* pp. 303, 315. The latter committee contained fifteen merchants, fifteen mechanics, and sixty-nine planters.

47. According to Frakes, *Laboratory for Liberty,* p. 122.

48. Ibid., p. 128; Edwin Hemphill and Wylma Ann Wates, eds., *Extracts from the Journals of the Provincial Congresses of South Carolina, 1775–1776* (Columbia, S.C., 1960), pp. xxii, xxiv. Committee service figures for the next two paragraphs are compiled from the *Journals* index entries on pp. 269–99 (excluding local and district committees and commissions that included men who were not members of the legislature).

49. For this episode, see Wallace, *South Carolina: A Short History*, pp. 265–67.

50. Methodology and terms for tables 6.1, 6.2, and 6.3 can be found in the Appendix: Statistical Methods.

51. Nadelhaft sees the constitution of 1790 as "a victory for emerging powers." *The Disorders of War: The Revolution in South Carolina* (Orono, Maine, 1981), p. 202. For other views, see William A. Schaper, "Sectionalism and Representation in South Carolina," American Historical Association, *Annual Report, 1900,* vol. 1 (Washington, D.C., 1901), p. 380; Marvin R. Zahniser, *Charles Cotesworth Pinckney: Founding Father* (Chapel Hill, N.C., 1967), p. 109; Raymond G. Starr, "The Conservative Revolution: South Carolina Public Affairs, 1775–1790" (Ph.D. dissertation, University of Texas, 1964), pp. 280–82.

52. *Journals of the House, 1791,* p. ix.

53. Ibid., p. xxv; Nadelhaft, *Disorders of War,* p. 211.

54. Schaper, "Sectionalism and Representation," p. 378.

55. *The City Gazette,* cited in Nadelhaft, *Disorders of War,* p. 208; Schaper, "Sectionalism and Representation," p. 377.

56. Fletcher M. Green, *Constitutional Development in the South Atlantic States, 1776–1860: A Study in the Evolution of Democracy* (Chapel Hill, N.C., 1930), p. 121; [Timothy Ford], *The Constitutionalist, Or An Enquiry How Far It Is Expedient And Proper To Alter The Constitution of South-Carolina* (Charleston, S.C.: Markland, M'Iver & Co., 1794), Early American Imprints, Evans no. 26987, p. 53.

57. *Journals of the House, 1791,* January 14, 1791, pp. 36–37.

58. Nadelhaft, *Disorders of War,* pp. 208–9.

59. [Robert Goodloe Harper], *An Address to the People of South-Carolina by the General Committee of the Representative Reform Association, at Columbia . . .* (Charleston, S.C.: W. P. Young, 1794), Early American Imprints, Evans no. 27092.

60. *Journals of the House, 1792–94,* pp. xxiii-xxiv, December 13, 1793, May 5, 1794, pp. 397–99, 523–25. Richard Walsh, ed., *The Writings of Christopher Gadsden, 1746–1805* (Columbia, S.C., 1966), "A Steady and Open Republican," *Gazette of the State of South-Carolina,* July 17, 1784, p. 207.

61. [Ford], *The Constitutionalist.* For the sources of this and following attributions, see Pierce Welch Gaines, comp., *Political Writings of Concealed Authorship Relating to the United States, 1789–1810, with Attributions* (Hampden, Conn., 1972; original ed., New Haven, Conn., 1959).

62. Ibid., p. 4.

63. Americanus cites Rousseau on p. 10, but does not specify the text.

64. Ibid., pp. 6–8.

65. Ibid., pp. 15–18; and compare Americanus with Madison on slaveholding and the divisions in American society, ch. 5, above.

66. Ibid., p. 21.

67. J. R. Pole, *Political Representation in England and the Origins of the American Republic* (London, 1966), pp. 171–89. Quotation is from p. 176.

68. [Ford], *The Constitutionalist,* pp. 31–36.

69. August L. Spain, *The Political Theory of John C. Calhoun* (New York, 1951), esp. ch. 5, "The Concurrent Majority."

70. *The Works of John C. Calhoun,* ed. by Richard K. Crallé (New York, 1851–67), I. 28. Glimmers of an interest group basis for society can be found in Christopher Gadsden's thought in 1784. He opposed the principle of instructing assemblymen for fear that organized, politicized societies (lobbies) such as the violently anti-Tory Marine AntiBritannic Society would successfully bind members. They should instead present their views in constitutional forms, such as the petition, so that legislators could calculate a *"general combined* interest of *all* the state *put* together, as it were upon *an average"* (226). Richard Walsh, ed., *The Writings of Christopher Gadsden, 1746–1805* (Columbia, S.C., 1966), pp. 203–4, 217, 223, 225–26.

71. Spain, *Calhoun,* pp. 130, 133.

72. See Lacy K. Ford, "Republican Ideology in a Slave Society: The Political Economy of John C. Calhoun," *JSH* 54 (1988): 418–22, for Calhoun on the necessity of equality between interests.

73. John C. Calhoun, quoted in Schaper, "Representation and Sectionalism," p. 435.

74. *Unification of a Slave State: The Rise of the Planter Class in the South Carolina Backcountry, 1760–1808* (Chapel Hill, N.C., 1990).

75. *South-Carolina State Gazette,* in Schaper, "Representation and Sectionalism," p. 377.

76. Howard K. Beale, ed., *The Diary of Edward Bates, 1859–1866,* Annual Report (1930), American Historical Association (Washington, D.C., 1933), IV. 139.

77. "A Steady and Open Republican," *Gazette of the State of South Carolina,* July 17, 1784, quoted in Richard Walsh, ed., *The Writings of Christopher Gadsden* (Columbia, S.C., 1966), p. 207.

Chapter Seven

A COMPARATIVE VIEW

1. The discussion of the first five paragraphs of this chapter is based on Jack P. Greene, "Changing Interpretations of Early American Politics," in Roy Allen Billington, ed., *The Reinterpretation of Early American History: Essays in Honor of John Edwin Pomfret* (San Marino, Calif., 1966), pp. 151–77 (quotation from p. 163).

2. The most recent colony-by-colony studies for the colonial and revolutionary periods are published in the History of the American Colonies series (Millwood, N.Y., 1973–86), Milton M. Klein and Jacob E. Cooke, eds.

3. Marc Egnal, *A Mighty Empire: The Origins of the American Revolution* (Ithaca and London, 1988), p. xi.

4. Michael Zuckerman, *Peaceable Kingdoms: New England Towns in the Eighteenth Century* (New York, 1970), pp. 177, 184–85, 243–47.

5. Benjamin W. Labaree, *Colonial Massachusetts: A History* (Millwood, N.Y., 1979), pp. 125–44.

6. Alison Olson, "Eighteenth-Century Legislatures and Their Constituents," *JAH* 79 (1992): 555–56.

7. Richard Walsh, ed., *The Writings of Christopher Gadsden, 1746–1805* (Columbia, S.C., 1966), pp. 225–26. Gadsden thought instructions would "put the legislature into *leading strings*" of a "designing few."

8. Oscar and Mary Handlin, eds., *The Popular Sources of Political Authority: Documents on the Massachusetts Constitution of 1780* (Cambridge, Mass., 1966), pp. 1–54; Walsh, *Writings of Christopher Gadsden*, p. 244n.

9. The discussion on Massachusetts and local authority in this and the following paragraphs is drawn from J. R. Pole, "Shays's Rebellion: A Political Interpretation," in Jack P. Greene, ed., *The Reinterpretation of the American Revolution, 1763–1789* (Westport, Conn., 1968), pp. 416–34.

10. Robert A. Becker, "Salus Populi Suprema Lex: Public Peace and South Carolina Debtor Relief Laws, 1783–1788," *SCHM* 80 (1979): 65–75.

11. The "Beardian" argument that the legislation may have also helped indebted lowcountry planters should not detract from the fact that the legislation staved off social disorder, a far greater threat to elite power in this unstable period. Nadelhaft, *The Disorders of War: The Revolution in South Carolina* (Orono, Maine, 1981), pp. 99–104, 111–24.

12. Patricia U. Bonomi, *A Factious People: Politics and Society in Colonial New York* (New York, 1971); the quotation is on pp. 284–85; Michael Kammen, *Colonial New York: A History* (New York, 1975), pp. 191–215. Alan Tully, *Forming American Politics: Ideals, Interests, and Institutions in Colonial New York and Pennsylvania* (Baltimore, 1994).

13. See ch. 6, above. Alison Olson notes that colonial Pennsylvania's legislature "on occasion" tallied numbers of signatures on opposing petitions to assess public opinion in controversial issues. "Eighteenth-century Colonial Legislatures and Their Constituents" *JAH* 79 (1992): 558; also idem, *Making the Empire Work*, p. 162.

14. The discussion of the next seven paragraphs is based on Mark D. Kaplanoff, "How Federalist Was South Carolina in 1787–88?" in David R. Chestnutt and Clyde N. Wilson, eds., *The Meaning of South Carolina History: Essays in Honor of George C. Rogers, Jr.* (Columbia, S.C., 1991), pp. 67–103.

15. See ch. 5, above.

16. Although not the subject of his article, the aggressive political style of Carolina's leaders is noted by Kaplanoff in passing, pp. 77–78.

17. Butler's contemporaries in the Senate saw through him. William Maclay recorded in his diary that Butler made himself obnoxious to his fellow senators by "ever and anon declaring how clear of local Views [and] how candid and dispassionate he was." Cited in Gordon Wood, *The Radicalism of the American Revolution* (New York, 1992), p. 416 n. 12. Voter analysis by section is found in Nadelhaft, *Disorders of War*, p. 199.

18. Kaplanoff, "How Federalist Was South Carolina?" p. 86.

19. Ibid., pp. 86–87.

20. Pinckney quoted in ibid., p. 85; Nadelhaft, *Disorders of War,* pp. 194, 198.

21. Kaplanoff, "How Federalist Was South Carolina?" p. 87.

22. Nedalhaft, *Disorders of War,* p. 213. Additionally, removing the capital to Columbia weakened lowcountry attendance at votes for electoral college candidates and placed the legislature beyond the influence of Federalist Charleston's superior financial power.

23. J. R. Pole, *Political Representation in England and the Origins of the American Republic* (New York, 1966), pp. 109–24, 250–65. On colonial Pennsylvania's political culture, see also Tully, *Forming American Politics.*

24. On Quaker dissidents as lobbyists, see Douglas R. Lacy, *Dissent and Parliamentary Politics in England, 1661–1689* (New Brunswick, N.J., 1969), and Alison G. Olson, *Making the Empire Work: London and American Interest Groups, 1690–1790* (Cambridge, Mass., 1992), p. 116.

25. Richard Alan Ryerson, "Portrait of a Colonial Oligarchy: The Quaker Elite in the Pennsylvania Assembly, 1729–1776," and Alan Tully, "Quaker Party and Proprietary Politics: The Dynamics of Politics in Pre-Revolutionary Pennsylvania, 1730–1775," in Bruce C. Daniels, ed., *Power and Status: Officeholding in Colonial America* (Middletown, Conn., 1986), pp. 75–105, 106–45.

26. Ryerson, "Portrait of a Colonial Oligarchy," pp. 47, 187–90, 192, 194, 203.

27. Joseph E. Illick, *Colonial Pennsylvania: A History* (New York, 1976), pp. 320–21; O. S. Ireland, "The Crux of Politics: Religion and Party in Pennsylvania, 1778–1789," *WMQ,* 3rd ser., 42 (1985): 453–75.

28. Evangelism of the George Whitefield stripe was ignored or systematically discouraged in lowcountry South Carolina, especially as it proposed to preach to blacks in "great Assemblies." See Harvey H. Jackson, "Hugh Bryan and the Evangelical Movement in Colonial South Carolina," *WMQ* 43 (1986): 594–614.

29. F. N. Thorpe, ed., *The Federal and State Constitutions, Colonial Charters, and Other Organic Laws* (Washington, D.C., 1909), VI. 3241–48, 3249–57.

30. See ch. 5, above.

31. On the Drayton, Tennent, and Hart delegation to the upcountry, see David Duncan Wallace, *South Carolina: A Short History, 1520–1948* (Columbia, S.C., 1961), pp. 215, 265.

32. A convenient literature summary and discussion can be found in Herbert Sloan and Peter Onuf, "Politics, Culture, and the Revolution in Virginia," *VMHB* 91 (1983): 259–84.

33. Jack P. Greene, "'Virtus et Libertas': Political Culture, Social Change, and the Origins of the American Revolution, 1763–1766," in Jeffrey J. Crow and Larry E. Tise, eds., *The Southern Experience in the American Revolution* (Chapel Hill, N.C., 1978), pp. 55–108.

34. Rhys Isaacs, "Evangelical Revolt: The Nature of the Baptists' Challenge to the Traditional Order in Virginia, 1765–1775," *WMQ,* 3rd ser., 31 (1974): 345–68; Jacob M. Price, "Buchanan and Simson, 1759–1763: A Different Kind of Glasgow Firm Trading to the Chesapeake," *WMQ* 3rd ser., 40 (1983); 3–41; T. H. Breen, "The Culture of Agriculture: The Symbolic World of the Tidewater Planter, 1760–1790," in David D. Hall, John M. Murrin, and Thad W. Tate, eds., *Saints and Revolutionaries: Essays on Early American History* (New York, 1984), pp. 247–84.

35. Strong and Onuf, "Politics, Culture, and Revolution," pp. 269–70.

36. Ibid., pp. 281–82.

37. Ibid., pp. 278–82.

38. Becker, "Salus Populi," pp. 65–68.

39. Walter B. Edgar and N. Louise Bailey, eds., *Biographical Directory of the South Carolina House of Representatives*, vol. II, *The Commons House of Assembly, 1692–1775* (Columbia, S.C., 1983), pp. 525–27, 573–76, 578–81.

40. *The Development of Creole Society in Jamaica, 1770–1820* (Oxford, 1971). George Metcalf, *Royal Government and Political Conflict in Jamaica, 1729–1783* (Longmans, 1965), contains useful factual material for this study.

41. See n. 2, this chapter.

42. Jack P. Greene, "Colonial South Carolina and the Caribbean Connection," *SCHM* 88 (1987): 192–210. See also Warren Alleyne and Henry Fraser, *The Barbados-Carolina Connection* (London, 1988).

43. Greene, "Caribbean Connection," pp. 197–98, 202–3; Brathwaite, *The Development of Creole Society*, pp. 63–65.

44. Quoted in Greene, "Caribbean Connection," p. 207.

45. Jamaica experienced about twenty-eight riots and disturbances in the period up to emancipation, in one of which over a thousand Negroes were killed. Frank Cundall, *Political and Social Disturbances in the West Indies* (London, 1906), p. 3.

46. Greene, "Caribbean Connection," p. 205.

47. ST to Robert Taylor, Kingston, Jamaica, October 3, 1795, Simon Taylor Papers, Institute for Commonwealth Studies, London.

48. Brathwaite, *The Development of Creole Society*, pp. 112–13.

49. Advertisement in *The [Kingston] Royal Gazette* (1819), quoted in ibid., p. 115.

50. Ibid., pp. 116–17.

51. See ch. 3, above. Douglas Hall, *A Brief History of the West India Committee* (St. Lawrence, Barbados, 1971), p. 4.

52. "Minutes of several meetings at Pitcairn's Tavern in St Iago de la Vaga [Spanish Town], Jamaica on 4th, 10th and 11th December," read at a meeting of the [London] Jamaica Planters held at Stephen Fuller's (Agent for Jamaica) lodgings in Southampton Street, Bloomsbury, February 27, 1773, Minutes of the West India Committee, March 2, 1773, original manuscripts at the Library of the University of the West Indies, St. Augustine; microfilm copy at the Institute of Commonwealth Studies, London University. On Samuel Vaughn, see Brathwaite, *The Development of Creole Society*, pp. 64–65.

53. Resolution of the Jamaican Assembly, October 29, 1753, and Governor Charles Knowles's Speech on Dissolving the Assembly, November 8, 1754, in Frederick Madden and David Fieldhouse, eds., *The Classical Period of the First British Empire, 1689–1783: The Foundations of a Colonial System of Government* (Westport, Conn., 1985), II. 420 (doc. 246–b); 368 (doc. 225) and n. 3.

54. Resolution of the Assembly, November 7, 1754, in Madden and Fieldhouse, eds., *The First British Empire*, II. 367 (doc. 225–c).

55. Jamaicanus [Charles Knowles], *The Association Develop'd* (Jamaica, 1755; reprinted London, 1757).

56. Trelawney to Knowles, October 23, 1751, cited in Metcalf, *Royal Government*, p. 104.

57. *The Association Develop'd*, pp. 5–7.

58. *An Historical Account of the Sessions of Assembly for the Island of Jamaica: Which began on Tuesday the 23rd of September 1755, containing a vindication of his Excellency Charles Knowles, Esq., then governor of that Island* (London, 1757), p. 71. This pamphlet, authored by a Knowles supporter, includes a section written by Knowles himself that develops the arguments set out in *The Association Develop'd*.

59. *The Association Develop'd*, p. 8.

60. *An Historical Account*, pp. 11–16.

61. *The Association Develop'd*, pp. 16, 25, and passim.

62. Metcalf, *Royal Government*, p. 107.

63. *An Historical Account*, pp. 72–75. The address was never sent since the appointment was never made.

64. His words also indicate that the Association enjoyed some longevity. Governor Charles Knowles's speech on Dissolving the Assembly, November 8, 1754, in Madden and Fieldhouse, eds., *The First British Empire*, II. 368 (doc. 225–d).

65. *An Historical Account*, pp. 19–34, 71–75. A letter signed by the sixteen seceding associators included only one original member (Charles Price) and four with the same surnames as original members (p. 34). Original merchant members Edward Manning, Henry Archbould, and Philomen Pinnock had withdrawn during the capital relocation battle in 1754.

66. Metcalf, *Royal Government*, p. 137. On divisions within the legislature under former Governor Trelawney, see [James Smith], *A Letter from a Friend at J_____ to a Friend in London: Giving an Impartial Account of the Violent Proceedings of the Faction in that Island* (Arch. Willock, Kingston, 1747; reprinted for John Creole, in Jamaica-Street, Rotherhithe, [1748]).

67. Metcalf, *Royal Government*, p. 122.

68. Brathwaite, *The Development of Creole Society*, pp. 135, 266–95.

69. One who did, planter Hugh Bryan, found himself forced or persuaded to recant. Harvey Jackson, "Hugh Bryan and the Evangelical Movement in South Carolina," *WMQ*, 3rd ser., 43 (1986): 594–614.

70. Brathwaite, *The Development of Creole Society*, pp. 47, 107, 297.

71. Greene, "South Carolina and the Caribbean Connection," p. 210.

72. Ibid. This is Greene's reading of Drayton. It is just as possible that Drayton meant that by more than tripling its white population (from 25,000 in 1750 to 87,000 whites in 1780), South Carolina had achieved the critical mass necessary to mount an effective fighting force.

73. Max Farrand, ed., *The Records of the Federal Convention of 1787* (New Haven, Conn., 1966), II. 364.

74. Wallace, *South Carolina: A Short History*, p. 185; Peter H. Wood, *Black Majority: Negroes in Colonial South Carolina from 1676 through the Stono Rebellion* (New York, 1974), p. 36; Weir, *Colonial South Carolina*, p. 194. On the Assembly divisions of the 1740s, see ch. 2, above.

75. Weir, *Colonial South Carolina*, pp. 188–91.

CONCLUSIONS

1. Gordon S. Wood, *The Radicalism of the American Revolution* (New York, 1992). Quotation from p. 368.

2. See Robert M. Weir, "The South Carolinian as Extremist," in *"The Last of American Freeman": Studies in the Political Culture of the Colonial and Revolutionary South* (Macon, Ga., 1986).

3. Philip Shriver Klein, *Pennsylvania Politics, 1817–1832: A Game Without Rules* (Philadelphia, 1940).

4. Michael Zuckerman, *Peaceable Kingdoms: New England Towns in the Eighteenth Century* (Philadelphia, 1970), pp. 256–58.

5. February 22, 1787, cited in Robert A. Becker, "Salus Populi Suprema Lex: Public Peace and South Carolina Debtor Relief Laws, 1783–1788," *SCHM* 80 (1979): 73.

ESSAY ON SOURCES

PRIMARY SOURCES

In trying to extract a state of mind from a phylogeny of political behavior, it is particularly frustrating that the actors themselves never seemed to see the tendency of their own habitual actions. Perhaps it is because they did not deem their methods important in any sense except an instrumental one. They were not political scientists. They left us no neat contemporary passages to indicate any awareness that the routine tactics of lobbying for imperial trade concessions might play a role in settling a future politics. That this kind of imprinting did in fact happen in South Carolina must be inferred from the tendency of evidence that is often episodic and scattered. Primary evidence for the inception of this politics in South Carolina can be found in the petitions and memorials to the Board of Trade in the Colonial Office Papers from the early eighteenth century. By 1767 in the Daniel Moore case (George Rogers Jr. et al., eds., *The Papers of Henry Laurens* [Columbia, S.C., 1968–]; and Treasury Papers, series 1/459–61), we can see this politics domesticated to provincial turf when Charleston lobbyists sought to rid the colony of a corrupt customs official. From that point on, refined and matured by events in the revolutionary crisis and newly won Independence, this formula for political problem-solving became the politics of choice for Carolina leaders.

In a commercial state like South Carolina, the school for such a politics lay in the first instance in the transatlantic network of planters, merchants, lawyers, agents, members of Parliament, and others interested in promoting the colony's trade. Although the London merchant lobbies have received the most historical attention in light of their pro-American activities in 1775, the Bristol-Carolina lobby provides a more specific setting for analyzing the long-term role that the commercial lobby played in developing South

Carolina's unique politics. Edmund Burke, a pioneer in adapting commercial lobby strategies to political ends, and his campaign manager, Bristol-Carolina merchant Richard Champion, linked South Carolina's political leaders to the Rockingham Whigs throughout the revolutionary crisis.

Essential background on Bristol politics came from an excellent unpublished thesis by W. R. Savadge Jr., "The West Country and the American Mainland Colonies, 1703–1783, with Special Reference to the Merchants of Bristol" (B. Litt. thesis, Oxford University, 1952). Material to reconstruct a background for the slow refinement of commercial strategies into an opposition politics for Carolina leaders came from the archives of the Bristol Merchant Venturers Society, Central Library and Bristol Public Record Offices, England; T. W. Copeland et al., eds., *The Correspondence of Edmund Burke* (Cambridge, Eng., 1958–63); South Carolina agent Charles Garth's letters to the South Carolina Commons House of Assembly published in the *South Carolina Magazine of History* 31(1930): 233–39 and in the published Henry Laurens papers (above); John Almon's correspondence, 1766–1805, at the British Library; and the published debates respecting America in the British House of Commons (R. C. Simmons and P. D. G. Thompson, eds., *Proceedings and Debates of the British Parliaments Respecting America, 1754–1783* [Millwood, N.Y., 1982–]).

I relied on prosopographic material to reconstruct the Carolina-Bristol transatlantic lobby, in both its assumptions and processes, as a school for Carolina politicians. The lobby's evolving character (a process speeded up as the imperial crisis deepened), its attitudes, methods, and applications had potential to shape a dual instrument for South Carolina's leaders: an internal politics whose fundamental feature was conflict resolution, combined with the necessarily aggressive external politics of a weak minority power. Without claiming the lobby experience as either the sole or (unsupported by social factors) sufficient explanation for South Carolina's political culture, I found it an essential determinant, especially for the processes of internal conflict resolution.

The main manuscript sources for this reconstruction are as follows: at the Bristol Public Record Office, Richard Champion's Letterbooks, I–IV, 38083(1–4), Sarah (Fox) Champion's Letterbook, 38083(5), and at the New York Public Library, Letterbook V, collected and published as *The Letterbooks of Richard Champion (1743–1791)*, British Records Relating to America in Microform (BRRAM), W. E. Minchinton, gen. ed. (East Ardsley, 1985). Selections from the letterbooks have been edited by G. H. Guttridge, *The American Correspondence of a Bristol Merchant, 1766–76: Letters of Richard Champion* (Berkeley, Calif., 1934), although Guttridge makes mistakes in his attributions for Champion's unsigned correspondence; Hugh Owen, *Two Centuries of Ceramic Art in Bristol, being a History of the Manufacture of the true Porcelain by Richard Champion* (London, 1873), reproduces several letters from letterbooks that are now lost. Important Champion correspondence can be found in the Rockingham Papers, Sheffield (Eng.) Public Library, the Portland Papers, University of Nottingham, England, and *The Correspondence of Edmund Burke, 1744–1782*, edited by T. W. Copeland et al. (Cambridge, Eng., 1958–63). I am grateful to the Sheffield Central Library for allowing me access to the Rockingham Papers.

For the Charleston side of the network, manuscript materials on John Lloyd are found in three small collections: the John Lloyd Papers at the South Caroliniana Library, Columbia, S.C.; the John Lloyd and Thomas Farr Letters at the South Carolina Library Society, Charleston, S.C.; and the Harford Lloyd Papers, Gloucestershire Public Record Office, Gloucester, England. Important Farr correspondence among the records of the Society of Merchant Venturers in Bristol, England, proved invaluable for reconstructing activism by Champion, Lloyd, Farr, and other Carolina traders of the Carolina-Bristol lobby in events from the Stamp Act to the Revolution.

To demonstrate this politics at work in South Carolina from 1767 on, I looked at several key events. The composition and methods of the enforcement committee during the 1769 Nonimportation Movement show a lobby taking on the role of a legislature. The writings of William Henry Drayton in *The Letters of Freeman, Etc.: Essays on the Nonimportation Movement in South Carolina*, edited by Robert M. Weir (Columbia, S.C., 1977), come closest to recognizing that a new politics is afoot in revolutionary South Carolina. Volume 1 in the series, *The Letters of Delegates to Congress, 1774–1789*, edited by Paul H. Smith (Washington, D.C., 1976–), is the main source for South Carolina's short secession from the Continental Congress in the 1774 rice nonexportation controversy. South Carolina's aggressive position on the slave trade section of the Constitution is found in Max Farrand, ed., *The Records of the Federal Convention of 1787* (New Haven, Conn., 1966). Accounts of leading South Carolina Federalists' brokerage of state interests to win ratification can be drawn from Jonathan Elliot, ed., *The Debates in the Several State Conventions of the Adoption of the Federal Constitution* (Washington, D.C., 1854).

The argument ultimately turns on the claim that the newly independent state legislature adapted this politics to promote conflict resolution and a form of interest representation that saw it through the troubled 1780s. Michael E. Stevens, Christine M. Allen, and et al., eds., *The State Records of South Carolina: The Journals of the House of Representatives* (Columbia, S.C.,

1977–88), is the key source here. The formulation of these trends in the 1790s into theory and argument can be found in the pamphlet exchanges of [Timothy Ford], *The Constitutionalist, Or An Enquiry How Far It Is Expedient and Proper To Alter The Constitution of South-Carolina* (Charleston, 1794), [Robert Goodlow Harper], *An Address to the People of South Carolina* (Charleston, 1794), and [William Henry Dessausure], *Letters on the Question of the Justice and Expediency of Going into Alterations of the representations of the legislature of South-Carolina as Fixed by the Constitution* (Charleston, 1795).

Although South Carolina's was among the last of the colonial lobbies to emerge and to peak in influence (making differences in timing relevant), this "school for politics" was not a unique experience. To show how and why the lobby's strategy fell more readily into South Carolina's social and political context than elsewhere, and to demonstrate that it produced a politics that worked differently in South Carolina than elsewhere, required a comparative chapter. I drew the comparative framework from Jack Greene's taxonomy of colonial politics, which he based on degrees of factiousness ("Changing Interpretations of Early American Politics," in Roy Allen Billington, ed., *The Reinterpretation of Early American History: Essays in Honor of John Edwin Pomfret* [San Marino, Calif., 1966]). Evidence for the comparison of conflict resolution methods, and the political cultures that supported those methods, came nearly entirely from secondary sources. The major exception (owing to a dearth of published studies) was the comparison of South Carolina's early politics with that of Jamaica. The pamphlets of the Gov. Charles Knowles controversy, for example, Jamaicanus [Charles Knowles], *The Association Develop'd* (Jamaica, 1755; reprinted London, 1757); and *An Historical Account of the Sessions of Assembly for the Island of Jamaica: Which began on Tuesday the 23rd of Sept. 1755, containing a vindication of his Excellency Charles Knowles, Esq., then governor of that Island* (London, 1757), at the British Library, and the Minutes of the West India Committee, Library of the University of the West Indies, St. Augustine (microfilm copy at the Institute of Commonwealth Studies, London University), are the chief sources here.

Such a study that is particular to one state could not be persuasive without material specific to that state alone and to its leading personalities. Newspaper essays and items contribute in immediacy what they lack in continuity of argument. South Carolina is fortunate in having an unbroken run of newspapers from the 1720s. A project indexing these newspapers (along the lines of the *Virginia Gazette* index) would put a rich tool within the reach of all historians of early America.

What is true for newspapers may also be said of private correspondence. The commentary and observations found in Anna Deas, ed., *The Cor-*

respondence of Mr. Ralph Izard of South Carolina, 1774–1804, with a Short Memoir (New York, 1844), Richard Walsh, ed., *The Writings of Christopher Gadsden, 1746–1805* (Columbia, S.C., 1966), and especially George Rogers Jr. et al., eds., *The Papers of Henry Laurens* (Columbia, S.C., 1968–), remind us that history is made and interpreted by human beings.

SECONDARY SOURCES

All new works owe a large intellectual debt to the scholarship on which they build. The insights of J. R. Pole on the general subject of interest representation (*Political Representation in England and the Origins of the American Republic* [New York, 1966]) continuously affirmed my sense that South Carolina's legislative politics in the 1780s and its early experience with commercial interest group politics were connected. Working out the history and character of interest group politics took me to the work of several scholars. Best known of the general studies are Michael Kammen's two books, *Empire and Interest: The American Colonies and the Politics of Mercantilism* (Philadelphia, 1970) and *A Rope of Sand: The Colonial Agents, British Politics, and the American Revolution* (Ithaca, N.Y., 1968), and Jack M. Sosin's *Agents and Merchants: British Colonial Policy and the Origins of the American Revolution, 1763–1775* (Lincoln, Nebr., 1965). These volumes are still the starting point for any survey of the field.

A few specific studies helped refine my understanding of how these groups operated to influence political decision-making. Walter Minchinton's volume on the Merchant Venturers of Bristol, *Politics and the Port of Bristol in the Eighteenth Century: The Petitions of the Society of Merchant Venturers, 1698–1803*, Bristol Record Society 23 (1963), and also his article on the Bristol lobby, "The Political Activities of Bristol Merchants with Respect to the Southern Colonies before the Revolution," *Virginia Magazine of History and Biography* 79 (1971): 167–89, examined the petition as an instrument of political pressure. Studies of the powerful West Indian lobby such as Lillian M. Penson's "The London West India Interest in the Eighteenth Century," *The English Historical Review* 36 (1921): 373–92, and "Early Years of the West Indian Committee," *West India Commercial Circular,* May 13, 1920, follow that well-known group's political history, but give little actual analysis of its methods.

Alison Olson's string of articles on interest group politics is the best introduction to the methods of this politics available. They include "The Virginia Merchants of London: A Study in Eighteenth-Century Interest-Group Politics," *WMQ*, 3rd ser., 40 (1983): 361–88; "The London Mercantile Lobby and the Coming of the American Revolution," *JAH* 49 (1982): 21–40; "The Board of Trade and London-American Interest Groups in the Eighteenth Century," *Journal of Imperial and Commonwealth History* 7 (1980): 33–50; "Parliament, the London Lobbies, and Provincial Interests in England and America," *Historical Reflections* 6 (1979): 367–86. Her acute analyses of how these lobbies actually worked supplied the point of departure for this study.

Olson notes in her subsequent monograph, *Making the Empire Work: London and American Interest Groups, 1690–1790* (Cambridge, Mass., 1992), that in showing how informal mercantile, ecclesiastical, and ethnic ties (what we now call "voluntary associations") supplemented formal governmental ones in colonial America, she had to give short shrift to the political cultures in which these interest groups functioned. My study of the origins of South Carolina's early politics attempts to weld its interest group patterns to more fundamental impulses in the culture, a connection suggested in Robert M. Weir, *Colonial South Carolina: A History* (Millwood, N.Y., 1983). Weir's work on the social origins of South Carolina's early political culture (especially "'The Harmony We Were Famous For': An Interpretation of Pre-Revolutionary South Carolina Politics," *WMQ*, 3rd ser., 26 [1969]: 473–501; and *'The Last of American Freemen': Studies in the Political Culture of the Colonial and Revolutionary South* [Macon, Ga., 1986]) supplies essential context for the argument of this study, which extends the grounds over which political culture may find its sources.

The attempt to understand how this politics might have influenced South Carolina's behavior in the early Republic has been aided by the work of several scholars. Jerome J. Nadelhaft, *The Disorders of War: The Revolution in South Carolina* (Orono, Maine, 1981), supplies essential political background for the 1776–90 period as this politics realigned legislative procedures to meet the strains of a widened political community. How this politics persisted and intensified in the changing political conditions of the early nineteenth century is the subject of George C. Rogers Jr., "South Carolina Federalists and the Origins of the Nullification Movement," *South Carolina Historical Magazine* 71 (1970): 17–32; Mark D. Kaplanoff, "How Federalist Was South Carolina in 1787–88?" in David R. Chestnutt and Clyde N. Wilson, eds., *The Meaning of South Carolina History: Essays in Honor of George C. Rogers, Jr.* (Columbia, S.C., 1991), pp. 67–103; and Robert M. Weir, "The South Carolinian as Extremist," *South Atlantic Quarterly* 74 (1975): 86–103. Rachael N. Klein's *The Unification of a Slave State: The Rise of the Planter Class in the South Carolina Backcountry, 1760–1808* (Chapel Hill, N.C., 1990) locates the bridges necessary to transmit these patterns and values as power permanently shifted to the upcountry. As a coda, Lacy Ford's *The Origins of Southern Radicalism: The South Carolina Upcountry, 1800–1860* (Oxford, 1988) documents the growth of a popular republicanism that made the radical practices original to this politics relevant to common whites, supplying a compelling rationale for plain folks to join elites on a trajectory that ended in secession and Civil War.

INDEX